Christian Men of Science

ELEVEN MEN WHO CHANGED THE WORLD

Christian Men of Science

ELEVEN MEN WHO CHANGED THE WORLD

George Mulfinger & Julia Mulfinger Orozco

AMBASSADOR INTERNATIONAL

Greenville, South Carolina • Belfast, Northern Ireland

Christian Men of Science

© 2001 Julia Mulfinger Orozco
Second printing, 2004
Printed in the United States of America

Cover design by A & E Media — Paula Shepherd
Internal layout by Sam Laterza
Internal illustrations by Mark Mulfinger
Edited by Rebecca Moore

ISBN 1 932307 22 2

Published by the Ambassador Group

Ambassador Emerald International
427 Wade Hampton Blvd.
Greenville, SC 29609
USA
www. emeraldhouse.com

and

Ambassador Publications Ltd.
Providence House
Ardenlee Street
Belfast BT6 8QJ
Northern Ireland
www. ambassador-productions.com

The colophon is a trademark of Ambassador

To

Joan Elizabeth Wade Mulfinger

Her children arise up, and call her blessed; her
husband also, and he praiseth her. . . . A woman
that feareth the LORD, she shall be praised.

Proverbs 31:28, 30

Contents

FOREWORD

I knew George Mulfinger (now with the Lord) as a devout Christian physicist and astronomer for many years. We served together as Board members in the early years of the Creation Research Society, and I was aware of his deep interest in the many founding fathers of modern science who were, like himself, committed to Jesus Christ as Savior and Lord and to the Bible as the written Word of God.

Although his unexpected early death prevented him from completing the book he had planned on this important theme, I am glad that one of his lovely daughters (George was also a devoted family man, with a wonderful Christian wife and many fine children) has taken on the task. Julia Mulfinger Orozco, now a pastor's wife in Mexico, has done a most commendable job in bringing the lives of these great Christian men of science of the past to the attention of young people today. Furthermore, son Mark Mulfinger has produced the excellent illustrations.

These modern-day young folks have been misled throughout their educational careers with the false notion that science must be based solely on naturalism, that the truth of supernatural creation by God in the beginning has been replaced by the "scientific" philosophy of evolution of all things, and that the Bible is not the inerrant revelation of God but only a pious book of now outmoded religion.

The truth, however, is that most of the great founding fathers of modern science (including those whose careers and testimonies are summarized in Julia's book) were Bible-believing men of science and sincere practicing Christians in their lives.

She has also, for some odd reason, included chapters on two Christian men of science who are still living. Although neither my friend, Dr. Walter Brown, nor I feel that we are in any sense comparable in stature to Robert Boyle, Michael Faraday, and the other great men of the past whom she has profiled in this book, we are of course honored to be included. Perhaps this will at least serve to alert the reader to the fact that there are literally thousands of scientists living today (evolutionist propagandists to the contrary notwithstanding) who are also Bible-believing creationist scientists.

It is worth mentioning also that Walt Brown and I, as well as George Mulfinger and Julia Mulfinger Orozco, are committed to the Biblical doctrines of a literal six-day creation and the global flood of Noah's day. The Biblical and scientific importance of these two great historical events may not have been as fully understood and appreciated in earlier generations as they are today, when there are so many "young-earth" books and periodicals available. Consequently, some of these great scientists of the past may not have been as committed to these truths then as I hope and believe they would be if they were living today. Nevertheless, they were men who were committed Christians, believing in the Bible, in God as Creator, and in Christ as their Savior and Lord. We Bible-believing creationist Christians today are grateful to be in their spiritual and scientific lineage.

I do trust that Julia's book will prove a great blessing and encouragement to many in this current generation.

HENRY M. MORRIS

PREFACE

August 1967

Most of us have been brainwashed into believing that any scientist worth his salt is an atheist. The truth of the matter is that some of the greatest experimentalists and theoreticians have been Bible-believing Christians. We should study these men—men who have been properly oriented to God's Word and His creation. They had unusually keen minds to use in carrying out the Lord's will for their lives, and they could rightly interpret the scientific evidence.

Unfortunately, our knowledge of these men is eroding as libraries gradually discard the older biographies written by Christians. They are being replaced by more up-to-date books, written for the most part by biographers with an antireligious mindset. The newer biographies tend to describe the man's scientific work adequately, but they fail dismally in communicating the true picture of the man himself and the motivation for his work.

It should be abundantly clear at the outset that we don't endorse the popular idea of categorizing a man as a Christian by default; that is, if he is not a Jew, a Buddhist, or a Moslem, then he must by the process of elimination be a Christian. Rather, a true Christian holds his beliefs as a result of something that has taken place in his life, not his failure to subscribe to some rival creed. In other words, by the event referred to in the Scriptures as the "new birth" (John 3), God has regenerated the individual so that now, "in Christ, he is a new creature" (II Corinthians 5:17).

We included each man based on these two questions: (1) Did he profess Christ as his Savior? (2) Did his life manifest the fruit of the Spirit, the good works evidenced by true Christians? It is quite possible that we do not agree with each man about every point of Biblical doctrine or that we do not necessarily agree with each man's denominational affiliations. But we can appreciate the testimonies of these men while not insisting that they conform to our every standard. Each man in this book showed a genuine love for Christ and was willing to live by His teaching.

We gradually shortened a long list of candidates by carefully studying their biographies. In some cases the task was rendered relatively easy by the writings of Christian biographers who had known their subjects personally. In cases where a doubt remained, we removed the names from the list. Thus it is possible that we could have assembled a more extensive and more impressive roster, but we felt that the more conservative list would carry a stronger testimony. Obviously, this list is by no means comprehensive. There were many more scientists who were Christians.

Undoubtedly a number of fine men have been overlooked in compiling this present book. For every person included in the book, a dozen or so had to be excluded—sometimes just for lack of information, not necessarily on the basis of negative information. We assume part of the blame for this injustice. But there are some grievous gaps in the literature, a fact that prevented our discerning the beliefs of many of the scientists of the past. There are other instances in which the beliefs of the man are simply unknown. In some cases, the biographers have seemed indifferent to the spiritual side of the man. They are mystified (or embarrassed) by the references to God and His Word and leave them out of the life account.

We made a sincere effort to distill each chapter to a readily readable length, retaining those things that should interest the Christian reader. We left out the tedious scientific details that would appeal only to students of science, and we abbreviated the descriptions of the technical processes leading to many of the discoveries and inventions. Only enough details are included to give the reader some insight into the difficulties that had to be surmounted. In many cases it then becomes apparent how the man's spiritual resources were in fact responsible for his success.

There is a mistaken notion that perhaps scientists of the past could believe in God as our Creator and Jesus as our Savior, but certainly not today. But just as God told Elijah that there were 7,000 prophets who had not bowed the knee to the false god Baal (I Kings 19), so there are many prominent men of science who are still faithful to the truths God has revealed to us in the Holy Scriptures. There are still many exemplary scientists who have Christ as their Savior and who believe in a literal six-day creation, the Genesis Flood, and all the other fundamentals of a Bible-oriented science. Hundreds of groups have been organized around the world to promote Biblical creationism and to help curb the pervasive propaganda that science "proves" evolution. Many Christian men of science are focusing their efforts in the creation-evolution debate because evolution has now become such a vital issue, undermining faith in God.

George L. Mulfinger
Greenville, South Carolina

August, 2001

I first learned about this book after my high school graduation cere-
mony. That was the day Dad announced that I would be writing a book
with him, and he took me into his study to show me the manuscript of
Christian Men of Science. He pulled a black notebook off his shelf and
showed me the chapters he had finished—all neatly typed on pages that
were beginning to yellow with age. He had started writing it the year I
was born—1967—and he had been too busy to finish it. Now eighteen
years had gone by, and he had decided that I would be the one to finish
it with him. As he flipped through the pages, he told me that the first
summer he had worked on it, he finished only two men. I laughed out
loud, thinking that was very slow writing.

We had meetings about the book, and we decided that I would write
about each man's personal life and he would write about his scientific
life. He gave me my first assignment, and fifteen years later, I finally finished it! Now I realize how quickly he had finished those first two
biographical sketches. When I had laughed, I had had no idea what intense research was hidden behind a short sketch.

We had assumed, of course, that we would be working on the book
together. But my father died of cancer when I was twenty. I picked up the
manuscript where he left off, and using his excellent notes and bibliogra-
phy, I have finished it for him. (My pace has been about the same as his.
It has taken me over fifteen years to finish it!)

Dad began this project because he couldn't find a book like this in
bookstores—a book that emphasized the Christian testimonies of well-
known scientists. He wanted to demonstrate that scientific advances are
not stifled by belief in God as Creator and Jesus as Savior. On the contrary, some of the most significant advances in modern science have been
made by men with a Christian worldview during a time when a Biblical
perspective still permeated mainstream culture. Unfortunately, our culture has moved far away from its Biblical basis and for the most part, the
study of science no longer serves to reveal God's wonders to man. Yet
there is a growing group of scientists who are working to bring science
back to its correct Biblical foundation. I have chosen two of these men to
profile, but there are many, many more who could not be included because of time and space constraints.

After all these years, we still recognize many of these names and remember the impact these men made on scientific thought. It is shameful,
though, that while we remember the scientific contributions of these men,
for the most part we have lost the memory of their Christian testimonies.

In their lifetime, they were known as strong Christians, and their public testimony was a great asset to the cause of Christ. These men would be disheartened to know that while their science may be remembered, their faith has been largely forgotten. We want to remedy that oversight and bring back the full memory of these men—their scientific work *and* their Christian faith.

Christian biography is a fascinating, edifying study. We can see God's dealing with a person all the way through his life—how he came to know Christ, what choices he made, and what his virtues and faults were. These men undertook their researches and scientific work in the context of real life. They faced the same problems that are common to all Christians—demanding family responsibilities and work pressures, temptations and difficult moral decisions, poor health and personal tragedies. A study of how these great men approached these matters is a most valuable undertaking.

I have spent many years studying these men, and I feel that they are now dear friends. I still feel a tremendous personal loss when I read that each man has died. I look forward to renewing my acquaintance with them when we are in heaven, praising our Lord together. But, until that day comes, I would like you to meet my friends through the pages of this book.

Julia Mulfinger Orozco
Hermosillo, Sonora, Mexico

ACKNOWLEDGMENTS

My father, George Mulfinger, wanted to thank the following people for helping him in the early stages of this book: Dr. Stewart Custer and Miss Margaret Bald helped him obtain books. Muriel Larson offered her encouragement and example as a Christian writer. Dr. Edward Panosian and Mr. Everett Cox answered questions on matters of church history and church creeds. Dr. Joseph Henson and Dr. Emmett Williams contributed through helpful discussions of Bible Science matters.

I also want to express my appreciation to the many people who helped me through different stages of the preparation of this book. Those who prayed for me during this project are too numerous to mention, but I value those prayers more than any other help I received, and I realize that the Lord has answered and brought this book to publication. I especially thank my church families in Greenville and Mexico for their prayers.

I am deeply grateful to my husband, Paco, who has patiently endured this project for the first twelve years of our marriage. He drove me many times to the library at the University of Arizona so I could get the books I needed. (Living in Mexico, I have not had the luxury of a local library.) Paco read the manuscript several times and gave advice and encouragement. He and our daughter Alejandra were my first readers.

My mother, Joan Mulfinger, answered many questions along the way. And my siblings all contributed in useful ways. I want to thank Mary, Martha, Daniel, Sharon, Rachel, and Joanna for reading parts of the manuscript and making suggestions. Linda transcribed one of the interviews for me and saved me a great deal of time. Ruth, Sara, and Joanna helped me obtain books and copied research material. And Mark, of course, did the artwork. Even my brothers-in-law helped out. Tim Kain copied research material; Andy George and Achim Gerber helped with research; Andy Wortman, a librarian, helped me obtain hard-to-find books; Tom Pryde and Terry Ritschard gave computer help; and Francisco Orozco gave me the official biographies of Kepler and Kelvin—treasures for my bookshelf. The help and support of my family has been invaluable.

Rachel Richmond, Mrs. Jacquelyn Cochran, and Jacquelyn's sons Benjamin and Jonathan read the manuscript for age-level appropriateness. My friend Marjorie Garrett read the entire manuscript and offered excellent suggestions. Bob Ray, Retired Commander in the United States Naval Reserve, helped me understand the Navy while I was writing the Matthew Maury chapter.

Bevan Elliott gave valuable comments from a scientist's viewpoint and helped with research. Bevan is part of the current generation of Christian men of science. Perhaps he will write a sequel to this book. (As a musician, Bevan would be well-qualified to write the sequel that my father had planned called Christian Men of Music.) Dr. Hugh Clarke and Dr. Andrew J. Fiedler "introduced" me to Dr. Howard Kelly during premed forum. Dr. Clarke is a vibrant Christian and a neurosurgeon. He encourages the premed students with examples of Christian doctors. Dr. William McCandless and his wife read the chapter on Dr. Kelly. Dr. McCandless is a retired gynecologist and a gracious Christian gentleman; his medical knowledge was a valuable asset. To all of these I am sincerely grateful.

I extend my heartfelt appreciation to Dr. Steve Phillips and his wife Sharon for their hospitality during the interviews for the chapters on Dr. Kelly and Dr. Morris. I also want to thank the following people who kindly helped with research questions: Dr. Kent Hovind, Dr. Stan Eby, Dr. Stuart Patterson, Dr. Eugenio Medina, Dr. Emmett Williams, Mrs. Vivian Knutson, Mrs. Debi Pryde, and Tim and Lois Mills.

For the last three chapters, I had the tremendous advantage of working with living people. The Wegter family introduced me to Mrs. Laetitia Coolidge, Dr. Kelly's youngest daughter. Mrs. Coolidge graciously answered all my letters and let me visit her twice so that we could talk about her father. She was in her nineties when we spoke, and her memories of her father were still sharp and fresh. She takes after her father in her love for books and her love for the Lord. She was still reading commentaries when she was ninety-three years old. And, like her father, she loves to give away her favorite books. She gave me D. Martyn Lloyd-Jones on Ephesians when I went to visit her!

I want to thank Dr. Walt Brown and his wife Peggy for their kindness and hospitality. They gave extensive interviews and allowed me access to their files. Dr. Brown read many of the chapters of this book and made suggestions that I incorporated into the manuscript.

My special thanks goes to Don Rohrer of the Institute for Creation Research, who gave me two dozen books written by Henry Morris to help me with my research. Although Dr. Morris was reluctant to be included in this project, he allowed me to interview him and gave me access to personal papers. He also graciously agreed to write the foreword, even though he thought it a bit awkward since he is profiled in the book.

I am also deeply grateful to the following people who contributed significantly to the completion of this book: Dr. Alan Cairns, our minister and friend, realized the potential of this manuscript and recommended it to his publisher. He has given invaluable encouragement and direction during the writing and publishing. Dr. Dan Hurst, my writing professor in college, allowed me to work on a chapter of this book for a class project. My father had recently died, and I was overwhelmed by the thought of this book. I didn't know where to begin. His kindness and encouragement came at a crucial time in my life. Malcon Bechelani, our family's personal computer technician (he volunteers for this thankless task), cheerfully rescued this manuscript from several computer black holes. Many times he went far beyond the call of duty when I needed help.

I would also like to thank Bob Jones University Press. Several of these biographies appeared in abbreviated form in the *Science for Christian Schools* Series and in *Faith for the Family*. Information taken from these publications is used with permission of Bob Jones University Press, Greenville, South Carolina.

I am sincerely grateful to Rebecca Moore who patiently and skillfully edited the manuscript. And I heartily thank the staff at Ambassador-Emerald for their work, especially Samuel Lowry, whose generosity made this publication possible.

The fact that this work has made it to publication is a tremendous testimony to God's grace. Many obstacles came up over the years, and it became abundantly evident that the Lord brought this to completion, not us. May God be pleased to use this book for His glory to encourage others in their Christian walk.

Johannes Kepler (1571-1630)

JOHANNES KEPLER
(1571-1630)

The Father of Modern Astronomy
The Father of Modern Optics

Knowest thou the ordinances [laws] of heaven?
Canst thou set the dominion thereof in the earth?
Job 38:33

Johannes Kepler held his mother's hand as they walked through the dark streets of the village. When they reached the top of a hill outside the village gate, Frau Kepler pointed to the sky and showed her six-year-old son the Great Comet of 1577. That giant dagger of light in the night sky made a deep impression on his young mind.

A few years later, his father woke him up one night to show him an eclipse of the moon. By the time Johannes had put on his coat and had gone outside, a chunk of the moon was already missing. The eclipse progressed slowly, lasting several hours. He shivered in the night air, watching as the moon slipped quietly into the earth's shadow. He stood fascinated as the lunar disk darkened and took on an eerie coppery tinge. "Why does the moon change colors during an eclipse?" he wondered.

He listened as his parents talked to several of the neighbors. They were trying to figure out what this eclipse meant. It was a bad omen, they decided. Maybe a plague was coming. Or perhaps a war, they said. But Johannes wasn't interested in what it meant. He wanted to understand how it happened. As he stood there watching the shadow slowly leave the moon's surface, he made up his mind to learn more about the heavens.

And learn more he did. Johannes Kepler became the celebrated German astronomer who is best known for his three laws describing the motions of the planets around the sun. These famous laws of planetary motion laid the foundation for calculating orbits for satellites and mapping routes for space travel. Sir Isaac Newton once commented, "If I have seen further, it is by standing on the shoulders of giants."[1] One of these giants was Johannes Kepler.

An unhappy childhood

Johannes Kepler was born in 1571 in the picturesque German village of Weil, located near the edge of the Black Forest. He was the first-born child in a very unhappy marriage. His father, Heinrich, who never studied or learned a trade, was vicious, immoral, and unkind to his family. He was a professional soldier and was away from home most of the time. He finally abandoned his family completely. Katharina, Johannes's mother, was gossipy, quarrelsome, and unpleasant. She often left her children and traveled with her husband because she couldn't bear to stay at home with her mother-in-law. Johannes and his three siblings were left with the Kepler grandparents and the dozen or so aunts and uncles in a small cottage. The family was loud, quarrelsome, and unhappy.

Johannes was born prematurely and was always frail and sickly. He contracted smallpox when he was four and almost died. The illness crippled his hands and left him nearsighted and suffering from multiple vision in one eye. It is ironic that he should become one of the great leaders in the field of astronomy—a calling in which good vision plays such an important role.

The Kepler family was one of the oldest Protestant families in the village. But even Johannes's grandfather, Sebald Kepler, who served as mayor of Weil, was unable to establish a Protestant church there. The Kepler family and other Protestant townspeople had to attend services in one of the nearby villages while their Catholic neighbors attended the lovely Gothic church with the three steeples. Although the Keplers were zealous about their Lutheran religion, they were unsympathetic to the frail, sickly Johannes and treated him harshly.

In his loneliness and unhappiness, Johannes found a Friend in heaven because he didn't have one on earth. He later said that it was only by leaning on God's power that he was able to come through such a maze of unpleasant experiences with an attitude of humble acceptance and thanksgiving. On the other hand, his brother Heinrich, who had had the same negative influences in his upbringing, turned out to be a completely unstable character—according to some accounts, he was a psychopath.

A brilliant scholar

At the age of seven Johannes entered the Latin school at Leonberg. Latin was stressed in those days because it was the international language of scholars. Here Johannes learned to read, write, and speak Latin fluently. He welcomed the distraction of school because it took his mind off his unhappiness at home.

Johannes's brilliance was soon obvious, but family finances forced him to leave school for several months at a time to work on a farm. As a result, it took him five years to complete the three-year course of study. His teachers had noticed his outstanding work and Christian testimony, and when he finished at the Latin school, they encouraged him to go on and study for the ministry.

He passed the entrance examinations and began his studies at the Lutheran lower seminary of Adelberg when he was thirteen. Here he endured a rigid schedule of study, beginning with psalm singing at four or five o'clock in the morning (depending on the season) and continuing through the day with Latin, Greek, rhetoric, grammar, logic, music, and Bible study. The young scholars wore long sleeveless coats and conversed with each other in Latin. Kepler completed the two-year curriculum and moved on to the higher seminary of Maulbronn, where he received his bachelor's degree when he was seventeen.

The Great Comet of 1577 sparked within Kepler the desire to learn more about the heavens.

During his seminary years, he memorized several of the long psalms and other large portions of Scripture. Whenever he had a moment to reflect, he pondered controversial theological questions. He often saw merit on the other side. His classmates and teachers criticized him because he was sympathetic toward the Calvinists, a group that the Lutherans opposed as strongly as they opposed the Roman Catholics. His sympathy with the Calvinists brought him trouble throughout his life. The Lutherans always viewed him suspiciously because he could not wholeheartedly agree with all their doctrine, yet he never thought of separating from them. He always thought of himself first of all as a Christian and then as a Lutheran. "I tie myself to all simple Christians," he said, "whatever they are called, with the Christian bond of love."[2]

As a teenager Johannes was prone to outbursts of temper, and he often suffered the consequences for his lack of self-control when he spoke. He had a brilliant mathematical mind, but he wasn't good at sticking to a task because his mind was constantly interrupted by new ideas and new goals. He was plagued by poor health and had to follow a careful diet, or his stomach and gall bladder trouble would flare up. His frequent headaches and mysterious fevers and rashes often interrupted his studies.

As a student at the Stift—the seminary connected with the University of Tübingen, Johannes was required to take two years of liberal arts studies. Here he studied mathematics and astronomy under Michael Maestlin, a fellow Christian who became a major source of inspiration for Kepler's work. Maestlin still taught the old geocentric (earth-centered) theory of the solar system that had been popularized by Ptolemy's *Almagest.* The newer theory of Copernicus (sun-centered) was still banned by the theological men at the university because it seemed contrary to Scripture. It is hard to appreciate just how radical the Copernican theory appeared at first. Maestlin couldn't teach it publicly, but privately he exposed his students to the ideas of Copernicus in a way that kindled their imagination. When Maestlin saw how interested Johannes was in this new theory, he lent him his own copy of Copernicus's book. Johannes instinctively preferred the ideas of Copernicus; he was not satisfied with the earth-centered theory because he felt it was "clumsy."

"Something special may be expected of him"

Kepler's first two years at the Stift had been covered by a scholarship that included all expenses plus a generous stipend. At the end of this time he took a cumulative examination in which he scored second out of fourteen candidates. The university senate decided to continue his scholarship with these words of commendation: "Because the above-mentioned Kepler has such a superior and magnificent mind that something special may be expected of him, we wish, on our part, to continue to that Kepler his stipend, as he requests, also because of his special learning and ability."[3] This assessment of his capabilities was certainly prophetic.

A surprise offer

When he graduated from the School of Arts at Tübingen in 1591 (the equivalent of our master's degree), he felt certain that he was destined for the Lutheran ministry. With that in mind, he enrolled at the Theological Seminary and continued his advanced studies.

However, in 1594, before he was able to complete his final examinations, an unexpected opportunity arose. The death of the mathematics and astronomy teacher at the Protestant seminary in Graz (the capital of the Austrian province of Styria) had created a vacancy that was most difficult to fill. The senate of the University of Tübingen immediately recommended Kepler because of his extraordinary mathematical ability.

This offer took the young divinity student completely by surprise. He had been most successful in his theological studies and felt assured of a good position in the Lutheran Church. Now came the prospect of an appointment of lower esteem and considerably less pay in faraway Austria.

It was a difficult decision that required much thought and prayer. On the one hand he had a great talent for the subjects he was asked to teach, and he was aware of his innate abilities in these areas. On the other hand, he had a high regard for theology and the ministry and was reluctant to cast aside so many years of study when his work was so near completion. He finally decided to accept the position with the understanding that he could return to Tübingen to finish his studies at some later date.

But, as it turned out, he never did. Looking back later in life, he was able to see clearly the Lord's leading in this decision. It was an important turning point, not only in his own life but also in the history of astronomy.

Teaching at Graz

In Graz, Kepler was lonely. He had come from a prestigious university where he was surrounded by professors and friends who appreciated his brilliance and could converse with him and exchange ideas. Now he found himself in a much narrower intellectual world. To satisfy his hunger for scientific dialogue, he began associating with other scientists by letter.

At this time, before scientific journals, scientists exchanged their ideas through correspondence. At first Kepler wrote mainly to his beloved professor, Maestlin; but later he corresponded with many prominent scientists, sharing his wealth of original ideas. One letter to Galileo says, "There will certainly be no lack of human pioneers when we have mastered the art of flight. In the meantime, we shall prepare for the brave sky-travelers maps of the celestial bodies."[4]

In addition to his classroom duties, Kepler's appointment included the responsibilities of district mathematician. This involved the annual chore of drawing up the calendar for the upcoming year. The calendar included weather forecasts, eclipses, sowing and harvesting prospects, and other assorted predictions. It probably resembled our *Farmer's Almanac*. In all, he produced a total of six calendars while in Graz, covering the period from 1595 to 1600.

Kepler's views on astrology

Kepler was not the avid follower of conventional astrology that some of today's popularizing writers would have people believe. He was not a seer in any sense of the word, and he cautioned against making decisions based on astrological predictions.[5]

He did believe that the heavens imprinted a certain character on a person.[6] It was the standard explanation in those days for differences in personality: people thought that the position of the heavenly bodies at the time of birth determined personality traits.

Kepler undoubtedly would have regarded as so much unenlightened nonsense the brand of astrology perpetrated today by the syndicated horoscope writers, who believe that the fate of men is determined and ruled by the heavenly bodies.[7] Kepler was opposed to all superstitious and occult uses of astrology. Even then he thought there was much trash in the science of astrology and a lot of it should be thrown out.

He believed, however, that celestial bodies exerted a more subtle influence on the earth's affairs. He explained how the moon's attraction caused the tides on the earth, but his explanation was opposed at first by other astronomers, even Galileo. For many years Kepler kept a weather journal, trying to determine how the heavenly bodies influenced the weather. It seems a bit tedious to establish a relationship between the weather and the position of the stars and planets. But at this point in history, not even the motions of the heavenly bodies were understood, much less their possible influence on the earth and its inhabitants. There was still ample room for speculation.

A new model of the solar system

At Graz, Kepler produced his first serious scientific treatise—an ambitious geometric description of the solar system. He was standing in front of his classroom sketching a figure on the blackboard when the idea for this geometric design hit him. He eagerly pursued his new and unorthodox ideas and came up with a geometric model of the solar system based on the heliocentric theory of Copernicus. What he produced was a strange combination of inscribed spheres and polyhedrons. As is frequently the case in the creative arts and sciences, the early efforts, even of the most gifted, leave something to be desired. The model did not accurately fit the measured planetary distances of the day; but the idea caught the fancy of his old astronomy teacher, Maestlin, who helped him get it published.

The book, called *Mysterium Cosmographicum* (The Mystery of the Universe), was well received. Kepler shrewdly placed it in the hands of several leading astronomers (including Galileo and Tycho Brahe), and his name became known in the important scientific centers of Europe.

The scientific historians note with interest that, throughout the pages of this book, Kepler poses some very valid and penetrating questions that had apparently never been asked before. These questions guided his thinking for the rest of his life.

Kepler wanted to include a chapter showing how the sun-centered theory of Copernicus did in fact harmonize with Scripture. The Tübingen administrators, though, felt that the issue was still too explosive, and they dissuaded him from including the chapter in his book. But he included it in his later writings.

Marriage

The same year *Mystery* appeared in print, Kepler married a young widow of twenty-three named Barbara Müller. She was the oldest daughter of a wealthy mill owner. Herr Müller opposed the marriage because he thought a lowly schoolteacher would not be able to provide for his daughter; he had no appreciation for scholars and thought only about money.

Unfortunately, Frau Barbara never understood the importance of Kepler's work or appreciated his genius. She took offense when people called them Mr. and Mrs. Stargazer. Kepler couldn't understand why she didn't just laugh it off as he did. In all fairness to her, it was hard being married to a great man who was absorbed in his studies. They suffered many things together—financial pressures, poor health, bouts of depression, and the deaths of three of their five children.

Kepler was thrilled when his first son, Heinrich, was born the year after his marriage. But the happiness did not last long; the baby died after two months. The next year little Susanna came into their family, but she lived only a month. Both children died of cerebral meningitis. Without children of his own, Kepler became very attached to his seven-year-old stepdaughter, Regina.

Religious persecution

Late in 1596, a few months before Kepler's marriage, Archduke Ferdinand of Hapsburg assumed the rule in Styria. He was a young, energetic disciple of the Catholic Jesuits. He quickly passed new laws that oppressed the Protestants.

The Archduke regarded the Lutherans as heretics, and after conferring with the Pope in 1598, he vowed to banish Lutheranism from his district. He banned the singing of hymns and the use of Lutheran Bibles and other "heretical" literature. He ordered all babies to be baptized as Catholics, and all weddings and burials had to be performed by the Catholic clergy. When Kepler's little daughter Susanna died, he had to pay a fine because he evaded the Catholic clergy for her burial.

The Archduke closed Kepler's school and expelled the Protestant clergy from the district. Then his persecution moved to the citizens. He gave non-Catholic citizens the choice of converting to Catholicism or leaving the district. However, leaving the district meant losing one's property. Many were tempted to remain and become proselytes. Kepler's own father-in-law, Herr Müller, whose life had been devoted to acquiring material possessions, turned Catholic rather than leave his wealth.

Frau Barbara hoped to inherit her father's property, and she certainly didn't want to leave her family. Herr Müller was the guardian for little Regina, and he told Kepler that Regina would stay if they left the district. Kepler worried, though, that she would be brought up Catholic if he left her with her grandfather.

Even though his wife's family had turned Catholic, Kepler refused to give in. In July of 1600 more than a thousand residents of Graz were called individually before the town magistrate for interrogation about their faith. The Archduke himself attended these sessions, and most of those called were intimidated into submission. Kepler was among a small group of sixty-one individuals who chose to exile themselves and retain their religious freedom. He was given forty-five days to evacuate his family and was forced to pay a tax on all his belongings.

His true character is evidenced during this distressing period. He was surrounded by troubles of his own—financial difficulties, anxiety about his future employment, and the problem of where and how to move his family—but he still found time to offer consolation and encouragement to others. At considerable personal risk he wrote and distributed letters among his fellow believers, consoling them and strengthening them in the faith.[8]

A providential invitation

Earlier the same year Kepler had accepted an invitation to visit Tycho Brahe in Prague. Recognized as the world's leading astronomer, Tycho (as he is called) had for twenty years made remarkably accurate observations of the positions of the planets. Now someone needed to make sense out of the massive columns of figures he had assembled. Kepler longed to have access to these observations, and Tycho was eager to add a theoretician of Kepler's caliber to his staff of assistants.

Fortunately, as imperial mathematician to Rudolph II (emperor of Bohemia and several neighboring countries), Tycho had been given free rein in choosing his collaborators. Tycho persuaded Kepler to come work for him, and Kepler was relieved to have a place to go. He packed his household goods in two wagons and moved to Prague with his wife and stepdaughter. At the last minute, much to Kepler's relief, Herr Müller did not object to letting Regina go.

Collaboration with Tycho Brahe

Now Kepler could begin the great work of deciphering Tycho's data. Although the invention of the telescope was still nine years away, Tycho had measured planetary positions to an accuracy of two minutes of arc (about 1/15 the moon's diameter) using instruments of his own design. The exactness of these measurements and their continuity over so many years played a crucial role in the development of the laws of planetary motion.

Kepler knew that these observations contained the material to build a new structure for astronomy. Tycho had the raw material, and even the workers; but he lacked an architect to use it all according to a plan. Kepler believed that he was the architect. He was convinced that God had controlled all the events to bring him and Tycho together. "If God is concerned with astronomy, which piety desires to believe," he told a friend, "then I hope that I shall achieve something in this domain, for I see how God let me be bound with Tycho through an unalterable fate and did not let me be separated from him by the most oppressive hardships."[9]

But the relationship between the two men was not always peaceful. They were opposites in every way. Tycho was an overweight, overbearing nobleman with a magnificent salary. Kepler was a wiry, intense man from an undistinguished family, always one step from poverty. The one similarity between the two men was their love for mathematical precision.

Inevitably, there were disagreements and quarrels. Tycho was stingy with his observations and never let Kepler see more than the data that he needed at the moment. Kepler felt that Tycho guarded his observations too selfishly. Why not exchange his data with other astronomers in the interest of furthering science?

Kepler's temper and Tycho's arrogance made an explosive combination. When the first quarrel occurred between the two men, Tycho was not content with Kepler's verbal apology; he wanted a written one! After these quarrels, it was invariably Kepler who begged forgiveness and effected a reconciliation. But, on the whole, there was good will on both sides. Tycho recognized Kepler's brilliance and extraordinary talent, and Kepler never forgot that Tycho had befriended him and generously took him in when he had been expelled from Graz.

There was, however, one conflict between the two that was never resolved—their opposing views on the heliocentric theory of Copernicus. Kepler endorsed it. But Tycho attempted to devise a compromise system combining the best of Ptolemy with the best of Copernicus. Convinced that the earth was too massive to move, he reasoned that the sun and moon revolved around the earth but the other planets orbited the sun. This scheme, called the Tychonian (or Tychonic) system, betrayed a faulty understanding of the sun's gravitational influence on the planets. Since the time of Newton, it has not received any serious scientific recognition.

When they first met in 1600, Tycho was fifty-three; Kepler, twenty-eight. One might expect that they were destined to spend many years studying the heavens together. They were not. Tycho's sudden and unexpected death from a bladder ailment in 1601 cut the length of their association to a brief eighteen months. Since Kepler was sick with a fever for many months when he first arrived in Praque and since he traveled for a portion of this time, their actual time of contact was very short.

Before the funeral had even taken place, Kepler received word from the emperor that he had been appointed to succeed Tycho as imperial mathematician. With mixed emotions he gave thanks to God for this honor but still retained his characteristic humility. In a letter to Maestlin he wrote, "I scorn with secret pride all honors and offices and, in addition, if it is necessary, also those things which they bestow. I count as the only honor the fact that by divine decree I have been put near the Tychonic observations."[10]

Kepler's productive years in Prague

In Prague Kepler found a climate of religious tolerance and intellectual stimulation. Rudolph II, a zealous patron of the arts and sciences, had surrounded himself with an impressive array of artisans and learned men. When he invited scholars and artists to his court, he didn't care about their religious beliefs. Rudolph was a bit eccentric and neglected his political duties to engage in his hobbies. He spent colossal sums of money collecting artwork and treasures and stocking his gardens with exotic animals; yet he never had enough money to pay the intellectuals he employed at his court.

Within this circle of outstanding minds drawn from all over Europe, Kepler enjoyed scholarly friendships. The majority of these men were Catholics, but there was a greater spirit of toleration here in Prague. They rejected Kepler's theological views but held him in great esteem and affection.

Court life, though, did not enchant Kepler. Social prestige and political power held little attraction for him—he thought it was distracting. He wanted only to carry on his work in peace and quiet. Kepler learned how to move in tricky political situations with astute diplomatic skill. He was fairminded and tolerant and had a good sense of humor. He found that "humor is by far the best seasoning of any debate."[11]

The favorable atmosphere of Rudolph's court contributed to Kepler's productivity during his years in Prague. These are considered to be his most creative years—from 1601 until the death of the emperor in 1612. These were also happier days in Kepler's household. Three more children were born, and they all survived infancy—another daughter also named Susanna, and two sons, Friedrich and Ludwig.

The condition of astronomy in Kepler's day

It is difficult for those who live in the Space Age to picture the sorry condition in which Kepler found astronomy. The ancients had piled error on error, and a large body of misinformation had been handed down through the Middle Ages. The basic framework of Ptolemy's geocentric theory had gone unchallenged until the Renaissance. Finally, in 1543, Copernicus stunned the world with *De Revolutionibus*, the book describing his radical new scheme to simplify calculations of the heavenly motions by placing the sun at the center.

But even though this first modern effort at a heliocentric theory did represent a major breakthrough, it still retained some of the old misconceptions. Copernicus pictured the planets as moving at a constant speed in circular orbits. Traditionally men believed that everything in the celestial realm partakes of divine perfection. The circle, considered to be the most perfect geometric figure, was thought to be the only allowable shape for an orbit. Now Kepler, using the greatly increased accuracy of the Tychonic data, discovered that the orbits are actually not circular in shape and that the planets do not travel at a constant speed.

The first two laws of planetary motion

Kepler's first two laws addressed the shape of the planets' orbits and the speed of the planets. These two laws, conceived between 1601 and 1606, were published in 1609 in his *New Astronomy*. The work behind these laws was tedious and time consuming.

When Kepler arrived in Prague, Tycho had assigned him the task of interpreting the observations on the planet Mars. Tycho's senior assistant, Longomontanus, had failed in this effort, and the responsibility now fell to the refugee from Graz, who was more capable and more dedicated.

It was providential that this particular planet was chosen, since its orbit deviates noticeably from a circle. Again he gave God the credit: "I believe it was an act of Divine Providence that I arrived just at the time when Longomontanus was occupied with Mars. For Mars alone enables us to penetrate the secrets of astronomy which otherwise would remain forever hidden from us."[12]

Kepler tackled Mars, predicting in his youthful optimism that he could finish his interpretation in eight days. But he underestimated the difficult calculations involved. It actually took him closer to eight years. After filling nine hundred pages with cumbersome calculations, he was prepared to announce his celebrated law of areas: *An imaginary line from the center of the sun to the center of a planet always sweeps over an equal area in equal time.* This relationship is known as Kepler's second law, although chronologically it preceded the first law. It has a surprisingly wide range of applicability, holding true in principle for artificial satellites revolving about the earth and even for asteroids and comets orbiting the sun.

Up to this time the exact shape of the planet orbits had eluded him. Despite his best efforts, he was unable to fit Tycho's data on Mars into a circular orbit. It worked only in a crude sort of way. At some points there were discrepancies of as much as eight minutes of arc (about 1/4 the moon's diameter). Yet the Tychonic observations were known to have a maximum of only *two minutes* of error.

Kepler now doubted the time-honored dogma of circular orbits. He recalculated using an egg-shaped orbit. Failure again. (The egg-shaped digression took up a year of his life.) But he didn't give up. He displayed remarkable patience and mental stamina.

Finally he hit upon the idea of an elliptical (oval) orbit. After several more months of painstaking calculations, he at long last obtained detailed agreement at all points along the orbit. Triumphantly he wrote his well-known "first law": *Planets move in ellipses with the sun at one focus.* With this great innovation he was able to do away with the epicycles (circles upon circles) that had plagued all previous systems, including, even, that of Copernicus!

The effort involved in formulating these two laws is revealed in a letter he wrote to a fellow astronomer: "I have spent so much pains on it that I could have died ten times. But with God's help I have held out and have come so far that I can be satisfied with my discovery and rest assured."[13]

Kepler had shown that the motions of the planets are precise, predictable, and obedient to definite rules. He was well ahead of his time. He had no rivals who claimed to have anticipated him. In fact, to the other astronomers of his day, the area and ellipse laws were new, unorthodox, and baffling.

Even Galileo preferred to adhere to the old circular orbits. But Kepler's great Italian contemporary was busy making other advances in astronomy. In 1609, the same year Kepler's *New Astronomy* appeared in print, Galileo constructed an astronomical telescope and became the first man to verify the truth of the Biblical statement that "the host of heaven cannot be numbered."[14] He was amazed when he scrutinized the vast expanse of the Milky Way and saw that the stars were indeed innumerable—as the grains of sand upon the seashore.[15] With this telescope Galileo quickly made other discoveries—the four largest moons of Jupiter, the phases of Venus, and the craters and mountains of the moon.

The Father of Modern Optics

Intrigued by the telescope and its possibilities, Kepler took a renewed interest in the field of optics. Several years earlier he had written a highly original treatise entitled *Astronomia Pars Optica*, which included a discussion of the inverse square law for light intensity, the use of a pinhole arrangement for viewing solar eclipses, and an explanation of why lenses can correct nearsightedness and farsightedness. Spectacles had been used for several centuries, but no one knew why they worked until Kepler explained it. In this treatise, Kepler was the first one to explain the process of vision that involves an upside-down image striking the retina.

Kepler imagined he was making celestial maps for brave sky travelers.

Then, in 1610, came a more advanced work, *Dioptrice*, in which he analyzed various combinations of lenses and their application to optical instruments. These two superb works have justly earned him the title of the "Father of Modern Optics." He was thus the founder of two new sciences—physical astronomy and instrumental optics—a truly astounding feat.

Financial trouble

Working for Rudolph II should have been the end of Kepler's financial difficulties. On paper his salary was adequate; but the emperor was notoriously slow in paying salaries. Kepler never received his entire salary, and he was always forced to beg for what was due him. But the worst part of having low funds was that he couldn't afford a regular assistant. He lost a lot of time in the routine mathematical calculations he had to do. "Sometimes an arithmetic mistake, made in a hurry, holds me back for a long time," he moaned.[16] It would have been ideal to have an assistant who could free him from the drudgery of the voluminous calculations. But only for short periods could he afford that luxury.

Family tragedy

The year 1611 brought great tragedy to the Kepler household. The soldiers who were fighting in the city brought sicknesses with them. Early in the year, all three of the Kepler children came down with smallpox. The oldest and the youngest recovered; but the favorite child, six-year-old Friedrich, died. He had shown great promise and talents and the parents were heartbroken.

Soon afterward an epidemic of Hungarian spotted typhus swept through the city of Prague. Frau Barbara could not be kept from visiting the sick, and she contracted the fatal disease herself. She had already been in poor health for several years, and now this sickness caused epilepsy and affected her mind. It was very disturbing for Kepler to see her suffer so much. She was weakened by her sadness over her son's death, and she soon passed away.

During this time of severe grief Kepler was sustained by trusting the promises of Scripture. The passage beginning with Romans 8:26 proved to be particularly precious to him. He comforted himself thinking how much better the Shepherd of their souls was caring for his loved ones in heaven.

A few years later, Kepler's sister wrote that his mother had been accused of practicing witchcraft. When he got this news, he felt that his heart would burst. He knew that she would be put to death either by hanging or by being burned at the stake. That year, six women had been sentenced to death as witches in her town. At this time in Germany, witch hunting was bordering on hysteria.

It all started as a quarrel between two old women. Frau Kepler offended an old friend, and she retaliated by saying that Frau Kepler made her sick with an herbal drink. The townspeople added their own fabrications, and soon it mushroomed into a full-blown witch trial. Somehow she was responsible for the death of children in the town, the sickness and death of livestock, the schoolteacher's lameness (although he had fallen and then was crippled), and various pains that the townspeople felt when she walked by. She had been raised by a relative who was a witch, and the townspeople held this against her.

Kepler left his work for a whole year and traveled to Württemberg to defend his mother against this "old female babble." Frau Kepler spent a year in chains while Kepler, with some legal assistance, wrote briefs in his own hand.

Frau Kepler refused to be intimidated into a confession. Even when they brought her into the torture room, telling her that she would be hung if she did not confess her sins of witchcraft, she insisted that she was innocent. She fell on her knees, calling God as her witness that she had done no wrong. After this dramatic scene, the officials declared her innocent.

Her son had saved her from certain death by hanging, and his stubborn loyalty throughout the ordeal was touching. But Frau Kepler didn't have much time to enjoy her freedom; she died six months later.[17]

Teaching at Linz

To further aggravate matters, Rudolph II had been deposed and Kepler was soon forced to seek employment elsewhere. He chose a position as district mathematician and teacher at Linz, located in Upper Austria on the Danube River. It was similar to his earlier appointment at Graz. Again he had the opportunity to influence young people "with admiration for the works of God and to ignite them with love for God, their Creator."[18] It had been his long-standing conviction that the primary goal of science should be to lead men to God.[19]

Why study nature?

The lack of religious peace in his homeland greatly disturbed Kepler. He prayed for God to grant peace in his country so that men would leave fighting and spend their energies studying the arts and sciences, to "learn the praise of God their Creator from these arts."[20]

To anyone who questioned the usefulness of studying astronomy, Kepler gave this answer: He reminded him that the Apostle Paul presented God to the heathens by showing them the Book of Nature. And King David received the ideas for his songs when he admired the skies: "The heavens declare the glory of God." To Kepler the study of nature is a valuable tool for elevating worship of God. "Our worship is all the more deep," Kepler insists, "the more clearly we recognize the creation and its greatness."[21]

Marriage again

At the age of 42, Kepler remarried. When he decided that he would marry again, he considered eleven candidates! His own hesitation and uncertainty frustrated him. Which one should he choose? He finally came back to the fifth lady he had considered. His new bride was Susanna Reuttinger, a twenty-four-year-old orphan whose father had been a cabinetmaker. She had no wealth or social position, but she had the simple virtues that Kepler was looking for.

This marriage was happier than the first. She suited Kepler well and made a peaceful home for him where he could complete his work undisturbed. Money problems did not worry her because she came from a humble background. She also loved the stepchildren, Susanna, eleven, and Ludwig, six. This new union was blessed with seven children, but five died at an early age.[22]

Kepler tried to give his children a thoroughly Christian upbringing, and he held regular family prayers. Once he wrote a tract for his family called "A Lesson from the Holy Sacrament of the Body and Blood of Jesus Christ Our Saviour." It was a sort of catechism, divided into questions and answers. He had his children memorize the answers, hoping that through this "the power of the Holy Ghost would be more fruitful in continuing right true Christianity with them." A copy of this tract is still preserved in the library at the University of Tübingen.[23]

Third law of planetary motion

In the context of severe family trials and political unrest, Kepler devised his third law of planetary motion. His mother's ordeal was dragging on, and his daughter Katharina died shortly before her first birthday. He was so upset that he put aside his work on the astronomical tables that he was compiling because he couldn't concentrate on the complicated mathematics. Instead, he turned his mind to the thoughts that brought him comfort.

When he contemplated the harmony of the heavens, much like the harmony found in music and geometry, he felt solace and strength. He had been mulling this over for almost twenty years—looking for the order that he believed God had established when He created the world. Twenty years earlier when he was grieving over the death of his first daughter, he had first found solace in his contemplations about harmony in creation.

Out of these thoughts grew a major work called *World Harmony*. Here he announced his third law of planetary motion. As with the first two laws, countless computations were required. He had for some time been looking for a relationship between the periods of the planets (the time required to complete one trip around the sun) and their distances from the sun. It was clear that the greater the distance from the sun, the greater the period. But was there an exact mathematical function that related them?

On May 15, 1618, it came to him in a flash: *The squares of the periods of revolution are to each other as the cubes of the mean distances from the sun.* He felt exuberant and fancied that he had been given a morsel of heavenly knowledge that had, up until now, been denied to man. "I feel carried away and possessed by an unutterable rapture over the divine spectacle of the heavenly harmony."[24]

While this law may be difficult for lay people to comprehend, it is extremely important, because it formed a foundation for Newton's law of gravitation, which was to come half a century later.[25] (Kepler clearly anticipated this law when he postulated a force that the sun exerted on the planets.) In Newton's writings, he readily acknowledged Kepler's contribution: "And the same year I began to think of gravity extending to the orb of the Moon, and . . . from Kepler's Rule [Third Law] . . . I deduced that the forces which keep the Planets in their orbs must [be] reciprocally as the squares of their distances from the centers about which they revolve."[26] Newton stood on Kepler's shoulders and saw further.

Hobbies

As a diversion from his usual pursuits, the versatile astronomer enjoyed studying Biblical chronology. By comparing and correlating ancient records, he determined that the actual birth of Christ was several years earlier than had been thought—probably around 4 or 5 B.C. This view, that the present numbering system had been erroneously calibrated when it was instituted in the sixth century A.D., is almost universally accepted today. He also made a detailed analysis of the chronology of Christ's public ministry. His Old Testament studies led him to place the date of the Creation at 4977 B.C., almost a whole millennium earlier than the date calculated by Archbishop Ussher.

He also exposed the fallacies of secret groups and superstitious teachings: he opposed Rosicrucianism, theosophy, numerology, and other pseudoscientific cults of his day.[27] He disagreed in principle with all secret organizations, believing that their teachings should be exposed to the light of day so that men could assess their true worth. His stature as a scientist and his Christian testimony lent authority to his tracts and other writings on these issues.

Textbook

Still another major work, *Epitome of Copernican Astronomy*, came from the Linz period of his life. This was a massive and erudite treatise in three volumes. (Kepler could never be concise. One of his colleagues complained that it took a lifetime to digest one of Kepler's major works.[28]) This work was a milestone in the history of science comparable to Ptolemy's *Almagest* or Copernicus's *De Revolutionibus*. Here was the first systematic exposition of astronomy recast in the new heliocentric framework with all the Keplerian refinements. But the title was misleading—perhaps he should have called it the "Epitome of Keplerian Astronomy."

Religious persecution

Once again religious persecution dogged him. The Counter Reformation, aimed at establishing Catholicism as the sole religion of the land, became more oppressive in Linz. It had even reached the point where a Jesuit priest reprimanded Kepler for holding family devotions and secretly instructing his children in doctrine. Defending his God-given responsibility in this matter, he replied simply, "I act as father of the family."[29]

Then for a time the Jesuits sealed up his personal library, and he was allowed to use only a few scientific books. This was a severe torture for him. He loved all his books, but he sorely missed his Greek Bible and his German Bible. The ban was lifted, though, after a few weeks when a Jesuit friend of his from another city intervened for him.

The situation became thoroughly unbearable when war broke out and Bavarian soldiers had to be quartered at his very house. They interrupted his work in the day and his sleep at night. But Kepler kept working; now more than ever he needed the consolation of his studies to cope with the stress around him.

The Lutheran peasants in the surrounding areas had revolted and attacked the city. Since Kepler had chosen a house just inside the moat on the city wall, he now found himself in the middle of intense fighting. The siege went on for more than two months. Eventually the ranks of the peasants became depleted, and imperial relief troops drove away those who remained. Meanwhile a fire had swept through Kepler's section of the city, and the printing house was destroyed. The first part of his book that had been printed was lost.

The Rudolphine Tables

The book was the long-overdue *Rudolphine Tables*. These were the astronomical tables begun by Tycho and commissioned (although never actually funded) by the now-deceased Rudolph II. Fortunately, the manuscript was not destroyed in the fire. Kepler was able to pick up the pieces and flee the city with his family and possessions in search of another printer. His quest took him to the city of Ulm in his native Germany, less than fifty miles from Tübingen.

At great personal expense he at last saw the printing of the *Tables* completed in 1627. This work had occupied him off and on for over twenty years. He likened it to carrying a fetus inside him for more than twenty years. And now as it neared completion, he said that the labor pains tormented him. For many months he had to go to the printer's house every day and supervise the typesetting.

Astronomers, astrologers, and mariners around the world warmly welcomed the *Tables*. It was the standard for the next hundred years. It furnished data for calculating the positions of the planets, moon, and sun for each day of the year. It also contained the newly devised Naperian logarithms, which Kepler incorporated because he saw how they would simplify astronomical calculations. Kepler had extended Tycho's original catalog of 777 star positions to 1005.

Later years

The remaining three years of his life were restless ones. After completing the printing at Ulm, he wandered in search of employment. He had flattering offers from England and Italy (including the chair vacated by Galileo at the University of Padua); but he was over fifty years old now and preferred to stay in his own culture. For a time he was employed as private mathematician to Wallenstein, the emperor's leading general; but this relationship dissolved when the general's military fortunes took a turn for the worse.

Providing for his growing family weighed heavily on Kepler. Another daughter had been born in 1630. How would he provide for his children and wife in this war-torn land? Where could they find a safe permanent home? His choices were limited: he could live in a city that had been destroyed or move to another one that was about to be destroyed. Everywhere he looked, his prospects seemed bleak.

All through his adult life he suffered because his employers never had money to pay him. The excuse was always that the war expenses ate up all the money in the treasuries. The emperor still owed him more than twelve thousand gulden for past services. (This represented many years of pay. His original salary in Rudolph's court had been five hundred gulden per year.) He also had been unable to collect the interest on some Austrian bonds he owned.

He decided to go in person to request the money that was owed him. He traveled by horseback in the rain and slush of winter. Shortly after arriving in Regensburg, he became ill with a severe fever and was confined to bed at the house of a friend. At first Kepler thought it was just another one of his frequent illnesses.

But it soon became obvious that he would die. When a pastor came to visit him and asked him what his hope for salvation was, Kepler answered confidently that his only refuge and consolation lay in the work of Jesus Christ. The physicians prescribed bleeding (a typical treatment of that time), and Kepler became worse, slipping into delirium. He died on November 15, 1630, shortly before his fifty-ninth birthday.

But his life's work had been completed. Already in his *World Harmony* he had expressed a sense of fulfillment and gratitude to the Lord for allowing him a generous measure of success. "See, I have now completed that work to which I was summoned. In doing so I have utilized all those powers of my mind which Thou hast loaned me. I have shown man the glory of Thy works, as much of their unending wealth as my feeble intellect was able to grasp. My mind has been ready to correct the path and be punctilious about true research. If I have let myself be led astray by the astounding beauty of Thy work and become audacious, or if I have found pleasure in my own fame among men because of the successful progress of my work, which is destined for Thy fame, forgive me in Thy kindness and mercy."[30]

Thinking God's thoughts

It is refreshing to study Kepler's God-centered approach to the science of the heavens because it represents such a complete contrast to the astronomy of today. He believed that a scientist who correctly studies God's world is thinking God's thoughts after Him. "Those laws are within the grasp of the human mind," Kepler said. "God wanted us to recognize them by creating us after his own image so that we could share in his thoughts. . . . Only fools fear that we make man godlike in doing so; for the divine counsels are impenetrable, but not his material creation."[31]

Kepler saw himself as an instrument in God's hands for revealing more of the details of His handiwork to men. "Since we astronomers are priests of the highest God in regard to the book of nature," he wrote, "it befits us to be thoughtful not of the glory of our minds but rather, above all else, of the glory of God."[32]

Kepler's name lives on in history. His name has been immortalized by his three laws of planetary motion, a prominent crater on the moon has been named in his honor, and his native Germany has paid him homage by erecting monuments in Regensburg and Weil der Stadt. Any fame he achieved, however, was simply a by-product of his efforts to glorify God's name. "Let also my name perish," he said, "if only the name of God, the Father . . . is thereby elevated."[33]

---

[1] Margaret Maria Gordon, *The Home Life of Sir David Brewster* (Edinburgh: Edmonston and Douglas, 1870), p. 299.

[2] Max Caspar, *Kepler* (London and New York: Abelard-Schuman, 1959), p. 218.

[3] Ibid., p. 44.

[4] John Hudson Tiner, *Johannes Kepler, Giant of Faith and Science* (Milford, Michigan: Mott Media, 1977), p. 152.

[5] Caspar, pp. 58-60.

[6] Kepler said "In what manner does the countenance of the sky at the moment of a man's birth determine his character? It acts on the person during his life in the manner of the loops which a peasant ties at random around the pumpkins in his field: they do not cause the pumpkin to grow, but they determine its shape. The same applies to the sky: it does not endow man with his habits, history, happiness, children, riches, or a wife, but it molds his condition. . . ." Arthur Koestler, *The Watershed: A Biography of Johannes Kepler* (Garden City, N.Y.: Anchor Books, Doubleday and Co., Inc., 1960), p. 42.

[7] Caspar, pp. 58, 95, 183-85, 204, 278-79, 329, 354. See also Koestler, pp. 90-91. See also: Gerard de Vaucouleurs, *Discovery of the Universe*, (New York: Macmillan, 1957), p. 53.

[8] Caspar, p. 113.

[9] Ibid., p. 123.

[10] Ibid., p. 159.

[11] Carola Baumgardt, *Johannes Kepler: Life and Letters* (New York: Philosophical Library, 1951), p. 83.

[12] Koestler, p. 124.

[13] Caspar, p. 170.

[14] Jeremiah 33:22.

[15] Genesis 22:17.

[16] Baumgardt, p. 139.

[17] Caspar, pp. 240-56.

[18] Ibid., pp. 219-20.

[19] Ibid., p. 374.

[20] Ibid., p. 306.

[21] Baumgardt, p. 33.

[22] His sons Fridmar and Hildebert died in a plague a few years after Kepler himself died.

[23] Caspar, p. 224.

[24] Ibid., p. 267.

[25] Kepler's three laws can be derived from Newton's second law of motion and Newton's law of gravitation. Newton's laws, formulated decades later, are more general and powerful.

[26] Arnold B. Arons, *Development of Concepts of Physics* (Reading, Mass: Addison-Wesley, 1965), pp. 297-98.

[27] Caspar, pp. 290-93.

[28] Koestler, p. 189.

[29] Caspar, p. 317.

[30] Ibid., p. 375.

[31] Baumgardt, p. 50.

[32] Caspar, p. 88.

[33] Ibid., p. 373.

Robert Boyle (1627-1691)

ROBERT BOYLE
(1627-1691)

The Father of Chemistry

For God giveth to a man that is good in his sight
wisdom, and knowledge, and joy.
Ecclesiastes 2:26

A steady rain fell as the elegant coach lumbered across the Irish countryside. The coach was transporting Robyn, the four-year-old son of the Earl of Cork, to a family gathering. Several servants riding horseback accompanied the coach as they traveled to Dublin. It had been raining for several days and the muddy roads slowed the party down. When they came to a swollen creek, the horses hesitated. The driver of the coach was impatient to be out of the chilly rain, and he urged his horses into the swift water. Midway across the creek, the coach bogged down. The driver muttered under his breath and got down into the chilly water to give the coach a push. After several heaves, he realized it wouldn't budge.

The other horsemen waited on the bank, watching the driver slosh unsteadily through the rushing water and come to stand on the bank beside them. The men had dismounted and were discussing how they would move the coach. Robyn was still in the coach with the young footboy who was in charge of him. The two boys squatted on the seat, trying to keep their feet dry as they watched the water seeping through the joints of the carriage.

The men decided to leave them in the coach until the water went down a bit. But one of the servants disagreed and said that he couldn't leave the boys in there alone. He mounted his horse and went upstream a little way. He plunged in, and the current dragged his horse swiftly downstream until he came alongside the stranded coach.

He peered into the carriage and instructed the boys to climb out through the window. He held Robyn in his arms and swung the other boy on the saddle behind him. Then he headed back toward the bank. As they struggled up onto the bank of the creek, they turned in time to see the capsized coach being swept downstream. The men on shore watched in horror as the horses were dragged downstream with the coach. Losing the coach was unfortunate, but losing the horses would be a tragedy. The horses, though, struggled violently and broke their harnesses. They swam to shore, frightened but safe, while the coach was swept downstream in the swift current.[1]

The Good Samaritan on horseback realized that he had just saved the life of young Robyn. But he had no idea what a service he had done for mankind and for the progress of science. For Robyn would grow up to become Robert Boyle, the "Father of Chemistry."

A legacy of wealth and intelligence

Robert Boyle was born in the province of Munster, Ireland, in 1627. He was the fourteenth in a family of fifteen children. His father, the Earl of Cork, was said to be the wealthiest man in all of Great Britain. The Earl professed to be a devout Christian, and he carefully attributed his great prosperity to the goodness and providence of God. Perhaps the Earl was truly a regenerate man, but his priorities in life were sadly mixed up. He used his influence as the Lord High Treasurer of Ireland in an industrious and perhaps unscrupulous way to amass his personal fortune.

He paid dearly for his love of money and discovered, as the Bible says, that those who would be rich pierce themselves through with many sorrows. His teenaged children, with few exceptions, earned the reputation of being wild and dissipated. The Earl thought that these excesses were just a normal part of growing up in a wealthy family, and he indulgently excused his children and paid their debts.

The Earl extended his influence by having his children marry into wealthy, influential families. But this meant that he never considered character when he contracted marriages for his children—he cared only about the wealth and status of the other family. As a result, the in-laws of the family were generally lazy and irresponsible, expecting their rich father-in-law to support them and bail them out of trouble.

Besides the wealth, influence, and good connections that the Boyle children inherited from the Earl, they all inherited his brains. The Earl had devoted his brilliance to building a fortune; but the children devoted this same brilliance to politics, military careers, writing, and intellectual pursuits. Robert's mother died of consumption when he was four years old, and he was always sorry that he had no memories of her. He felt that losing his mother at this early age was his greatest misfortune.

The custom of the day among the wealthy families was to send the infant boys away to be brought up in a peasant home. There the boy would have the advantage of fresh air and plain wholesome food. Ideally, he would grow up to be a stronger man than if his wealthy mother had pampered him. Robert defended this practice when he grew older and said that the genteel "used to breed their children so nice and tenderly, that a hot sun, or a good shower of rain, as much endangers them, as if they were made of butter, or of sugar."[2]

When he was a boy, Robert used to make fun of other boys who stuttered. He thought it was great fun to imitate them. But he imitated them so often, that stuttering became a habit for him. And it was not an easy habit to break. He finally learned to start each sentence slowly, and it seemed to others that he was a hesitant speaker. (Years later, he still spoke with the same deliberateness.)

During his early childhood, Robert was taught at home by tutors. At the age of eight he was sent to study at the fashionable Eton College with his older brother Francis. Here they learned more than academics—they learned the social graces that were so important to the seventeenth century aristocracy.

As sons of nobility, they were given special treatment. They sat at one of the head tables with the chaplain and were waited on by the less affluent students. They enjoyed more luxurious living quarters than the regular students and a generous allowance of spending money. The Boyles also had their own valet and tutor. In spite of his privileged status, young Robert managed to avoid arousing the envy of his peers. He was very popular with the students and teachers, even more so than his brother, who excelled in sports.

Robert was a brilliant scholar and would much rather study than play. He was so studious that he had to be forced to participate in sports. During his three years at Eton, Robert developed a great love for knowledge and began his lifelong habit of reading constantly. He always had a book with him and would read even while he was walking.

When Robert was eleven years old, the Earl removed his two sons from Eton after learning that things were not spiritually right at the school. It was a comfort to the aging Earl to have Robert around him again. Robert was his favorite son, the "Benjamin" of his father's old age. He made a good companion for the elderly man because he resembled his father most in character. It was a welcome relief to the Earl to have a son who was not constantly in trouble.

When the Earl placed the boys back in the hands of a private tutor, he selected a Frenchman of extraordinary qualifications for this assignment and arranged for the instruction to take place in Geneva, Switzerland. The curriculum included languages, rhetoric, mathematics, history, Bible, Calvinistic catechism, tennis, and fencing. Two chapters of the Old Testament were read and discussed after the noon meal, and two chapters of the New Testament were studied each evening. But even with this daily exposure to the Scripture and the godly example of his instructor, Robert still was not a Christian.

The day of judgment

One hot summer night in Geneva, when Robert was thirteen years old, he was awakened by a thunderstorm. The noise of the violent winds almost drowned out the thunderclaps, and the heavy showers of rain seemed to quench the lightning bolts. The flashes of lightning appeared to the frightened boy to be the very fire that God had sent to consume the world. *This must be the day of judgment!* he thought in a panic. Up to this point in his life, he had considered himself a "good" boy because he dutifully attended church and studied his Bible. He had a compliant temperament and found that obedience caused less trouble than rebellion. He figured that of all his family, he must be a Christian because he acted most like one and didn't cause trouble like his older brothers and sisters.

But at that moment, believing that the world was ending and he would be facing God's judgment, Robert realized that his religion was not genuine and his

Robert would read even while he was walking.

sins had never been forgiven. *I am totally unprepared to meet God*, he thought in horror. He sank to his knees beside his bed and made a solemn promise. "If you spare my life, O God, I promise that I will be a true Christian." He repented of his sins and resolved to accept Christ's payment for his sins. As the storm died down, he fell into an exhausted sleep.

In the morning, he looked out at the cloudless sky and remembered how afraid he had been in the night. He blushed at the thought that it had taken this fright to awaken him spiritually. But he had no desire to change his mind. In the sober light of the day, he renewed the vow he had made the night before. This was clearly the turning point in his life, and he never regretted this decision to follow Christ.

The year after his conversion he traveled with his tutor to Italy. On this trip, after the initial exuberance of coming to Christ, he fell into a deep depression. He convinced himself that Christ's forgiveness did not include him because he was too great a sinner. He took long walks by himself in the countryside and didn't tell anyone about his distress—not even his brother. There were times when Robert was so disturbed that he contemplated suicide to escape his misery. The only thing that kept him from that drastic step was his conviction that God firmly prohibited "self-dispatch."[3]

After many months of suffering, God restored to him the sense of His divine favor during a communion service. Robert was still prone to these occasional clouds of despair, and he used to say that this disease of his faith was much like a toothache; for though a toothache is not fatal, it is still very troublesome. But Robert believed that all things work together for good for those who love God, and he saw that these doubts and despair had driven him to study the fundamental doctrines of Christianity to see whether his belief was really grounded in truth. And from this study he gained a solid foundation for his faith. [4]

Even as a teenager, Robert wanted to serve God with his whole heart. Once when he was talking with a group of teenagers, one of them said, "Wouldn't it be grand if we could sin all our lives and know for sure that we would have leisure to repent on our deathbeds?" But Robert replied that he wouldn't like to have freedom to sin, even on those terms. He would hate to deprive himself of the satisfaction of serving God.[5]

Preserved by divine providence

As a young man Boyle counted some six instances when God had miraculously spared his life. Viewing these events in their proper perspective, he determined to live a life worthy of God's special providence.

His first narrow escape occurred when he was rescued from the stranded coach. As a young boy at Eton, he was twice almost brought to an early grave by accidents involving horses. On another occasion an entire wall collapsed on him while he was lying in bed, but he escaped without injury. His most frightening memories, though, centered on the times he was inadvertently given the wrong prescription. For the rest of his life, he feared physicians more than he feared disease. Boyle's interest in medicine dates back to these mishaps. He figured that if he studied medicine for himself, he wouldn't have to use doctors.

In his autobiography, he said that he "would not ascribe any of these rescues unto chance, but would be still industrious to perceive the hand of heaven in all these accidents." He was quick to recognize "so gracious and so peculiar a conduct of Providence" in his rescues.[6]

Returning to England

While Robert was studying abroad, his father died. He returned to England, a bewildered seventeen-year-old who had been away from home so long that he felt like a foreigner in his own country. By now he had been speaking and thinking in French for so long that he easily passed as a Frenchman. With both his parents dead and his older brothers off in Ireland fighting in a rebellion, Robert felt there was no place that he could call home. For several months he stayed with his older sister Katherine in London.

Katherine was thirteen years older than Robert and had always enjoyed mothering him. She had a special fondness for him, perhaps because they were so similar in temperament. She and Robert were not rebellious and extravagant like the other Boyle children. Besides her beauty and intelligence, Katherine was noted for her extraordinary memory. She could hear a sermon, then come home, and after dinner write the sermon verbatim.

She suffered in one of the worst marriages that her father had contracted. Her husband, Viscount Ranelagh, was described by a contemporary as "the foulest churl [a surly, ill-mannered person] in Christendom, whose best point was that he was nightly dead drunk and so probably not quarrelsome."[7] The Viscount died young and gave Lady Ranelagh many years of peaceful widowhood.

Lady Ranelagh's influence in society was a great asset to Robert. She introduced him to her friends who were intellectuals and scientists, and Robert became active in this learned group of men who called themselves "The Invisible College." ("Invisible" in the sense that they had no regular place to meet and no formal organization.) This group attracted Robert because they insisted that the study of science must not be a mere intellectual exercise to puff up their egos but that it must be useful to mankind. The older men were impressed by this serious teenager who had read so widely and displayed such an excellent grasp of scientific concepts.

Materially, Robert was well taken care of—he had inherited estates in both England and Ireland. But his father's financial affairs were in a muddle, and it was some months before Robert was able to claim what was rightfully his. Eventually he moved into the family manor called Stalbridge in Dorset, England.

At this time there was great religious and political turmoil from the civil war between King Charles and the Parliament. Robert found that living at his estate was a fortunate necessity because the location provided him protection from the unrest. He was lonely there, but he found diversion in his studies and his writing. As an independently wealthy aristocrat in his twenties with no family to support, he could afford to spend his time doing the things that interested him most—studying theology, dabbling in science, and writing.

From this period of his life came such works as *Style of the Scriptures, Ethics, Occasional Reflections, Some Motives and Incentives to the Love of God*, and a religious novel entitled *Martyrdom of Theodora and Didymus*. Most of his writing at this time was religious because he studied a subject for his own edification and then wrote about it. He intended these writings to be circulated just among his immediate circle of friends; but years later, after succumbing to pressure from his friends, he had several of them published.

Occasional Reflections was a series of meditations that Robert wrote after he determined to find a lesson of providence in everything that happened to him. He found many lessons from his observations of nature during his daily walks. He wrote these lessons down in short essays, initially for his own devotional aid. He lent these essays to his sister Katherine, and she passed them around to her friends. When she saw how well-received the meditations were, she persuaded him to publish them, and this book became very popular in Boyle's day.

A scientist emerges

Boyle's two great loves in life were theology and science. His love for theology began when he became a Christian, and for the rest of his life, he never tired of this subject. The first hint of his analytical tendency was his discovery of the fascinating world of math as a teenager. He enjoyed

Around the table, the Invisible College discussed "experimental philosophy."

extracting square roots and cube roots of large numbers or posing complicated algebra problems to work out in his head. (He used these mental math exercises to keep his mind occupied so it wouldn't wander into daydreams.)

His love for science began when he was a teenager traveling in Italy. While he was staying in Florence, the famed Galileo died in a town not far away. After hearing this sad news, Boyle decided to read his works. He taught himself to read Italian and eagerly studied Galileo's writings on the "new mechanics" and the heliocentric theory. Boyle chose to become a follower of "the great star-gazer" because his arguments made sense and because he had the courage to stand up to the authoritarianism of the day.

Later, Boyle's scientific inclinations were further stimulated when he listened to the discussions of the Invisible College. These scientists motivated Boyle to read all the standard scientific works. But it seems that it was Boyle's poor health that moved him to enter the field of chemistry. When he became ill, he took a great interest in recipes for remedies, and he collected these recipes all his life. At that time, there was no standardization in medicine, and each doctor was his own chemist, mixing up his own remedies.

Boyle was fascinated with these remedies and wanted to examine them chemically. When he was twenty-one, he set up a laboratory at his manor in Stalbridge. Installing chemical equipment was frustrating and expensive. He took great pains to buy a furnace in France and have it shipped to his home, only to have it delivered to him broken in pieces.

When he finally got his laboratory set up, it was stocked with a charcoal burner, a dependable balance, basic chemicals, and glass containers. As he progressed, he designed and constructed his own equipment. At this point, he was just an enthusiastic amateur repeating experiments that he had read about. But he developed a skillful, rapid technique in the laboratory and began recording his observations with precision.

When he was in his mid-twenties, he had to visit his estates in Ireland to take care of business. His stay stretched into two years, and he sorely missed his laboratory. Since it was impossible to get chemistry equipment where he was, he decided to study anatomy with his new friend, Dr. Petty—a brilliant physician who later became one of the founders of the Royal Society.

Boyle soon became proficient in animal dissections and found himself on the frontier of biological knowledge. He was thrilled to observe first-hand the intricate mechanism for blood circulation, and he wrote to a friend, "I have seen (especially in the dissections of fishes) more of the variety and contrivances of nature, and the majesty and wisdom of her Author, than all the books I ever read in my life could give me convincing notions of."[8]

Dr. Petty was just one of the many physicians who became Boyle's friends. Even though he mistrusted doctors because of what he had suffered from them, he enjoyed exchanging ideas and remedies with them and found their friendship stimulating. Boyle was well-read in medicine and perhaps even better prepared than the physicians of his day, because in his opinion, they had the disadvantage of being encumbered with a medical practice and the daily interruptions of patients; but Boyle was free to study and perform his experiments all day long.

Dr. Petty once told Boyle in good humor that Boyle suffered from three diseases. The first one was that Boyle read too much—twelve hours a day, according to Dr. Petty! The second disease was that he feared contracting the diseases that he studied about (an ailment, Dr. Petty said, that afflicts most people who study diseases). The third disease that Boyle suffered from was the tendency to self-medicate, especially with untried medicines.

Poor health

Boyle's tendency to self-medicate began when he was diagnosed with kidney stones at the age of twenty. He had never been a robust child and was prone to recurrent fevers and colds; but after the kidney ailment, he never enjoyed good health. He took care of his health with the same fastidious care that he employed in the laboratory and in managing his estates.

His friends teased him about the elaborate pains he took with his health—the different cloaks he would wear depending on the temperature and the concoctions he would drink. But those who teased him overlooked the fact that he had found a way to stay productive in spite of his weak constitution. He adopted a simple diet that seemed to help him more than any of the remedies he inflicted on himself. His rule was to eat only for nourishment and not for pleasure. He insisted on exercising even when he was very weak because he thought that staying in bed would make the pain unbearable. Pale and thin, Boyle lived with such fatigue and weakness that it is amazing that he could accomplish anything, let alone his astonishingly prolific writing and profuse experimenting.

Because of eye trouble that developed as he grew older, he couldn't read or observe for long periods and had to rely on laboratory assistants and secretaries. His secretary did more than just take dictation; he would also read out loud for Boyle. It disturbed Boyle that he couldn't proofread everything that he dictated, and he often felt that errors were made because he was not doing the work himself.

Boyle studied diseases of the eye with great interest and collected recipes for eyewashes. It is a wonder that these very cures didn't make him blind. He told one friend that he had found relief for a while using powdered dung blown into his eyes!

Years at Oxford

After spending ten years on his estate, writing and dabbling in his own experimenting, Boyle decided to pursue science formally. When he was twenty-seven years old, he moved to Oxford at the invitation of Dr. John Wilkins, the Warden of Wadham College. This move brought Boyle into a very favorable intellectual and spiritual climate. Under the chancellorship of Oliver Cromwell, Oxford had become the most prominent center of learning in England, easily surpassing both London and Cambridge. Boyle was not a student in the ordinary sense, but he pursued his own studies and thrived in the scientific atmosphere. For six years he was an apprentice to the scientific leaders of the day, and at the end of this period his rise to fame was phenomenal.

Many of the members of the Invisible College were now at Oxford, and they continued the discussions that Boyle had attended in London. This group included mathematicians, chemists, theologians, and physicians—many of them godly men who exerted a beneficial influence on the group.

At their weekly meetings, they discussed the latest developments in "experimental philosophy," the term used at that time for experimental science. This group formed the nucleus for the better-known Royal Society, chartered in 1662 as the Royal Society of London for the Promotion of Natural Knowledge. Boyle was destined to become the most illustrious of the twelve original members, and he was the dominant personality in the organization until Isaac Newton came into prominence some years later. (It was Boyle who encouraged and financed the publication of Newton's *Principia*.)

Boyle championed the society's empirical scientific method, the practice of science based on observation. They followed Francis Bacon's teaching that facts must be collected from reliable observations before conclusions could be made. This has now become the standard way to practice science, and it is hard to imagine any other way. But it was very different from Aristotle's approach to science, a method based on logic, speculation, and tradition.

Boyle's first scientific paper

Boyle's first scientific paper, *New Experiments Physicomechanical Touching the Spring of the Air and Its Effects*, was published in 1660 when he was thirty-three. It brought him immediate and lasting worldwide fame. His financial resources had enabled him to purchase a good assortment of equipment and to hire the needed laboratory assistants. He summarized this series of experiments at some length in his flowery literary style, drawing a number of ingenious conclusions that corrected errors that had persisted since the time of Aristotle.

One such erroneous doctrine that Boyle refuted in his paper concerned the possibility of producing a vacuum. The traditional saying that "nature abhors a vacuum" had been so firmly ingrained into scientific thinking that producing a vacuum was almost unanimously held to be an impossibility. With the help of Robert Hooke, an ingenious inventor and fellow scientist whom he had hired as a mechanic, Boyle perfected a vacuum pump that was remarkably successful for its day.

In testing the pump initially, they observed several small laboratory animals expire as the air was pumped from the container in which they were confined. In another famous

Boyle's vacuum pump

experiment he placed a loud clock inside a glass container that was connected to a pump. The ticking of the clock, clearly audible at first, became fainter and fainter as the pressure in the chamber was progressively reduced. Boyle thus became the first to realize the importance of air as a medium for the transmission of sound waves.

Boyle's paper also included an explanation of the mercurial barometer. In 1643 Torricelli, a student of Galileo, had performed his famous experiment leading to the invention of the barometer. He filled a yard-long glass tube with mercury and inverted it into a dish of mercury. The liquid in the tube dropped to a height of about thirty inches, leaving a space above it. The obvious question arose: Why should it stop there and not all fall into the dish? Fransiscus Linus, a contemporary of Boyle, postulated an invisible cord called a funiculus that connected the top of the mercury column to the top of the glass tube. The idea sounded ridiculous and even amusing to Boyle, but his correspondence with Linus was conducted on a courteous and scholarly level.

The true explanation is found, remarkably enough, in the Bible! Job 28:25 states the fact that air has weight, and it is this weight pushing down on the mercury in the dish that supports the column of mercury in the tube. Yet common sense would dictate that air is weightless. If it does have weight, it seems logical that it would fall to the ground. But another factor enters in at this point—the fact that the air molecules are in such violent motion that they can never settle. Boyle actually realized these facts about air; he was well over a hundred years ahead of his time in recognizing the importance of molecular motion as an explanation for the heat of a gas as well as its pressure. In the second edition of his paper in 1662, Boyle presented the definitive proof that air, like other material bodies, has weight.

But the third and perhaps the most important aspect of the paper was the experimental work leading to what is now called Boyle's Law. Boyle devised the apparatus that he would need—a J-shaped tube sealed at the lower end but open at the top. By pouring in mercury from the top, he was able to trap a quantity of air in the lower portion of the tube. After leveling the mercury on the two sides, he began increasing the pressure on the trapped air by adding more and more mercury. It was "not without delight and satisfaction" that he observed the volume of the air to be down to exactly half of its original quantity when the pressure on it had been doubled.[9] And at four times the pressure, the volume was down to one-fourth of its original value. After data had been collected for about two dozen in-between points, the relationship emerged that is so familiar to every student of science: the pressure multiplied by the volume is equal to a constant.

The Father of Chemistry

In 1661, Boyle published his best-known scientific work, *The Sceptical Chymist.* (The title refers to the critical scrutiny to which he subjected the earlier theories of the composition of matter.) This treatise was a major milestone in the history of chemistry and earned Boyle the title "The Father of Chemistry." It met with immediate and enthusiastic acceptance because it represented both a collection of a large body of empirical information and a new philosophical approach to its interpretation.

In this work he rejected several theories of the composition of matter: the earth-air-fire-water theory of those who accepted Aristotle's teaching, the mercury theory of the early alchemists, and the sulphur-salt-mercury theory of the Iatrochemists. As an alternative he proposed a "corpuscularian hypothesis" that is astonishingly similar to modern atomic theory. And in the second edition of the book published twenty years later, he offered his famous definition of an element as a substance "incapable of decomposition by any means with which we are now acquainted."[10] This astute wording even allowed room for nuclear disintegrations, which have been studied only in recent decades.

As "the father of chemistry," Boyle guided the great transition from alchemy to chemistry. Before his time, men spoke of "elixirs" and "essences"; after his work had made its impact on the scientific world, men spoke in terms of "elements" and "compounds." As a result of Boyle's contribution, the "spagyrists" and "hermetick philosophers" gave way to the chemists of the eighteenth century—men like Lavoisier and Dalton who were able to launch out in new directions, unhindered by the errors of previous generations.

Two other important treatises that Boyle published were *Experiments and Considerations Touching Colours* (1664) and *New Experiments and Observations Touching Cold* (1665). These studies undoubtedly influenced Newton's later work on optics and heat. The same year that the latter treatise appeared, Oxford University awarded Boyle the honorary degree Doctor of Physic.

Impressive output

Boyle disliked the dull, tedious writing that scientists used. He wanted to make scientific knowledge available to laymen, so he wrote in ordinary language, not the mathematical jargon that scientists were prone to use. He used his skill as a writer to bring his scientific observations to life with striking metaphors and descriptive language. He was very interested in reader response and tried to make his writing more readable by putting in illustrations, marginal references, and brackets to show material that could be skipped by the hurried reader. He strived for clarity, but often he added new material as the manuscript went through revisions, and his final drafts tended to be sprawling and shapeless. By modern standards, he seems to ramble, because scientists have now adopted a more efficient and concise way of reporting results.

His writing covered many subjects because he was a well-rounded man who was not afraid to study any discipline. He published theological works, medical and scientific works, and philosophical works. As a philosopher, he is undervalued and unappreciated, perhaps because his other accomplishments have overshadowed this achievement. In Europe, they thought of him as "the English philosopher" because of his subtle, sophisticated philosophical arguments.

The sheer volume of his writing is impressive. The most recent collection of his works covers fourteen volumes, and his correspondence fills another six volumes. And what he published was not the extent of his writing. There were many works that the public never saw. When he was thirty-two, he decided to publish something every year. There were few years that he didn't meet this goal. Almost every year he published something—a new work, a reprint, or a Latin translation. (Some of this writing had been done earlier in his life, but he did not decide to print it until later.)

At first he wrote his manuscripts in notebooks, but a few were stolen by a thief who hoped to find marvelous alchemy secrets. Boyle then started keeping his notes on loose sheets of paper and filing them into piles. These papers accumulated rapidly because he was careful to jot down every idea that came to him so that it wouldn't be lost. Often a sheet would be misplaced, and the entire household would be searching for it. Sometimes several years would go by before it surfaced again; in the meantime, Boyle would have to redo it from memory. (Once he lost an entire chapter; he couldn't replace it and had to put an explanatory note in the text.) He would review the heaps of paper when he had a bit of leisure time and would decide where to use the information.

He caused many headaches for his publishers. He delivered his manuscripts in bits and pieces, missed deadlines, and insisted on making changes and inserting new material when a book was already paginated.

Often there were mistakes in the final copy because Boyle did not proof-read thoroughly. His publishers tolerated him, though, because they knew that his work was brilliant.

Scientific innovations

A few innovations attributed to Boyle are not so well known. He was the first chemist to collect a gas over water—a procedure so common-place today that one scarcely feels it had need of an inventor. He was the first experimenter in England to use a sealed thermometer. He pioneered the use of indicators to distinguish acids from bases, and he laid the foun-dations of qualitative analysis for studying unknown substances by utilizing spot tests, precipitates, fumes, densities, solubilities, and flame tests.

He was also the first scientist to write up his experiments in a way that enabled other investigators to reproduce his results. (This was very differ-ent from the alchemists' secrecy.) He carefully described his apparatus, procedures, and observations. He also included details of his experiments that didn't work because he felt there were lessons to be learned from failed experiments. Boyle showed great ingenuity in designing and carry-ing out his experiments, and his inferences from his results showed remarkable insight.

Family life

Only Robert and his sister Mary escaped their father's atrociously arranged marriages. (Mary rebelled and married for love.) The Earl of Cork died while Robert was a teenager, but he had made arrangements for Robert's marriage to Lady Ann Howard when the two were quite young. In his will the Earl had left property to Lady Ann Howard on the condition that she marry his son Robert. But Robert had seen enough mis-ery in the arranged marriages in his family, and he felt that it was disaster to marry for any reason other than overwhelming passion.

Women found Boyle attractive because of his courteous manners and wit, not to mention his wealth and social standing. Boyle seems to have wooed a young lady who encouraged his attentions and then jilted him in the end. After this unsuccessful courtship, he was content to remain a bachelor. Several times his friends and family tried to set him up with a wife; but by this time, he felt that his life was dedicated to serving God through the study of science, so he never married. He was not a recluse, though. He entertained frequently and enjoyed the company of his friends, his brothers and sisters, and his nieces and nephews.

Obviously, growing up with the Boyle name was a great advantage for him. His high social standing opened doors for him wherever he went. But Boyle saw his nobility as a handicap to learning. He said that "being born heir to a great family is but a glittering kind of slavery."[11] He thought there were many lessons in life that he could never learn unless he associated with the lower working class. In spite of his aristocratic background, he was not a snob—he was a humble, affable person who made friends easily.

Perhaps Boyle's greatest asset, one that he exploited well, was his wealth. Wealth certainly had its advantages. He could pay for his own laboratory, his assistants, and the printing of his books when necessary. He could also afford to pay the Latin translators who prepared his books for the scholarly audience in Europe who read his books in Latin.

Boyle's faith

Boyle's Christian faith was the driving motivation for his work in science. He saw no inconsistency in dedicating himself to science while living the Christian life. "There is no inconsistence between a man's being an industrious virtuoso, and a good Christian," he wrote in his book *Christian Virtuoso*.[12] Boyle regarded his mission in life to be the use of science to support the Christian faith. Just as reading God's Word reveals God's character, Boyle felt that correct "reading" of God's creation would reveal God's perfection, intelligence, and benevolence. Boyle considered himself a "reader" of creation, pursuing the noblest aim of life, which was studying the nature of God and the attributes of God.

He thought that the correct study of science leads men invariably to God: "The vastness, beauty, orderliness, of the heavenly bodies; the excellent structure of animals and plants; and the other phenomena of nature justly induce an intelligent and unprejudiced observer to conclude a supremely powerful, just, and good author."[13] He was convinced that a layman's testimony for the Christian faith could have even more impact than that of a clergyman, so he dedicated his scientific endeavors to be a witness to God's creation and control of the universe.

Yet he was careful not to fall into the trap of exalting the creation above the Creator. God was always at the center of his study of science. He said, "Is it wise to dispute anxiously about the properties of an atom, and be careless about the enquiry into the attributes of the great God, who formed all things?"[14] He never allowed his scientific studies to take the place of God's revelation of Himself in the Bible.[15]

He was militantly opposed to any worldview that detracted from God as the Creator. He was especially vocal in his opposition to atheism. In the foreward to one of his books, he tells his readers that they know him as a naturalist and may be inclined to lump him together with the other infidel naturalists; but he says that "if I be a naturalist, it is possible to be so without being an atheist, or of kin to it."[16]

As he grew in the faith, Boyle became increasingly convicted of the fact that not only are Christians to "have no fellowship with the unfruitful works of darkness," but they are also to "reprove them" (Ephesians 5:11). His great reverence for the name of God moved him to write a treatise titled *A Free Discourse Against Swearing*. He took this treatise to heart and was never heard using even the mildest expletive. When he would say the name of God in conversation, he would first pause reverently.[17]

Boyle was strictly orthodox in his Christian beliefs. Concerning the Lord Jesus Christ, Boyle wrote of "His passion, His death, His resurrection and ascension, and all those wonderful works He did during His stay upon earth, in order to confirm mankind in the belief of His being God as well as man."[18] He did not claim to understand the triune nature of God but spoke of "the adorable mystery of the Trinity."[19]

He was thoroughly intolerant of preachers who spiritualized or allegorized important truths of the Bible rather than accepting them at face value. On one occasion he heard a sermon on Daniel 12:2—"And many of them that sleep in the dust of the earth shall awake, some to everlasting life, and some to shame and everlasting contempt." He was greatly disturbed when the preacher stated that the verse referred to religious doctrines—that some of them would survive the test of time, while others, devoid of merit, would fall by the wayside. Immediately after the service Boyle took issue with the preacher, declaring to him that this passage was one of the clearest statements of the resurrection in the entire Old Testament.[20]

As a young man, Boyle developed a deep distaste for the religious clashes that were going on. He despised the misery that the religious and political turmoil had inflicted on the people. He disliked controversy, especially religious controversy, and he was always courteous when he felt it necessary to disagree. "A man can be a champion of truth," he said, "without being an enemy of civility."[21] He felt that the political and religious turmoil could be calmed if only men could be persuaded to live truly Christian lives. To him, Christianity was simply the practice of holy living.

Boyle defended and upheld the great doctrines of Scripture in his words and actions. But his interest in theology was much more practical than mere studying and writing. He was very interested in the daily practice of the Christian life. His scrupulous honesty was just one example of his practical theology. He was so strongly opposed to taking oaths that he refused to be the president of the Royal Society because he would have had to take an oath. He never made vows because he had made a solemn and deliberate vow never to make a vow. (He made this statement with no hint at humor.)[22] He had a tender conscience and scrupulously tried to right anything that he perceived to be wrong in his dealings with others.

Although he sympathized with the Nonconformists who had left the Anglican church and often helped these ministers financially, Boyle was satisfied to remain in the Anglican Church his entire life. Some of his best friends were clergymen. One of his friends was Richard Baxter, the Puritan author who is still read today with admiration. Boyle at times commissioned his clergy friends to write books, and he supported them while they were writing.[23]

As a result of his faithfulness and his blameless testimony, he was repeatedly offered the highest positions in his church. He always declined these offers, though, saying that he could exert more influence for the cause of Christ as a layman.

Throughout his life Boyle read the Bible each morning in spite of illness, eye trouble, and other adverse circumstances. He followed a rigorous daily program of Scripture reading, meditation, self-examination, and prayer. He studied the Scriptures in their original languages and was intimately familiar with all the important theological writings of his day.

Boyle credits the famous Archbishop Ussher, his colleague at Oxford, with encouraging him to study the Bible in the original tongues. Boyle did not feel that he had any special gift for languages, and in fact, he called himself "one of the greatest despisers" of language study. But his great reverence for the Word of God gave him a deep desire to read it in the original tongues so that he was not at the mercy of translators. He became so familiar with the Greek New Testament that he could quote from it as readily as he quoted from the English New Testament. He cheerfully accepted the hard work that went into his language study. He disapproved of lazy persons who expected to understand the wonders of God's book on the easy terms that Adam obtained a wife—"by sleeping profoundly, and having her presented to him at his awaking."[24]

Boyle's godly influence was felt even after his death. In his will he provided funds for the "Boyle lectures"—a series of eight sermons to be delivered each year to demonstrate that Christianity is, in fact, intellectually defensible and far more reasonable than the various philosophies that seek to discredit it.

Boyle's evangelistic efforts

During his later years at Oxford, Boyle became intensely interested in worldwide evangelism. When he received a large windfall of money from additional Irish estates by decree of the king, he designated that income for evangelism and charity. One use of the money was to spread the gospel among the American Indians. The work that he supported was conducted by the missionary John Eliot. Eliot's correspondence with Boyle shows that it was a difficult field, a work that was beset with heartbreaking discouragements. Eliot valued Boyle's friendship and assistance highly, and in his letters, he addressed Boyle as "Right honourable, right charitable, and indefatigable, nursing father."[25]

Boyle also had a great burden for Orientals. As a director of the East India Company, he was able to effect some significant changes in the company's policies. His efforts helped develop the company into not only a successful business venture but also an agency to promote the spiritual welfare of the people of India. In addition he commissioned translations of the four Gospels and the Acts into Turkish, Arabic, and Malayan, and an Arabic translation of *The Truth of the Christian Religion* by Grotius.

But his greatest burden was for his fellow Irishmen. In spite of great opposition from the clergy, he financed new Irish and Welsh translations of the entire Bible so that the people themselves could have access to the Word of God. Thousands of these Bibles were distributed at Boyle's own expense throughout Ireland, Wales, and the Scottish highlands.

Boyle's compassion extended beyond the spiritual needs that he saw. When he saw material needs, he generously distributed his wealth to the poor people of both England and Ireland, regardless of their beliefs. But he was very secretive about his giving to charity, and he purposely never kept a record of it. Often the recipients didn't even know where their help had come from because he used his friends in the clergy to distribute it.

He lived modestly, without pomp. With all his wealth, Boyle never made a point to surround himself with luxury. Those who knew him in private said that he put on no airs in public. He was the same in private as he was in public. He didn't waste his time in foolish mirth, but he allowed himself a great deal of decent cheerfulness. Boyle's pastor summed him up this way: "His great thoughts of God, and his contemplation of his works, were to him sources of continual joy, which never could be exhausted."[26]

His last years

Boyle spent the last years of his life in London, from 1668 to 1691, where he lived with his sister Katherine, Lady Ranelagh. Here Boyle had a larger laboratory that looked out onto the pleasant countryside. Katherine's estate in Pall Mall, then a sparsely settled area, was ideally suited for entertaining the many visitors who came to see the renowned scientist. Foreign visitors believed that Mr. Boyle and his air pump were among the important sights to see in London! Eventually the demand on his time became so taxing that his doctor advised him to restrict the days and hours that he received callers. He maintained a second house across town to which he sometimes retreated to relax and collect his thoughts. Even with this second residence, he didn't have enough room to store all the apparatus and papers that he had collected. His own bedroom was crammed full of mathematical and chemical instruments, stacks of books, and bundles of papers.

In the Pall Mall residence Boyle had again selected an intellectually stimulating environment. His neighborhood was a focal point of English society and learning. One of his friends and neighbors was the noted physician Dr. Thomas Sydenham, who later became known as the "Father of English Medicine." Another was Newton's predecessor at Cambridge, Isaac Barrow.

A portion of Boyle's time was spent supervising a large laboratory that he had set up in downtown London. Operating it as a business venture, he hired a number of assistants, and for many years his establishment enjoyed a monopoly in the production of phosphorus.

When Boyle was forty-three years old, he suffered a stroke that caused paralysis. Over time, he slowly regained movement, but he occasionally had relapses. He tried many remedies but found that having someone bend his joints and help him exercise was the best help. His mind was as agile as ever, even though his body was failing. He continued to dictate to secretaries and to oversee his laboratory assistants as they carried on the experiments he designed.

Perhaps a normal man would have resigned from active life after so many years of poor health and the final blow of intermittent paralysis. But Robert Boyle still had work to do. For more than twenty years, he carried on his experimental work, published widely, answered his immense correspondence, and received visitors.

His health continued to deteriorate, and in 1691 he knew that he was near death. He carefully drew up his will so that his beloved charities would be carried on. When he bequeathed all his raw minerals to the Royal Society, his words to them reflected his attitude toward science: "Wishing them also a most happy success in their laudable attempts to discover the true nature of the works of God, and praying, that they and all other searchers into physical truths may cordially refer their attainments to the glory of the Author of Nature, and the benefit of mankind."[27]

Lady Ranelagh nursed her brother until she, too, became very ill. When she died a few days before Christmas in 1691, Boyle was crushed. A week after his sister's death, he died. He had feared that the end would involve a painful struggle, but he died peacefully in his sleep at the age of sixty-five. His death was a merciful release from his many ailments.

His loss from the scientific scene was felt acutely around the world. The funeral was, according to his wishes, simple and unpretentious. Gilbert Burnet, a bishop in the Anglican church, preached the funeral sermon. He had been Boyle's personal counselor for many years. The text he used came from Ecclesiastes 2:26– "For God giveth to a man that is good in his sight wisdom, knowledge, and joy." Without exaggerating and without using flattery, Burnet found much to praise in the life of this eminent giant of science. Here truly was a man who had contended earnestly for the faith, had ministered liberally to the needs of his fellow man both spiritually and materially, and had used his scientific genius to exalt the name of the Lord.

---

[1] Robert Boyle, *The Works of the Honourable Robert Boyle* (Bristol, England: Thoemmes Press, 1999), vol. 1 to which is prefixed the Life of the Author. Reprinted from the 1772 edition. Page xiv describes the rescue from the stranded coach.

[2] Ibid., p. xiii.

[3] Ibid., p. xxiii.

[4] Ibid., p. xxiii. See also More, pp. 44-46,161.

[5] Boyle, p. xxii.

[6] Boyle, pp. xvi – xvii.

[7] Louis Trenchard More, *The Life and Works of The Honourable Robert Boyle* (Oxford: Oxford University Press, 1944), p. 54.

[8] Ibid., p. 76.

[9] Dagobert D. Runes, ed., *Treasury of World Science.* (New York: Philosophical Library, Inc., 1962), p. 90.

[10] Philip Cane, *Giants of Science* (New York: Pyramid Publications, 1962), p. 74.

[11] Boyle, p. xiii.

[12] More, p. 164.

[13] Ibid., p. 184.

[14] Ibid., p. 185.

[15] Peter Alexander, "Introduction to The Works of the Honourable Robert Boyle," in *The Works of the Honourable Robert Boyle* (Bristol, England: Thoemmes Press, 1999), vol. 1 to which is prefixed the Life of the Author. Reprinted from the 1772 edition, pp. xi-xii.

[16] More, p. 140.

[17] His six directions for forsaking the vice of swearing are applicable to giving up any vice.

    1. Acknowledge swearing to be a sin.

    2. Pray zealously and incessantly for God's power to subdue this stubborn vice.

    3. Forsake the company of swearers.

    4. Pay a fine or inflict some type of punishment on yourself when you do swear. Be sure that the fine goes to help distressed Christians.

    5. Resolve to renounce the habit all at once, not gradually.

    6. Reflect on the vanity and foolishness of swearing.

[18] More, p. 171.

[19] Ibid., p. 181.

[20] Boyle, p. cxl.

[21] Antonio Clericuzio, "Carneades and the Chemists: A Study of *The Sceptical Chymist* and its Impact on Seventeenth-Century Chemistry" in *Robert Boyle Reconsidered*, Michael Hunter, ed. (Cambridge: Cambridge University Press, 1994), p. 81.

[22] Michael Hunter, "Casuistry in Action: Robert Boyle's Confessional Interviews with Gilbert Burnet and Edward Stillingfleet, 1691" (*Journal of Ecclesiastical History*, Vol. 44, No. 1, January 1993), p. 95.

[23] Boyle supported Bishop Gilbert Burnet while Burnet wrote his *History of the Reformation of the Church of England*. Boyle also commissioned Robert Sanderson to write *Ten Lectures on the Obligation of Humane Conscience* (1660) because Boyle was very interested in solving difficult questions of conscience. (From Hunter, "Casuistry in Action," pp. 82-83 [Sanderson], p. 87 [Burnet].)

[24] Boyle, p. l.

[25] Ibid., p. ccix.

[26] Ibid., p. cxliii, quoting Bishop Gilbert Burnet.

[27] Ibid., p. clx.

Sir David Brewster (1781-1868)

SIR DAVID BREWSTER
(1781-1868)

Experimental Physicist
Inventor

The Lord is my light and my salvation.
Psalm 27:1

David Brewster jogged half a mile down the road to his friend's house. He was done with school for the day and finally free to do what he really wanted. He found his friend James Veitch in his workshop, just finishing up his work for the day. James pointed to the plow he was making. "I figured out how to make it lighter," he said as he hung it up on the rack and turned to his workbench. Now that his work was done for the day, he could work on his hobby—making scientific instruments.

The young intellectuals of the neighborhood gathered in Veitch's workshop each afternoon to watch him work and to discuss science, mathematics, and theology. Even foreign visitors came to meet this remarkable "peasant astronomer" who made some of the best telescopes in Scotland and England. Sir Walter Scott lived in the area and often dropped by the workshop. He thought Veitch was one of the most impressive persons he had ever known. Veitch was just a humble plowmaker, but he had taught himself philosophy, astronomy, and mathematics.

The discussions in the workshop were deep, but the young intellectuals also had lighter moments. They enjoyed playing a prank with Veitch's electrifying machine. The boys put the conducting wires on a chair and waited until an unsuspecting visitor sat down. After they got him talking, a boy in another room cranked the machine until it discharged. The poor visitor jumped out of his chair with a startled exclamation. The boys never let on that they knew the cause of the shock. They pointed to a piece of quartz on the shelf and suggested that perhaps it had mysterious sparking qualities.

David Brewster was the youngest member of this mischievous group of intellectuals. His mother had died when he was nine, and he covered his grief by staying busy at Veitch's workshop. He spent most of his free time watching Veitch work and listening to the men talk. He often stayed until midnight if Veitch was testing a new telescope in his observatory.

When David was ten years old, he begged Veitch to let him build a telescope. Patiently Veitch guided him as he ground the lens. Then they built the tube and the stand. After several weeks of work, David finished the telescope. "Now we are ready to test it," James said, carefully dusting the lens one last time.

He helped David carry it outside and set it up on the dirt road. David knew the routine. He pointed his telescope to the designated tree half a mile away. He was relieved to see the leaves come into focus. Now to find a bird. He moved the tube slightly and a blackbird came into the viewfinder. He watched the bird for a moment. "It works!" he cried. "I see his eye! I see the sparkle in the bird's eye!"

David proudly carried his telescope home to show his father. He installed it by his favorite window upstairs—the window that often grabbed his attention and made him think about light and reflections.

Education

David Brewster was born in 1781 in Jedburgh, Scotland. His father was the rector of the local grammar school. He was a stern man and saw to it that his boys learned their lessons well. His neighbors used to say that he was the best Latin scholar and the quickest temper in Scotland.

David was a brilliant student. He was so precocious that he was allowed to enter the University of Edinburgh at the age of twelve! Here at the university David studied theology just as his older brothers had. His natural inclination was toward science, but Mr. Brewster had his heart set on having his four boys be ministers. They all dutifully obeyed their father's wish and prepared for the ministry.

David enjoyed the new learning opportunities, but he missed the carefree days at Veitch's workshop. Even though he was absorbed in theological studies, science still tugged at him. He often corresponded with his friend Veitch, and they shared their latest inventions and ideas. David continued to build instruments and dabble in astronomy, but he reminded his friend that science would have to take a back seat to theology.

David completed his master's degree when he was nineteen. He was still too young to preach, so he worked as a live-in tutor for several wealthy families. He often showed the children his experiments and let them feel the shock of his electrifying machine. They thought he was a fascinating teacher, but the housekeeper complained that he would burn the house down some day with one of his experiments. In one neighborhood where he worked, ghost stories circulated. The neighbors reported seeing a wizard in long flowing robes chanting under the stars. It was really just Brewster out late at night in his nightgown observing the stars!

This tutoring work occupied him for the next eight years, but he still had time to write and do scientific research. He received his license to preach as a Presbyterian minister when he was twenty-three years old and preached occasionally in Leith and Edinburgh. But he became so nervous every time he was to speak that he often felt faint. Preaching became extremely painful for him. Even extemporaneous praying bothered him.

With Veitch's help, Brewster built his first telescope at the age of ten.

Because of his theological training, he possessed a good intellectual knowledge of the Scriptures, and his messages were doctrinally sound. But he lacked the all-important "heart knowledge." His daughter wrote that his orthodoxy was obviously "a barren set of dogmas, giving neither joy, comfort, nor strength."[1] It was still to be many years before he experienced the new birth in his own life. Perhaps his spiritual condition also caused him to feel ill at ease in the pulpit. He finally chose not to enter the ministry as his life's work.

Writing career and marriage

As a teenager, David began contributing articles to the *Edinburgh Magazine*, a monthly periodical that combined science and literature. When he was twenty-one, he became the editor of this magazine. This was the first of several editorial jobs that he held during his life. In this job he wrote book reviews and reported on current events and scientific breakthroughs. He made many contacts in this job and soon knew most of the great scientists of the day.

Five years later he became editor-in-chief of the *Edinburgh Encyclopedia*. He jumped into this job with his customary enthusiasm and energy but soon found that it was more difficult than he imagined. The correspondence alone was a full-time job. He corresponded with 150 authors, trying to get them to turn in their articles on time. The authors regularly missed deadlines or forgot to send articles. Often Brewster had to supply the missing article. He ended up writing forty-one of the articles himself. The delays in publication affected the success of the encyclopedia, and it never was a serious rival to the *Encyclopedia Britannica*. Brewster worked on the encyclopedia for twenty-two years and saw eighteen volumes published. His work with the encyclopedia brought him recognition, but it was a disappointing financial failure.

In retrospect, perhaps the best thing about the encyclopedia was the indirect influence it had on the Rev. Thomas Chalmers, the Scottish theologian. Brewster and Chalmers were the same age and had been licensed to preach at about the same time. Chalmers was a brilliant mathematician but at the time was not too serious about theological matters. Brewster asked him to write the article on Christianity for the encyclopedia. While writing this article, Dr. Chalmers grasped the truths of the Christian faith as a deep reality. He went on to become a noted leader of the Evangelicals in the Scottish Presbyterian Church.

The impressive list of Brewster's published writings numbers over 1,000 items. (It is hard to know the exact number because his personal papers were destroyed in a fire after he died. Also, the sheer volume of his output makes it difficult to trace everything he wrote.) He gained a well-deserved reputation as a science historian. He wrote biographies of Galileo, Tycho Brahe, and Johannes Kepler. He was a great fan of Isaac Newton's and spent his life researching and defending Newton.[2] Brewster's biography of Newton and his *Treatise on Optics* are perhaps his best-known pieces of writing.

Brewster was also a prominent science journalist. His writing was clear and readable, and he succeeded in making science popular for the common people. He was also an excellent book reviewer and always included biographical information on the author. He had the pleasant task of reviewing Lieutenant Maury's *Physical Geography of the Sea*.

When he was twenty-nine, Brewster married Juliet Macpherson, the daughter of a fellow writer. The Brewsters had four sons and one daughter. Mrs. Brewster was a frail woman and almost died when her last child was born. For years she suffered with poor health and could not accompany her husband on his trips. He wrote to her almost every day when he was gone—chatty letters full of any detail that might interest her and cheer her up.

Brewster's scientific contributions

Brewster submitted his first scientific research report to the Royal Society of Edinburgh when he was thirty-one. The title of this paper was "On Some Properties of Light." He had been studying light since he was a teenager and had made his first discovery when he was eighteen years old. He turned out 314 more scientific reports during his long and productive career. His research covered topics related to light and vision—the polarization of light, double refraction, the theory of colors, the structure of the eye, lines of the solar spectrum, photography, optical illusions, and optical problems such as cataract, double vision, and color blindness.

Brewster's painstaking study of the sun enabled him to catalog 1,600 new dark lines in the sun's spectrum. His work in crystallography—the study of the crystals of various minerals—led to the founding of a whole new science called optical mineralogy. With this powerful research tool it became possible to identify hundreds of minerals by the behavior of light as it passed through them. His work in crystallography led him to formulate Brewster's Law, which describes the polarization of light. (To commemorate his work in crystallography, a mineral, brewsterite, has been named in his honor.)

He laid the foundation for modern biophysics with his experimental techniques to study the structure of the lens of the eye.[3] Using simple but insightfully designed experiments, he discovered the ball-and-socket joints between lens fibers. No one observed this structure again until it was "rediscovered" using the scanning electron microscope.

Brewster's work in optics and his careful study of the eye led him to suggest a cure for cataracts. This and several other applications to medicine prompted a group of German doctors to confer an honorary M.D. on Brewster. Of all the recognition that he received, he regarded this honor as his most satisfying.

For many years he experimented on a very limited budget. He made do with odds and ends that normal people would find no use for—bits of broken glass, scraps of tin and wire, and broken bottles. He did not have access to fine laboratory equipment until he was in his fifties, working at

St. Andrews University; yet he did some of his best work when he was in his thirties.

One of the greatest dangers he saw in experimenting was "taking for granted" the discoveries and assumptions of others. He often pointed out the blunders in the history of science and the delays in discovery because scientists assumed that a certain fact had already been proved.

Brewster found writing to be drudgery, but he thoroughly enjoyed his experimenting. He found beauty in such ordinary substances as soap bubbles and often entertained children with his bubbles. One night he woke up his wife to share his rapture over the beauty of a particular bubble. (It didn't occur to him that other people didn't share his enthusiasm about every little thing.)

His personality

Brewster threw himself wholeheartedly into everything he did. He worked at an intense pace, yet he knew when he needed to take a break. He took walks each day, and when he was much older and not able to walk far, he took daily rides in an open carriage. He also played an intensely competitive game of croquet, even when he was quite elderly. He enjoyed being outside and admiring God's creation, and he found something to comment on every few steps.

He was highly opinionated and quick to make his opinion known. His study in light and colors made him very opinionated about paintings. He thought many painters had an instinctive feel for color but could go much further if they had a real scientific understanding of the harmony of color. When he toured a gallery, he would often stand in front of a painting, shaking his head sadly and muttering, "Hideous."[4]

Financial difficulties

Brewster was, essentially, a self-employed scientific scholar. Other gentleman scholars had the benefit of being independently wealthy, but Brewster had no private means. His nervousness prevented him from lecturing as a university professor, so he was forced to operate outside the university scientific community. At times he found himself in embarrassing financial circumstances because his income as a writer was barely enough to support a family. He was an industrious worker, but he seemed to choose enterprises with poor remuneration: his inventions earned little money, and the encyclopedia turned out to be a financial failure.

At one crucial point, when the financial pressure was particularly heavy, his wife's sister invited the Brewsters to live with her because she was lonely after her husband's death. Brewster couldn't just live quietly at his sister-in-law's. Here he found a field ripe for reform and threw himself into managing her estate. He evicted unworthy tenants and put better men in their place. He planted trees, built a watercourse, and reclaimed waste ground. He made a few enemies in the neighborhood, but at the same time, the tenants were proud of their famous landlord, who by now was a well-known scientist. Sometimes they would come and ask to look through his telescope.

His reputation

Brewster's scientific work received almost immediate recognition because optics and studies on light were popular research fields. When he was thirty-four, he was elected a fellow of the Royal Society and soon was awarded most of the medals the Society gave. King William IV knighted him when Brewster was in his early fifties. He received numerous medals and honorary degrees from around the world.

During his lifetime, Brewster was considered the greatest living experimental physicist. His status as a celebrity brought him into contact with many famous people, and he enjoyed interacting with them. But he kept a true estimation of the significance of his contributions. He felt, to borrow the picture used by his hero Newton, that he was just a young boy who had collected a few shiny pebbles along the seashore and that the entire ocean of undiscovered truth still lay before him. He enjoyed the honors and fame that he received for his discoveries. But he hated to be flattered. "Oh, don't tell me any flummery," he would say.[5]

Although Brewster was timid about any occasion that involved extemporaneous speaking in public, he was a very social person and enjoyed the dinner parties that his rank in society now demanded. He liked conversing with others and delighted in explaining a fact of science to any listener who was truly interested and wanted to learn. Brewster gave the same enthusiastic explanation to a humble housewife that he would give to Prince Albert, the husband of Queen Victoria. Brewster often had a chance to visit with the Prince Consort because they moved in the same social and intellectual circles.

Brewster was genuinely interested in learning from the other person. One man remarked, "When I have been with other great men, I go away saying, 'What clever fellows *they* are;' but when I am with Sir David Brewster, I say, 'What a clever fellow *I* am.'"[6] One lady complained that it was no use to be admired by Brewster, because he admired everyone.

He cultivated friendships all over the world and carried on an immense correspondence. His correspondence included an impressive range of celebrities, but he was accessible to all degrees of people—not just the famous ones. Often everyday workmen would write to Brewster to ask a question or mention an interesting phenomenon.

Trials

Late one night Brewster's family heard his screams, and they rushed out of bed to see what had happened. They found him with his arms outstretched, screaming for water. He stumbled to the nearest basin of water and plunged his head in. He often experimented late into the night using a gas lamp for illumination, and this night while he was working with nitrogen dioxide, it exploded directly in his face.

His face and hands had been burned, but he was most worried about his eyesight. Losing eyesight is a tragedy for any human being, but for Brewster, his eyesight was the key to his discoveries. For several weeks he was blind and sat helplessly in the house with his eyes and hands bandaged. Gradually, though, his eyesight was restored.

Brewster always had a fear of water. He hated traveling by boat and avoided it whenever possible. When he was looking for a country home for his family, he turned down several possible dwellings because they were too close to water. He imagined that his children might drown. He finally settled on a country home two hours from Edinburgh that he named Allerly. The Tweed River ran nearby but was far enough away that Brewster felt safe.

As his boys grew older, he let down his guard and let them swim there occasionally. One day his son Charles went swimming alone. He was pulled from the river later that day, lifeless. This accidental drowning of his teenage son was a severe grief to the family. It was so painful for Brewster that he couldn't bear to mention Charles's name. The tragedy caused him to take a deeper interest in spiritual things for a time. But as the years passed, he settled again into his dry intellectual beliefs. He seldom attended church because his work kept him too busy to care for his own soul.

The kaleidoscope

Sir David Brewster is best remembered as the inventor of the kaleidoscope, a familiar device appreciated by children all over the world. Brewster first got the idea for his kaleidoscope while doing experiments in his favorite subject, the polarization of light. He called his invention

Brewster's kaleidoscope invention became a public craze.

the kaleidoscope, combining the Greek words for "beautiful," "a form," and "to see." Actually, the invention had little practical value, except for a pattern designer; but it won more lasting fame for Brewster than any of his other inventions.

The public's response to Brewster's invention was overwhelming. It has been compared to the Rubik's Cube craze of the 1980s, but even that comparison does not do justice to the overwhelming demand for the kaleidoscopes. In three months roughly 200,000 kaleidoscopes were sold in Paris and London.[7] His suppliers could not keep up with the incredible demand in both Europe and America. People lined up outside the supplier's office and left their money in advance hoping to get one of the next batch.

Everywhere in the streets both adults and children could be seen looking into the magic tubes, observing the symmetrical designs made by the motion of bits of colored glass. Brewster could have made a fortune if the patent had been managed properly, but the invention was pirated and Brewster saw little personal profit. The piracy irked him for the obvious reason that he needed the money, but he was also upset that the people were getting poorly constructed kaleidoscopes that were inferior in quality to his.

Even today kaleidoscopes are found all over the world. There are the inexpensive kaleidoscopes for children made with unbreakable Plexiglas. But there are also pricey models with elegant exteriors for those who want a collector's item.

Scientific instruments

Brewster had come a long way from the first simple telescope he built at Veitch's workshop. Now he was an expert lensmaker and improved the microscope, telescope, and other scientific instruments. He also improved the stereoscope by adding refracting lenses. He called it the Lenticular Stereoscope. This device used lenses to combine two photographs so that the eye sees a three-dimensional picture. (A child's View-Master toy operates on a similar principle.) This scientific toy was second in sales only to the kaleidoscope. Before the days of radio and movies, stereoscopes allowed people to sightsee around the world. Just as most houses today have a television, most homes before 1920 had a stereoscope.

Brewster also invented a device called the lithoscope (from the Greek words for "a stone" and "to see") that he used to examine precious stones. Several ladies who brought their jewelry to be examined by him were startled to discover that they owned pieces of glass that were brilliant fakes.

His most useful invention was the dioptric system for lighthouse illumination. The old system using copper reflectors threw such a divergent beam that the light could not be seen far out at sea. Brewster invented a lens, called the polyzonal lens, that produced a much stronger beam because it concentrated the rays of light into one plane.

He first suggested using this lens in combination with mirrors for burning purposes. But he soon realized the useful application for lighthouses. When he understood the life-saving potential of his invention, he became almost fanatical in his campaign to have this lighting system adopted in Britain and Europe. His persistence finally bore fruit. But it took more than fifteen years for the British to see the superiority of the system, even though several other countries were using it with great success.[8] With some improvements, this system has become the basis of all lighthouse systems. When Brewster died, his successor at the university said, "Every lighthouse that burns round the shores of the British empire is a shining witness to the usefulness of Brewster's life."[9]

British Association for the Advancement of Science

In 1831 Brewster helped establish the British Association for the Advancement of Science. This became an important research organization that still exists today. Brewster initially visualized an organization that would revive Britain's declining interest in science and that would lobby for government support of scientific research. In Brewster's writing he had often criticized the decline of science in England. He pointed out that other countries gave their scientists facilities and pensions to carry on their research for the good of the nation. But in England, each scientist struggled to keep himself afloat financially, and at the same time, to carry on his research. Even when England gave honors to her scientists, he argued, these honors never carried adequate monetary rewards.

Brewster also wanted the association to lobby for stricter patent laws. The scientists complained that the existing patent law afforded protection for literature but did not adequately protect scientific inventions and discoveries.[10] Brewster's own experience with the piracy of his kaleidoscope had a lot to do with his strong feelings on this subject.

In 1851 he was elected president of the Association. One issue of the journal published by this group contains a letter by Brewster describing a most unusual geological find. A large nail was discovered still partially embedded in a block of stone taken from Kingoodie Quarry in North Britain.[11] This find raised serious problems for the theory of long geological ages, which was rapidly gaining in popularity at that time. Obviously, the rock could not be millions of years old if it contained a nail known to be only thousands of years old at the most. Yet the scientific world chose to ignore this important discovery and several others like it. Within a few years the world had plunged headlong into enthusiastic acceptance of Darwin's theory, which was closely related to and dependent upon the theory of long geological ages. Brewster was a forceful opponent of Darwin's unscriptural theory and encouraged his readers to take a resolute stand against it. He pointed out that no evidence from either past or present supported the idea that one kind of living organism could change into another. In fact, he firmly stated that such a change could not happen.

St. Andrews University

To reward Brewster for his exceptional discoveries, the government appointed him the Principal of United College at St. Andrews University. This was the oldest university in Scotland, founded in 1411. Here was Brewster, at the age of fifty-six, beginning a new career as a university administrator.

This appointment finally put him in a secure financial position. He could now pursue his research without the nagging financial pressures that had always plagued him. Traditionally, this position had been an honorary post and no real work was expected of Brewster. But he couldn't preside over this institution without reforming the faults he found.

Brewster possessed that energetic personality that loves to correct errors. He also had the dogmatic assurance that his opinion was completely right. He could not agree to differ, and he had no use for a soft answer when he was in the middle of a controversy. He thought that the public was apathetic and that the only way to rouse them was to use violent language. Obviously, he lacked the diplomatic skills necessary for an administrative job. He pushed his reforms so rapidly and strenuously that the professors under him dug in their heels and opposed him vigorously.

But, even with all the opposition, he still managed to institute many needed reforms at the university. Brewster first tried to sort out the financial mismanagement he found. He discovered professors who were earning salaries but not lecturing at all! But he was particularly incensed with the method of obtaining honorary degrees and medical degrees. Anybody could pay a substantial fee and obtain a degree. This was a significant source of income for the university, so they were not inclined to give it up easily. Brewster insisted that degrees must be given based only on merit and that the university couldn't discriminate against a man because of his church connections.

As a boy, David Brewster had had the reputation of fearing no one on the playground, and that fearlessness was evident in him as a grown man. No one could intimidate him. But, even though his ideas were correct, "he was often wrong in his way of carrying out the right thing," as his daughter put it.[12] He earned the unflattering reputation of being contentious and quarrelsome. But he was not vindictive. In his mind he was attacking the error and not the man. As is often the case with quarrelsome people, he forgot the quarrel long before the other party did. Once a controversy passed, he often became friends with his opponent.

It never occurred to Brewster that most of his difficulties were his own creation. He never saw his own fault in the feuds he was involved in. But the grief he caused others was small compared to the grief he caused himself. People never saw the private shadow and gloom that a troublesome meeting caused him.

Each winter at St. Andrews, Brewster gave free lectures on optics and mineralogy. (Normally a professor charged fees for his lectures, and he could make more money if he attracted more students.) These lectures were open to the public as well as to the students. Brewster was friendly with his students, and he often invited them to breakfast and tea. If they were interested in his work, he showed them his experiments and explained his discoveries to them.

Brewster stayed at St. Andrews for twenty-one years. When he got news that he had been appointed the Principal of the University of Edinburgh, he struggled at the thought of leaving St. Andrews. By now, relations had improved, and he and his colleagues had developed a real affection for each other. He finally accepted the new position and spent his last years at his alma mater. Fortunately, his tenure at the University of Edinburgh was harmonious because he had mellowed considerably.

Free Church movement

Although Brewster was not preaching, he still maintained ties with the ministers of the Scottish Presbyterian Church. He often used his influence to help supply pulpits. In 1843 when a third of the pastors seceded from the Established Church and formed the Free Church, Sir David Brewster joined the group. For many of the ministers, it meant giving up their salaries and their manses; but they felt strongly that they were upholding the original intentions of the church. They opposed the state's interference in church business, and they were particularly bothered that individual churches had no say in who their pastor would be.

The leaders of the Free Church wanted to commemorate this important event with a painting. There were 470 people present, and the painter, David Octavius Hill, wondered how he would sketch so many portraits. Brewster suggested taking a photograph of everyone using the new calotype photography process. David Hill followed his advice and then spent twenty-three years painting the scene of the ministers signing the act of separation. After all that work, Mr. Hill would be disappointed to know that the photograph is remembered more than the painting.

Brewster was almost dismissed from his position at St. Andrews University because of his separation from the church. But the public outcry was so great that the government wisely backed down and let Brewster stay.

After this church separation, Brewster, now a man of sixty-two years, took a greater interest in spiritual things. He enjoyed a good gospel sermon and complained if the preacher tried to give a philosophical or scientific discourse.

He attended every meeting of the Free Church Assembly and served on several committees. His friendship deepened with Dr. Thomas Chalmers, who now was the spokesman for the Evangelicals, and they corresponded often about affairs of the Free Church.

Struggle for belief

Sir David Brewster's testimony demonstrates that it is possible to regard oneself as a Christian, even to be a preacher, and yet not be truly regenerated. For years Brewster dedicated his intellect to showing God's greatness through science, but his heart did not know Christ.

Like so many people who do not call on the Lord for salvation until they face a crisis, Brewster did not experience a turning point in his life until the death of his wife. She had been his companion for forty years, and losing her created a great turmoil in his heart and mind. Suddenly his dry orthodox beliefs offered no comfort for him. He looked around him at those who called themselves Christians, and he envied the peace and the assurance that they had. He had always thought it was utter presumption to have "assurance of salvation." Yet he longed for the certainty that his sins were forgiven so that he wouldn't fear death.

For a time he doubted the inspiration of the Bible, and he worried his family with his sophisticated arguments against inspiration. He also wondered how he could love Christ when he had never seen Him. He admired God for his marvelous works, yes. But love Him? That seemed impossible. Another huge stumbling block for many years was the people who professed to be Christians. He mistakenly thought that Christians should be perfect, and when he saw their glaring faults, he called them hypocrites. In fact, he said that he knew only two real Christians!

Although these stumbling blocks impeded his search, they did not stop him from the most important research of his life. Night after night, when his day's work was done, Brewster searched the Scriptures, trying to fill the void he felt. Often his family heard him late at night weeping and praying in agony.

When he remarried in 1857, at the age of seventy-five, his new wife joined him in this search. He spoke to her frequently about it, and his letters when he was away are full of allusions to "the great subject which interests us so much."[13]

Finally, after twelve years of searching, the doctrines he had learned so well in his youth made sense to him in a personal way. The doctrine of the atonement included him, Sir David Brewster. And Christ's work on the cross was sufficient to pay for all his sins—past, present, and future. When he accepted the work that Christ accomplished on Calvary as his covering for sin, a true peace entered his soul.

Now Brewster was able to testify that he saw all clearly. He finally had assurance of his salvation—the assurance that he used to ridicule. "It can't be presumption, to be *sure*," he said, "because it is *Christ's* work, not ours; on the contrary, it is presumption to doubt His word and His work."[14] Later he said, "Oh, is it not sad that all are not contented with the beautiful simple plan of God's salvation—Jesus Christ only—who has done all for us."[15] His favorite phrase was "the Lord our Righteousness."[16] It brought him great comfort that he could rest solely in Christ's work and not in his own good works. He would tell others, "The folly is trying to toil up the hill when God has sent a locomotive down for us."[17]

Those who saw him after this time could see that he was changed. His friends and family were amazed at his simple, childlike faith and his desire to see others share it with him. He was quick to see his own faults, where before he had been practically blind to them. He no longer criticized other Christians but quietly put up with their faults. Instead of barreling through with his opinions at all costs, he was much more reserved in contradicting others. Sometimes he would only show his disapproval with a grave shake of the head. His irritable temperament mellowed, and he made peace with his rivals. When he died, he could truthfully say, "I die at peace with all the world."[18]

Brewster's views on science

One time a friend secretly watched Brewster working with his microscope. Every few minutes, Brewster would lean back in his chair, throw his hands up, and exclaim, "Good God! Good God! How marvellous are Thy works."[19]

For most of his life, Brewster was not a born-again Christian. But, because of his background and knowledge of the Bible, he had a Biblical orientation to his science. He believed it was man's duty to use the tools God had given him to learn more about the Creation, and thus more about the Creator. These discoveries would bring men to a deeper worship of Him. "If the God of Love is most appropriately worshipped in the Christian Temple," he reasoned, "the God of Nature may be equally honoured in the Temple of Science."[20]

Brewster believed that the purpose of science was to discover God's design and control of the universe. He devoted so much time to studying the eye because he believed it was the pinnacle of God's creative work. He said, "Although every part of the human frame has been fashioned by the same Divine hand and exhibits the most marvellous and beneficent adaptions for the use of men, the human eye stands pre-eminent above them all as the light of the body and the organ by which we become acquainted with the minutest and the nearest, the largest and most remote of the Creator's work."[21]

Brewster campaigned for science education in the schools. To him, scientific instruction at a young age familiarized young people with the works of their Maker and prepared them to receive the higher revelation from God's Word. It would also enable young people to counter the objections against the Bible drawn from science.

Science and the Bible

Brewster believed that there was never any real contradiction between science and the Bible. He said, "It is difficult, if not impossible, to reconcile certain statements in Scripture with what is accepted by many persons as science, and imperfect and unsuccessful attempts to do this are more injurious than beneficial to religion. The only mode of dealing with this matter is to show that the science which is opposed to Scripture is not truth."[22] Unlike so many other scientists who reinterpreted Scripture to fit scientific "truth," Brewster held that any discrepancy between the Bible and science revealed either an imperfect knowledge of what the Bible says or a faulty interpretation of scientific observations.

He proudly showed a list of 717 scientific men who believed in Scripture. They affirmed that "it is impossible for the Word of God, as written in the book of nature, and God's Word written in Holy Scripture, to contradict one another, however much they may appear to differ."[23] He said it was unfair to assume that the study of science has a tendency to shake men's faith in the Word of God.

On his deathbed, he commented about the skepticism frequently found among scientists. He said, "Few received the truth of Jesus. But why? It was the pride of intellect—straining to be wise above what is written; it forgets its own limits, and steps out of its province. How little the wisest of mortals knew—of anything! How preposterous for worms to think of fathoming the counsels of the Almighty!"[24]

Final years

In Brewster's later years, he suffered mysterious bouts of fatigue and weakness and had to go to bed for several days at a time. Near the end of his life, his doctor found that he had a heart condition that had been undiagnosed for many years and that explained his episodes of fatigue. There were several times when he became so ill that his family thought he would die. But he would rally after a while and resume his experimenting and his duties at the university.

A daughter, Connie, was added to the Brewster home soon after he remarried, and she brought great happiness to Brewster in his old age. He taught her drawing, arithmetic, and astronomy and took her riding with him each day. He played dominoes with her each evening and then had her read to him from the Bible and sing hymns to him. His favorite hymns to hear were "Rock of Ages" and "There Is Life for a Look at the Crucified One."

Connie was a great comfort to Brewster. But she also caused him much pain because he worried so much about her health and safety. Once when they were visiting friends, whooping cough broke out in the house. Brewster carefully guarded his daughter so that she wouldn't contract the illness. It never occurred to him that he might become ill. He developed a severe cough that drained his strength completely. He couldn't do any work, so he amused himself in bed by calculating the seconds between each coughing fit and examining his symptoms with scientific precision.

Finally, when he was eighty-six, a bout of pneumonia weakened him so much that he knew he would die soon. His mind stayed clear, but every day his body became weaker. Each day he insisted on getting out of bed so that he could finish his business. He spent his last few weeks literally putting his house in order. He arranged his books and papers and gave instructions to a young friend about finishing a scientific paper that he had started. Then he dictated his final letters—touching farewell letters wishing his friends a life as long and full of blessings as his had been. He knew that God was calling him home, and he was ready to go. But he confessed to his family that it was wrenching to part with all the ones he had loved on the earth.

His testimony was solid, showing that all the years of doubt were passed. He looked back on his life's work with satisfaction, knowing that he had been useful to his generation and that the glory was due to God. He knew, though, that his honors or good deeds couldn't help him—nothing would help him in the hour of his death except the blood of Jesus. In spite of all the impressive knowledge that he had accumulated, "he rejoiced most of all in the '*knowledge* of *Christ* and in the power of His resurrection.'"[25]

Two days before he died, he said, "What should I have done now had I to find a Saviour at this time?"[26] His family stood around his bed encouraging him. One said, "You will see Charlie!" But he gently corrected them and said, "I shall see *Jesus*, who created all things; *Jesus*, who made the worlds."[27]

Before he died, he looked around at his family and said softly, "I have had the Light for many years, and oh! how bright it is! I feel *so safe, so satisfied.*"[28] Sir David Brewster had spent his life studying topics related to vision and light. Finally in his later years he saw the true Light, Jesus Christ. The fitting inscription on his tombstone reads, "THE LORD IS MY LIGHT."[29]

[1] Margaret Maria Gordon, *The Home Life of Sir David Brewster* (Edinburgh: Edmonston and Douglas, 1870), p. 313.

[2] He was grieved to come to the conclusion that Newton was in error about the person of the Lord Jesus. Brewster, who believed that the divinity of the Lord Jesus Christ was fundamental, said, "Yet how sad that Newton should have gone so far wrong! He was far from sound in his views of our Lord's person—in fact, they were of the Arian type." Gordon, p. 410.

[3] George Duncan, "Brewster's Contribution to the Study of the Lens of the Eye: An Experimental Foundation for Modern Biophysics," in *Martyr of Science: Sir David Brewster 1781-1868*, eds. A.D. Morrison-Low and J.R.R. Christie (Edinburgh: Royal Scottish Museum, 1984), p. 101-3.

[4] Gordon, p. 265.

[5] Ibid., p. 300.

[6] Ibid.

[7] A.D. Morrison-Low, "Brewster and Scientific Instruments," in *Martyr of Science: Sir David Brewster 1781-1868*, eds. A.D. Morrison-Low and J.R.R. Christie (Edinburgh: Royal Scottish Museum, 1984), p. 61.

[8] Several years after Brewster invented his lens, a Frenchman, Augustin Fresnel, independently invented an almost identical lens. The French quickly adopted his system in their lighthouses and it has been called the Fresnel lens ever since.

[9] Gordon, p. 381, footnote1.

[10] Brewster caustically said that the existing patent law "places the most exalted officers of the state in the position of a legalized banditi, who stab the inventor through the folds of an act of parliament, and rifle him in the presence of the Lord Chief Justice of England." (J. B. Morrell, "Brewster and the Early British Association for the Advancement of Science," in *Martyr of Science: Sir David Brewster 1781-1868*, eds. A.D. Morrison-Low and J.R.R. Christie [Edinburgh: Royal Scottish Museum, 1984], p. 25.)

[11] David Brewster, "Queries and Statements Concerning a Nail Found Imbedded in a Block of Sandstone Obtained from Kingoodie (Mylnfield) Quarry, North Britian," reported to the British Association for the Advancement of Science, 1844. There are other instances of man-made objects found encased in coal or inside deeply buried rocks. Examples include an 8-karat gold chain, a thimble, an iron instrument, an iron pot, three throwing-spears, a metallic vessel inlaid with silver, a coin, a screw, nails, and a tiny ceramic doll. Evolutionary dating techniques would date these man-made objects hundreds of millions of years *older* than man because the surrounding rock is supposedly hundreds of millions of years old. Obviously, something is wrong with evolutionary logic. For references to these finds, see Walter T. Brown, Jr., *In the Beginning: Compelling Evidence for Creation and the Flood*, seventh edition (Phoenix, AZ: Center for Scientific Creation, 2001), p. 78.

[12] Gordon, p. 427.

[13] Ibid., p. 320.

[14] Ibid., p. 323.

[15] Ibid., pp. 330-31.

[16] Ibid., p. 411.

[17] Ibid., p. 319.

[18] Ibid., p. 292.

[19] Ibid., p. 306.

[20] Ibid., p. 212.

[21] Nicholas Phillipson, "Sir David Brewster: Some Concluding Remarks," in *Martyr of Science: Sir David Brewster 1781-1868*, eds. A.D. Morrison-Low and J.R.R. Christie (Edinburgh: Royal Scottish Museum, 1984), p. 80.

[22] Gordon, p. 327.

[23] The Declaration reads as follows:

The Declaration of Students of the Natural and Physical Sciences

We, the undersigned Students of the Natural Sciences, desire to express our sincere regret, that researches into scientific truth are perverted by some in our own times into occasion for casting doubt upon the Truth and Authenticity of the Holy Scriptures. We conceive that it is impossible for the Word of God, as written in the book of nature, and God's Word written in Holy Scripture, to contradict one another, however much they may appear to differ. We are not forgetful that Physical Science is not complete, but is only in a condition of progress, and that at present our finite reason enables us only to see as through a glass darkly; and we confidently believe, that a time will come when the two records will be seen to agree in every particular. We cannot but deplore that Natural Science should be looked upon with suspicion by many who do not make a study of it, merely on account of the unadvised manner in which some are placing it in opposition to Holy Writ. We believe that it is the duty of every Scientific Student to investigate nature simply for the purpose of elucidating truth, and that if he finds that some of his results appear to be in contradiction to the Written Word, or rather to his own *interpretations* of it, which may be erroneous, he should not presumptuously affirm that his own conclusions must be right, and the statements of Scripture wrong; rather, leave the two side by side till it shall please God to allow us to see the manner in which they may be reconciled; and, instead of insisting upon the seeming differences between Science and the Scriptures, it would be as well to rest in faith upon the points in which they agree." (From Henry M. Morris, *History of Modern Creationism,* second edition [Santee, California: Institute for Creation Research, 1993], pp. 399-400.)

[24] Gordon, p. 410.

[25] Ibid., p. 251.

[26] Ibid., p. 331.

[27] Ibid., p. 415.

[28] Ibid.

[29] Ibid., p. 417.

Michael Faraday (1791-1867)

MICHAEL FARADAY
(1791-1867)

Experimental Physicist
Chemist

His delight is in the law of the Lord; and in his law doth he meditate
day and night . . . and whatsoever he doeth shall prosper.
Psalm 1:2-3

*Michael and Robert Faraday often visited their father's blacksmith
shop after school and helped with menial chores. One day after their
chores were done and they had grown tired of watching their father work
in the lower workshop, the boys climbed up the ladder and began playing marbles in the upper room. Then Michael thought of a new game.
They could pitch half-pence into a pot and see who got the most in. After
Michael won the first round, he told his brother that they could move the
line back and throw from farther away.*

*Michael was holding his half-pence, aiming at the pot as he took two
steps backwards. He completely forgot about the opening into the lower
workshop and fell down the hole. He would have landed on the anvil that
was directly below, but his father was bent over it, working. Michael
landed squarely on his father's back. He wasn't hurt, just stunned. His father dusted him off and said, "Well, Michael, my back saved yours."*

But Michael's care-free days of running around the blacksmith shop
were not to last. Mr. Faraday became ill and couldn't get out of bed to
continue working. He had been a healthy man in 1791 when Michael
was born. But when he became an invalid, the family had to move to the
slums of London. They lived in a few rooms in the top floor of an old
coach house.

Mrs. Faraday took care of her sick husband and her four children. She
gave her children the rich heritage of a godly upbringing, even though she
couldn't always give them the material things that they needed. She was
wise and calm and didn't let their desperate circumstances ruin her good
nature.

But there was so little money in the house that Mrs. Faraday finally decided to send her older boys to work so that they could support the family. When Michael Faraday was thirteen, his schooling ended and he went to work, first as a newspaper boy and then as an apprentice bookbinder. He had had only a basic grammar school education—just the basics of reading, writing, and arithmetic—and that was all the school training he would ever get.

The apprentice bookbinder

When Michael quit school to help support his family, he imagined that his life would be full of drudgery. But he found his life as an apprentice enjoyable. He had a kind master, and he was learning a useful skill. In the days before books were bound by machines, each book had to be put together by hand. Michael learned to sew the pages, pound them together with a wooden mallet, cut the leather for the cover, print the title on the spine, and put the book together. Two other boys worked as apprentices with Michael, and there was a good deal of friendly competition among the boys. Michael used to brag that he could pound 1,000 blows with the mallet without resting.

Mr. Riebau, the bookbinder that he worked for, saw how Michael eagerly read the books that came into the shop for binding. But he noticed that Michael had no discernment and would spend his time reading fantasies and novels. So Mr. Riebau guided him in choosing edifying literature.

Michael liked to read these books during his early morning walks. He would stop to read a page or two and then continue walking while he absorbed what he had read. One of the most exciting books he discovered at the book shop was *Conversations on Chemistry* by Mrs. Jane Marcet. He determined to find a way to do these experiments that she described. He somehow managed to set aside a few pence each week to buy chemicals, wire, and glassware for simple experiments. Mr. Riebau let him set up a little laboratory in the back room of the bookbinding shop. After Michael's work was done for the day, he would experiment in this laboratory.

When Michael was binding a volume of the *Encyclopedia Britannica*, he stopped to read the article on electricity. It opened a fascinating world for him—the history of electricity and the theories of electricity. It was illustrated with drawings of equipment and descriptions of experiments.

Michael wanted to copy these experiments and make his own electrical apparatus, but he was too poor to buy the equipment. He saved his money until he could afford two glass bottles that he had seen in a nearby shop. He turned the smaller bottle into a Leyden jar (a simple form of a capacitor, which builds up and stores an electrical charge), and the large bottle became the cylinder for his electrostatic generator.

He was now an amateur scientist, but he lacked two items that seemed so necessary to research—time and money. He often moaned about his lack of time and said, "Oh that I could purchase at a cheap rate some of our modern gents' spare hours."[1]

He had so many disadvantages to work against—he lacked the basic structure that formal schooling would have given him, he had little free time, and he had very little money to buy equipment. He would have agreed with Robert Boyle's words, "A philosopher must have a purse as well as a brain."[2] But even if he couldn't go to school, he was determined to learn. He read all the books that he could from the bookbinder's, and often at night he would copy a section of a book that he particularly liked.

One of the best books he had found was by Dr. Isaac Watts, the English pastor and theologian who was famous for the hymns he wrote.[3] But the book Michael found by Dr. Watts was not about hymns. It was called *The Improvement of the Mind*. It was a book written for young men, teaching them how to profit from lectures, reading material, conversations with people, and direct observation. Michael had seen how deficient his own education was and realized how bleak his prospects of improvement were. He knew that he could never go back to school because, by this time, his father had died, and he and his brother needed to support the family. But this book gave him hope that he could educate himself.

Michael followed Dr. Watts's suggestions rigidly. He started keeping a notebook in which he jotted down things he learned from his reading. When he was nineteen, he saw a notice in a shop window advertising a series of lectures, but he couldn't afford the fee. When he told his brother, Robert, about the lectures, Robert offered to pay for Michael to attend.

Each Wednesday evening, Michael heard lectures on a wide variety of scientific subjects. There were about three dozen working men in the audience, all with the same desire for self-improvement. Michael sat on the front row and took notes. When he got home, he quickly copied the notes. Then he used this clean set of notes to write out the lecture as he remembered it. But he was not just blindly transcribing the lectures. He could think for himself, and he jotted his questions and his disagreements in the margins of his notes.

This group that met every Wednesday called themselves the City Philosophical Society. The society later grew into a night school for working men. Michael asked some of these young men to help him fill in the gaps in his education. Six of them met together regularly to read to each other and to improve their pronunciation. When they had finished reading, they liked to sing, and Faraday sang bass in their informal choir.

One friend spent two hours a week with Michael, helping him with his spelling and grammar. Michael always had trouble with spelling and punctuation, even late in life, because he had not had a good foundation. After seven years of these grammar sessions, his writing had improved considerably.

He also asked his best friend, Benjamin Abbott, if they could correspond. It seemed rather odd since they saw each other often, but Michael wanted to practice writing down his thoughts. These letters show Michael's early interest in chemistry.

He bound his correspondence and his lecture notes into four neat volumes, and his boss often showed them proudly to his customers. One man was so impressed by them that he gave Michael four tickets to go to the Royal Institution lectures. So, when Michael Faraday was twenty-one years old, he attended four lectures by Sir Humphry Davy, the celebrity chemist who gave lectures at the Royal Institution.

The Royal Institution

The Royal Institution had been founded in 1799 by Count Rumford, a colorful, talented scientist and philanthropist. He wanted it to be an adult education center for the poor, a place where the working class could learn practical knowledge. But to bring in money to keep the institution afloat financially, Sir Humphry Davy turned it into a center for popular scientific lectures and a hub for chemical research.

Michael knew that Davy was a popular speaker, so he came early to get a good seat. He sat near the front, oblivious to the well-dressed crowd around him. Michael rested his hat on his lap and used it as a desk while he took notes. He listened spellbound as Davy lectured on gases, metals, and combustion.

When he got home, he wrote these notes out more fully in his neat handwriting and added diagrams of the experiments and an index. He bound them into a handsome volume, 386 pages long. He had made this volume for his own use; but later it would serve, in a sense, as his ticket of admission to the world of science.

These lectures made Michael want to pursue science seriously. But he figured that he would have to leave science to those who had time and money.

He completed his apprenticeship a few months later and found work as a bookbinder at a shop across town. It took him only a few months to decide that this was not the life for him. He found the business world cruel and unethical. *Perhaps,* he thought, *I could pursue science, even if only in some humble capacity.*

One day, he decided to take the bold step of writing to Davy, asking if he could work at the Royal Institution. He sent along the volume of lecture notes he had taken during Davy's lectures. Davy sent a kind reply and granted Faraday an interview. But there were no openings at that time. Michael was deeply disappointed. He wanted out of the business world, but he felt trapped.

A few weeks later, he was getting ready for bed after a long day's work. He heard a knock on the door and looked out the window. He saw a carriage standing outside. He walked downstairs to open the door, and a well-dressed messenger handed him a letter. Michael saw that the letter was from Sir Humphry Davy, and he quickly ran back up the stairs. He stood by his lamp and carefully tore open the envelope. It was a summons from Davy to come to the Royal Institution the next day!

Working at the Royal Institution

The next morning Michael dressed carefully and reported to the Royal Institution. Davy explained that there was an opening because the laboratory assistant had been dismissed for fighting with the instrument maker. He offered Michael the position of laboratory assistant. Michael happily gave up his life as a bookbinder and accepted the low salary that Davy offered him. For twenty-five shillings a week, Davy hired the man who was to become the most illustrious scientist ever to grace the halls of the institution. Davy himself was a brilliant researcher who discovered six of the chemical elements—sodium, potassium, calcium, barium, strontium, and magnesium. But in later years he often said, "The greatest of my discoveries is Faraday."[4]

So in the spring of 1813, Faraday began work as the laboratory assistant at the Royal Institution. His duties included setting up demonstrations, assisting during lectures, cleaning and returning the equipment to the storeroom after it was used, and keeping a record of repairs. His early Christian training stood him in good stead for his work. He put in more than a full day's labor and found additional projects to occupy himself.

Faraday worked in his basement lab at the Royal Institution.

Within a few days Faraday became proficient at several different chemical operations—extracting sugar from beet-root, the synthesis of carbon disulfide, and the preparation of the highly explosive nitrogen trichloride for Davy's latest research. Faraday was neat and thorough in the lab, and he quickly became indispensable to Davy.

European tour with Sir Humphry Davy

In the fall of 1813 Sir Humphry Davy, Lady Davy, and Faraday embarked on a tour through continental Europe. Faraday was twenty-two now, but he had never been more than a few miles from home in his entire life. He was fascinated with the scenery. Davy was happy to give impromptu lectures on geology and meteorology, and Faraday wrote these down in his journal.

Faraday worked as Davy's secretary for the trip, and he came into contact with some of the most distinguished scientists of the day. In France, Ampère showed them a sample of the newly discovered element iodine. Davy tested the substance with his portable laboratory and observed the violet vapors that were produced when the crystals were heated. In Italy they met Alessandro Volta who had constructed the first battery at the turn of the century. While they were in Florence, they burned a diamond with a large lens and analyzed the carbon dioxide formed from it.

Faraday's greatest difficulty on the trip was Lady Davy, the new bride of Sir Humphry Davy. She was wealthy and full of snobbish ways. At the last minute, their valet had been unable to travel; so she treated Faraday as the valet, and this grated on him. Besides being an insufferable snob, she talked incessantly. Faraday was so relieved when they were caught in a storm on a boat trip and the fright made Lady Davy unable to talk. He thought the few moments of silence were well worth the dangerous storm they had to endure.

The return trip took them through southern Germany, Switzerland, and Holland. By the time they arrived back in England in the spring of 1815, Faraday had gained more knowledge in a year and a half than most people would acquire in a full college curriculum.

Continuing education

When he returned from the trip, Faraday was given more duties and a slight raise. He moved into rooms on the upper floor of the Royal Institution, and that is where he lived most of his life. Although Faraday had never had a chance to formally study science at a university, he was, in effect, an apprentice in chemistry under Davy. He learned a great deal just from watching Sir Humphry Davy work.

In the evenings, Faraday filled in the gaps in his knowledge with a vigorous self-imposed reading program, using the library facilities of the Royal Institution. When he studied the history of chemistry, he tore apart *A Manual of Chemistry* by William Brande (another professor at the Royal Institution) and then rebound it with blank pages between each page of text. He used these blank pages to write down his own notes and references to other books. This library research occupied him for many years.

One morning, a terrific explosion resounded through the basement laboratory. Once again Faraday's test tube of nitrogen trichloride had exploded. The explosion drove pieces of his glass test tube through the window like bullets. Other pieces of the test tube landed in his eyes.

The doctor came and removed the pieces of glass and bandaged his eyes. But Faraday saw this as only a minor inconvenience. In a few days, he was back in the laboratory again. He took these occasional explosions in stride. An earlier explosion had ripped off a fingernail and torn open his hand. That time he had been wearing a glass mask to protect his eyes.

He was careful in the lab according to the standards of his day, but he unknowingly did things that are harmful. He often worked with big cups of mercury, and if some spilled, the vapors permeated the lab. He often used himself as a voltmeter, even though he had a measuring device. In the early years of electrical research, scientists were forced to use themselves as measuring devices. That was not necessary in Faraday's time, but he often applied current to his eyes, tongue, and arms to prove to himself the strength of the currents he was using.

Despite the occasional explosions, Davy recognized Faraday's competence in the lab, and he suggested research topics for him to pursue. Faraday soon built a reputation as a competent chemist with careful analytical skills. He was a stickler for accuracy, and he repeated his experiments over and over to check his results.

Davy always praised his work and publicly acknowledged the help that Faraday gave him with his experiments. Faraday had never thought of writing an original research paper. He was only twenty-five years old and still unsure of himself. But Davy urged him to write his first paper "at a time," Faraday said, "when my fear was greater than my confidence, and both far greater than my knowledge."[5]

Faraday always valued Davy's confidence in him. He found it hard to believe that he was now moving in the world of serious scientists. He did not trust his own theories, but he found confidence in pure facts—the solid, irrefutable results of his experiments. "Experiments are beautiful things," he said, "and I quite revel in the making of them. Besides they give one such confidence and . . . I am very glad to have them to fall back upon."[6]

Research policy

After returning to England, Faraday produced the world's first crude sample of stainless steel. But he made no attempt to capitalize on the discovery commercially. This was to become an enduring policy—whenever a discovery or an invention showed promise of bringing financial reward, he would leave it and go on to something else.

This doesn't mean that he scorned applied science. His work contributed to the development of India rubber, optical glass, alloys of steel, electroplating, patent locks, and artificial rubies.[7] He understood very well how scientific principles could lighten man's burden and have profitable economic results.

But he was content to let others pursue these applications. He felt sure that others would be able to find the practical applications of his work, and he didn't need to spend his time developing his discoveries. Thus he was always at the frontier of science, charting new territory. Others frequently reaped handsome profits from his labors, but this didn't seem to bother him. Sometimes he was pleasantly surprised to see what had been done with his work. When he saw what had been done with one of his inventions, he said, "I gave you this machine as an infant; you bring it back as a giant."[8]

He never took out patents. But he gave his brother his patent rights for a chimney that he had invented to ventilate oil burning lamps. Faraday's chimney invention was used in all lighthouses and even in Buckingham Palace.

Often, though, the usefulness of his inventions and discoveries was not immediately clear. When the prime minister was touring the Royal Institution, he pointed to Faraday's dynamo and asked what it was good for. "I know not," Faraday replied, "but I wager that one day your government will tax it."[9] At other times, when he was asked what electricity was good for, he would answer with Benjamin Franklin's humorous line: "What is the use of an infant?"[10]

Faraday's church and his Christianity

Throughout his entire life Faraday remained affiliated with the local Sandemanian church he had attended in his childhood. This was a closely knit group that had split off from the Presbyterian Church in Scotland.[11] They believed that the Bible was the only guide for life. The elders took turns preaching each Sunday because they did not have a pastor in this church. Later in his life, Faraday was an elder and preached in the congregations in London and Dundee.

In a typical church the members would stay after the Sunday morning service and eat the noon meal together. After the meal, there was another service followed by the Lord's Supper, which they observed each week. Members arrived home in the early evening, after spending most of the day at church. Then on Wednesday night they would assemble again for the midweek prayer service. Faraday faithfully attended all the services, even when the demands of research were heaviest.

The Sandemanians were very strict. One time Faraday had to miss church because Queen Victoria had commanded him to come to Sunday dinner. It was impossible for Faraday to attend the all-day services. For this breach in faithfulness, his name was removed from the church roll. Faraday, though, simply kept attending and was eventually reinstated.

His scientific colleagues respected him for his deep faith.[12] They noticed that he would leave an evening engagement early so that he could be at prayer meeting. Once after a lecture that he had given, the people couldn't find him to congratulate him. He had slipped out so that he could be at prayer meeting. Whenever he was out of town for the yearly meetings of the British Association, he would find the local congregation of his church and worship with them.

Marriage

Members of the Sandemanian Church were noted for their rigid separation from the world and from other religious denominations. They maintained close ties within the fellowship by intermarriage. True to form, Faraday chose his bride from his own local group. On June 12, 1821, when he was almost thirty years old, he married Sarah Barnard, the daughter of a silversmith who was an elder in the church. Up until this time, Faraday had considered women and love to be a bothersome entanglement. He was much too busy with his studies and his experiments.

But once he succumbed, he found himself very happily married. Looking back over his life many years later, he spoke of this as an event which more than any other contributed to his healthful state of mind and his earthly happiness.[13] Their home was a suite on the top floor of the Royal Institution. It was a happy and tranquil Christian home that was given purpose and direction by family worship services every evening. He and Sarah were together until his death, a span of nearly fifty years.

Sarah never pretended to understand her husband's work. (He did not talk much about his work anyway, because he preferred not to explain his thinking. He could spend hours in silence, not even speaking to his assistant, who was working right beside him.) She thought of herself as a pillow for his mind. When he was with her, he could let his mind rest from his work.

She doted on him and brought him his meals when he was so absorbed in the laboratory that he forgot to stop to eat. His laboratory was in the basement of the Royal Institution, and when the bustle of the day was over, she would go downstairs and find him. Sometimes she made an appointment with him to help her make home remedies. They would make lavender throat lozenges, which a niece said tasted much worse than those in the store. Once a year, the Faradays used the laboratory to brew a large batch of homemade ginger wine.

They never had children of their own, a sadness that Faraday considered his greatest misfortune. But they were very fond of children and often had two nieces live with them. The extended family often came over to celebrate special occasions. Whenever children came into the lab, Faraday introduced himself by throwing a bit of potassium in water and then enjoyed their excitement as they watched the potassium burst into flame and fizz and pop.

Profession of faith

A month after his marriage, Faraday made a public profession of his faith in Christ. From then on his spiritual growth was rapid, and in time he was appointed to the office of elder in the church. He was a diligent student of the Scriptures. His Bible contained nearly three thousand meticulously written notations in the margins—exegetical aids, comments, and cross-references.[14]

It is evident that the knowledge and wisdom gained from his study of the Bible found their outworking in his life. His actions in life were guided completely by God's will revealed to him as he read the Bible. He did not base his morals on any intuitive sense of right and wrong. The Bible was his only standard.[15]

He was an exemplary Christian both in the laboratory and in his testimony before the community. His good friend John Tyndall said, "I think that a good deal of Faraday's week-day strength and persistency might be referred to his Sunday Exercises. He drinks from a fount on Sunday which refreshes his soul for the week."[16]

The first electric motor

On Christmas day of the year 1821, just six months after his marriage, Faraday took his wife into the laboratory to show her the first electric motor. The contrivance appears strange to modern eyes. It consisted of a vessel filled almost to the top with mercury. He had attached a bar magnet to the bottom of the vessel with one pole projecting slightly above the surface. A copper rod suspended from above dipped into the mercury, making electrical contact with it.

Mrs. Faraday watched as the top end of the rod and the lower end of the magnet were connected to a voltaic pile. Instantly the rod started dancing around the magnet in a continuous circular motion. The magnetic field around the rod was repelling against the field of the bar magnet. Faraday had found a way to transform electrical energy into mechanical energy. This resulting "push" was to become the muscle of the motors of today's homes and industries.

False charge

When Faraday discovered the concept behind the motor ("electromagnetic rotation" was his term), he went to visit the scientist William Wollaston because he knew that Wollaston had been looking for a similar phenomenon but had not had success. Faraday wanted permission to mention what Wollaston had done so far and print it with his own work. But Wollaston was out of town. Faraday decided to go ahead and publish his paper, but without mentioning Wollaston's work since he did not have his permission.

As soon as his paper came out, there were rumblings in the scientific world that Faraday had *plagiarized* from Wollaston's work. This was a serious charge, and it completely disheartened Faraday. He had done his work independently and honorably. What he had discovered was different from Wollaston's work, but the distinction was unclear to casual observers.

Faraday had adopted the motto "Work. Finish. Publish." But now he wished that he had not been in such a hurry to publish. "I have regretted ever since I did not delay the publication, that I might have shown it first to Dr. Wollaston," he wrote to a friend.[17] It took several years for the charges of plagiarism to die down. Wollaston accepted his explanation, and Faraday's name was cleared; but it had been a painful lesson in scientific etiquette that he would never forget.

Productivity and thoroughness

In the next few years, Faraday's productivity increased sharply, and the scientific community recognized his brilliance. In 1824 he was made a Fellow of the Royal Society, one of the first of approximately ninety-five such honors and distinctions to be conferred on him during his lifetime.

His appointment as Director of the Laboratory of the Royal Institution in 1825 coincided chronologically with his discovery of benzene. What had begun as a routine analysis of the oil that collected in illuminating gas lines blossomed into the discovery of one of the most important hydrocarbons known to man. (Benzene is used today in the production of synthetic rubber, nylon, dyes, detergents, resins, pesticides, and plastics.)

Faraday was a master at planning and carrying out tedious operations. He worked with precision and patience in the laboratory and had incredible perseverance and stamina. Before he began any research, he thoroughly studied everything that had been done before him. First he would read everything that had been written about the subject, and then he repeated the experiments that had been done.

He noticed that scientists could inadvertently repeat one another's work if they did not make it a practice to stay current and read everything that had been done before in a field. This practice of background research gave him a thorough understanding of what had been done in electrical research up to this point. And when he decided to tackle the problem of electromagnetic induction, he found his answer in just a few weeks.

Cinderella of science

Faraday has been called the Cinderella of science because, against all odds, he educated himself and then became the greatest experimental physicist of all time. (Newton ranks as the greatest of the theoretical physicists.) Faraday's laboratory technique was unparalleled, but it is wrong to think of him only as a skillful laboratory manipulator. He also had a brilliant theoretical mind that could predict which experiments would be useful.

He was never one to jump to conclusions. He amassed a large body of evidence before he would commit to a position. And he was honest in reporting his negative results and his failures. In fact, he was not particularly disturbed by negative results. He could learn from being wrong just as easily as he could learn from being right. He was resigned to the inevitability of error, and he used to quote Bacon often: "Truth is more likely to arise from error than from confusion."[18]

Faraday didn't have the mathematical background of his formally trained colleagues. But, in the long run, this worked to his advantage because his mind was more open to unorthodox ideas. He wanted to be able to see a law, not just to state it or write it in a formula.

At times, though, he felt his mathematical disadvantage, especially when he couldn't grasp the meaning of another scientist's work because it was so technically written. In one of his letters to the young physicist James Clerk Maxwell, he said, "There is one thing I would be glad to ask you. When a mathematician engaged in investigating physical actions and results has arrived at his own conclusions, may they not be expressed in common language as fully, clearly, and definitely as in mathematical formulae? If so, would it not be a great boon to such as we to express them so—translating them out of their hieroglyphics, that we also might work upon them by experiment."[19] Faraday was sixty-six at the time he wrote this to Maxwell, and Maxwell was only twenty-six. But their mutual respect made this honest communication possible.

Humility

Faraday was a master of self-education.[20] He believed the first step to teaching oneself was humility. Self-education in his mind was linked to self-criticism. "I always tried to be very critical on myself before I gave anybody else the opportunity," he said, "and even now I think I could say much stronger things against my notions than any body else has."[21]

He also believed a good student must be aware of his own fallibility. He was deeply aware of his own propensity to error. In his Bible, he vigorously marked the passage from Job that reads, "If I justify myself, mine own mouth shall condemn me: if I say, I am perfect, it shall also prove me perverse."[22] It was these thoughts of his own fallibility that made him humble.

He never got over the wonder that God had allowed him—Michael Faraday, the uneducated son of a blacksmith—to glimpse the beauties of His creation. Even when he was an elderly scientist and his name was a household word and he had the worldwide respect of the scientific community, he did not think too highly of himself. When he was offered a knighthood, he turned it down. He felt that he should be just plain Michael Faraday to the end.

He had great respect for the younger generation of scientists coming up, and he cheerfully learned from them. His kindness and encouragement helped William Thomson (later called Lord Kelvin) and James Clerk Maxwell pursue electrical studies. When he was in his sixties, Faraday wrote to William Thomson after learning that Thomson had agreed to do a Friday evening lecture at the Royal Institution. "I cannot help but write to congratulate, not you, but myself on the delight I shall have," Faraday told him. "I wish I could continually sit under your wing."[23] Thomson was just thirty-two years old at the time, but Faraday was already his fan.

Supplementing his income

Faraday's income at the Royal Institution was modest, but he supplemented it for a time with outside consulting jobs. Sometimes he was even called on to give scientific testimony in court. Analytical chemists were a rare breed, and his meticulous services were often in demand. This consulting work was usually not exciting for him, but he carried it out with his characteristic thoroughness. None of his effort was wasted, though, because he was refining and perfecting his technique. He always helped the British government when they requested his services, but sometimes the work distracted him from his own research. The government asked him to analyze water samples and even to investigate drying different types of meat to be used by the British Navy. He groaned when he had to stop working on his electromagnetic researches so that he could analyze thirty-two samples of oatmeal for the Navy.

After the oatmeal research, he turned down all other consulting jobs. He had decided to devote himself wholly to his own researches, even though this meant a significant reduction in his income. But his dedication paid off. In a very short time, he obtained answers that had eluded the other scientists.

Difficulty with Davy

As Faraday's fame increased and his skill in the laboratory became apparent, it was inevitable, perhaps, that Sir Humphry Davy would feel envy. The chill that developed between the two men was a very sad chapter in Faraday's life.

When Faraday was thirty-three, he was nominated as a Fellow of the Royal Society. Davy was the president of the society that year, and he aggressively opposed Faraday's election. Faraday was finally elected, but Davy's opposition was disturbing and confusing. It seems that Davy was still upset over the Wollaston incident, even though Wollaston himself had accepted Faraday's explanation and had supported Faraday to be a Fellow.

Faraday and Davy were still cordial to each other after this incident, but the relationship was strained. Davy died five years later, and there is speculation that his declining health made him act at times in ungenerous ways. In later years Faraday always spoke highly of Davy and never wanted to hear anyone criticize him.

The discovery of electromagnetic induction

During his earlier electrical studies, Faraday had made this entry in his notebook: "Convert magnetism into electricity."[24] He knew that an electric current produced a magnetic field. *But was there a reciprocal relationship?* he asked himself. *Could a useful current be generated in some way from a magnet?*

He had an intuitive belief that there was symmetry in the design of the universe. It was this conviction that culminated in his prime achievement—

the discovery of electromagnetic induction in 1831. The key factor, which nobody had anticipated (with the possible exception of Joseph Henry in the United States[25]), was that there must be relative motion between the magnet and the conductor in which the current is being induced. As long as the motion was maintained, a steady current could be generated.

While he was working on this, he wrote, "I am busy just now again on electro-magnetism, and think I have got hold of a good thing, but can't say. It may be a weed instead of a fish that, after all my labour, I may at last pull up."[26] But this was no weed that he pulled up. It would be difficult to overstate the significance of this discovery. It laid much of the groundwork for James Clerk Maxwell's equations some years later, and it created the source of most of today's electricity. The great dynamos of modern hydroelectric plants are all descended from Faraday's quaint crank-operated generator—a device consisting of a twelve-inch brass disk that rotated between the poles of a horseshoe magnet. Up until this point in time, electricity had just been a scientific curiosity, but now it could be channeled into powerful technology.

As a by-product of this series of experiments, he also invented the transformer. In its original form there were two windings of insulated wire—primary and secondary—on a doughnut-shaped iron core. The transformer has proved to be a device unmatched in versatility and efficiency for use in communication, transportation, and power distribution. Its great beauty lies in the fact that it has no moving parts.

It had taken Faraday just a few weeks to discover electromagnetic induction when he put his mind to this problem. Then he spent the next thirty years working on the relation between electric and magnetic forces and how they were transmitted through space.

Contributions

Michael Faraday is rated by historians of science as the greatest of the experimental physicists. He is credited with the invention of the transformer, the electric motor, and the electric generator. He added a whole new list of words to our scientific vocabulary—*anode, cathode, ion, electrode, electrolyte, anion, cation,* and *electrolysis.* He had become frustrated because there were no words in the English language to describe the ideas that he had, so with the help of two friends, he coined the terms that he needed. Today, two of the basic units in physics are named in his honor—the *faraday,* a unit of electrical quantity, and the *farad,* a unit of capacitance.

In 1834, Faraday concluded a series of experiments leading to the formulation of his famous laws of electrolysis. Following up on research that Davy had begun, he passed electric currents through various solutions of metal salts. He found that the amount of metal plated out of solution depends on the quantity of electricity used and the equivalent weight of the metal.

He also made many important contributions to our knowledge of diamagnetism, polarized light, and the liquefaction of gases. His discovery of benzene laid the foundation for aromatic organic chemistry. And, perhaps most noteworthy of all, he initiated one of the most profound developments in the history of physics—field theory. From his brilliant and imaginative mind came the terms *magnetic field* and *lines of force*.[27] For a while, though, scientists considered his field theory completely unorthodox. Mainstream science didn't pursue this theory until two younger scientists, William Thomson and James Clerk Maxwell, showed the mathematical basis for it.

The frugal researcher

It would make a most interesting study to investigate Faraday's expenditures for research equipment. At that time in England there were no government grants for scientific pursuits, and he worked on a very limited budget from the Institution. The German scientist Hermann von Helmholtz said of him, "A few wires and some old bits of wood and iron seem to serve him for the greatest discoveries."[28]

One of his strongest virtues was the careful and prudent utilization of available materials. In the laboratory he waged war against breakage and waste. At the end of each day's experiments, he meticulously accounted for each item and returned it to its proper place.

Once when making measurements on the luminosity of a lighthouse in the English Channel near Dover, he used an ordinary black shawl pin as a photometer. (The light shone through the colored glass of the shawl pin, and he could calculate the brightness by the size of the image.) Although an assortment of fairly elaborate equipment had been taken along, those accompanying him on the expedition soon saw the superiority of his simpler, more reliable apparatus. Sir Frederick Arrow, one of the observers in the group, said later of the shawl pin, "Ever since I have used one as a very convenient mode of observing, and I never do so but I think of that night and dear good Faraday, and his genial, happy way of showing how even common things may be made useful."[29]

A demonstration of true faith

It has been said that true faith involves a willingness to trust one's safety and well being, both present and future, to the object of that faith. Preachers offer examples from the pulpit to illustrate this spiritual truth— such as the faith one has in the pilot of his plane or in a surgeon performing an operation. But how far will a man go to demonstrate his faith in a scientific principle?

In 1838, Faraday was willing to stake his life on his understanding of a corollary of Coulomb's law. According to Coulomb's law, two electrically charged objects are attracted or repelled by a force that diminishes as the square of the distance between them. A corollary of this law is that no charge can be detected on the *inside* of a charged object.

To prove his point, Faraday placed himself inside a twelve-foot wire cage. A high-voltage generator connected to the cage charged it to such an extent that it emitted sparks to the walls of the room in which it was located. Faraday felt nothing, and a sensitive electroscope inside the cage indicated no charge whatsoever. How could one demonstrate more sincerely that he believes something to be true?

In the same manner he held his faith in eternal verities with absolute assurance. A reporter once asked Faraday about his speculations on the hereafter. "Speculations?" he asked with astonishment. "I have none. I am resting on certainties. I know whom I have believed, and am persuaded that He is able to keep that which I have committed unto Him against that day!" [30]

Faraday's lectures

When Michael Faraday first came to the Royal Institution as the laboratory assistant, he helped in many demonstrations during the science lectures. He listened carefully during these lectures, but he was doing more than just learning science; he was observing the fine points of lecturing. From his own observation, he developed strong opinions on the mechanics of lecturing. He was interested in every detail—lighting, ventilation, the proper execution of experiments, and the manner of delivery. He was not a born speaker, but with practice and careful attention to detail, he made himself into one of the great lecture demonstrators of all time.

By the time he was twenty-four, he was giving lectures to the City Philosophical Society, the place where he had gotten his first exposure to science lectures. He was understandably nervous during these first lectures and wrote everything he would say in complete sentences, even down to his greeting—"Ladies and Gentleman"—because he was worried that his nervousness would make his memory desert him. As he gained confidence, he started using short notes and then abbreviated jottings. He finally pared down his notes to just two pages for a one hour lecture. On the right-hand side of the page he wrote his notes for the delivery, and on the left-hand side he jotted down the experiments and demonstrations.

He understood the short attention spans of the audience and said that the lecturer must make his subject irresistible. "I am sorry to say," he said, "that the generality of mankind cannot accompany us one short hour unless the path is strewed with flowers."[31] With his lavish use of demonstrations, he kept his audience enthralled. He thought it beneath the dignity of a lecturer to fish for applause with showy displays. But the applause at the end of his lectures was genuine and well deserved.

In 1826, Faraday began his famous Friday Evening Discourses. When he had been named the director at the Royal Institution the year before, he knew he needed to do something quickly to save the institution from bankruptcy. So he started the famous lectures that brought in revenue for the institution and made science popular. The purpose of his lectures was to show people the beauty and usefulness of science. He was at his best when he was showing his own researches. But he also reported on current researches of other scientists. The Faraday lectures were well attended and greatly appreciated. The audience of fashionable people often included such celebrities as Charles Dickens and Prince Albert. Faraday gave over 120 of these lectures himself and often invited other scientists to speak.

Once when he was escorting the guest speaker down to the lecture hall, the guest speaker was overcome by nerves and bolted down the stairs and escaped into the street. Faraday had to stand in for him that night and give an extemporaneous speech. From then on, the Royal Institution started a new tradition: when escorting a speaker to the lecture hall, the director would walk on the side nearest the outside door so that he could cut off a speaker's escape.

Faraday's favorite lectures were the ones he started for children. Though he never was blessed with children of his own, he had a great love for children. He always preferred lecturing to a young audience because the open-minded eagerness of a group of young people gave him a feeling of scientific fellowship. He addressed them as equals and loved the fact that they were still willing to be surprised and awed. They had not yet adopted the bored, reserved attitude of adults.

For almost two decades he delivered Christmas lectures for boys and girls who were home from school for the holidays. He covered electricity and magnetism, chemistry, gravitation, and other topics in physics. He taught the children to make observations and always to ask questions. "I hope you will always remember," he told the children, "that whenever a result happens, especially if it be new, you should say, 'What is the cause? Why does it occur?' and you will in the course of time find out the reason."[32]

The most famous of these was a series of six lectures delivered in 1860-61 entitled *The Chemical History of a Candle.* Starting with the very familiar and intriguing phenomenon of a candle flame, he led his young audience through many avenues of chemistry with several magnificent demonstrations to illustrate each lecture. The stenographic records of these lectures are still available today and are studied and emulated by science lecturers all over the world. This lecture series on the candle has been called Faraday's last testament. From that time on, his activities became more and more limited because of his failing memory.

The tradition of children's lectures still lives on at the Royal Institution. Each year over 35,000 school children come to lectures. And the Christmas series is now so popular that it is televised. Only children are allowed in the gallery for these lectures; the parents have to sit in the balcony.

Faraday's most famous lecture series: *The Chemical History of a Candle*

Loyalty to the Royal Institution

It is touching to see Faraday's loyalty to the Royal Institution. He always stayed with the institution, even in the lean years, because he appreciated the start it had given him in his scientific life. As his fame grew, he could have worked at more prestigious institutions and commanded a much higher salary. When the University of London offered him a post teaching chemistry, he turned it down, explaining that he wanted to help the institution through a difficult time.

When he was forty, his salary was one hundred pounds a year—really quite pitiful because he could have commanded five times that salary as a university professor. The institution wanted to pay him what he merited, but they could afford to give him only "house, coals, and candles" besides his meager salary.[33] There were times that finances were so slim at the Royal Institution that Faraday commented dryly that "we were living on the parings of our own skin."[34] But his salary and his fees for lecturing were adequate for the simple lifestyle he craved. And his wife was content with this.

He was always plain Michael Faraday with his simple tastes and his frugal ways. When he needed a book bound, he did it himself. (Some of his personal books that he bound are displayed at the Royal Institution.) He used his bookbinding skill all his life. When he borrowed a book, he would often return the book handsomely bound as a token of his gratitude. Even late in life, when he particularly respected an author, he would bind the book neatly to show how he valued it.

Health

Faraday was so driven in his work that he rarely let himself stop to rest. He said that it wasn't any religious motive that kept him from enjoying social activities. He simply needed more time to work, and he had decided to cut out all activities that weren't necessary, even those that were good and legitimate. He enjoyed music, but he rarely used his season ticket to the opera. He turned down most invitations to dinner, and preferred to stay at home in the evening with his wife and nieces.

He worked for intense periods in his laboratory until finally his health forced him to stop and rest. Occasionally the Faradays had to take a rest in the country so that he could recuperate. For most of his adult life, he suffered from memory loss, headaches, and giddiness. Some biographers have wondered whether this was mercury poisoning, because he was always using this element in his researches. Often cups of it would spill on the floor, and he breathed the vapors. His symptoms do fit mercury poisoning; or it could be that some other chemical exposure ruined his health.

For a while, the rests in the country would clear his head so that his headaches were less severe. He told a friend that he was leaving the city to try to rid himself of a headache that he had "*enjoyed* for the last four months."[35] But from the time he was forty-eight, his headaches were almost constant. For five years, he was unable to work because of this illness. He recovered more or less and was able to work in his laboratory again, but the residue of that illness still plagued him.

His memory trouble was already starting by the time he was in his midtwenties. He learned always to write things down to counteract his forgetfulness. He complained that his ideas were completely lost if he didn't write them down right away. As he learned more facts, his imperfect memory caused him real concern. He couldn't always access the data he had stored in his brain. He often made light of his poor memory, and it seemed to others that he was just an absent-minded professor.

As he grew older, he painstakingly kept a research diary and numbered the paragraphs so that he could cross-reference his work. Here he wrote down questions and ideas for research. When he answered his question, he drew a line through it with the date that he answered it. With this written record, he tried to counteract his growing forgetfulness.

His body was still strong, and when he took a rest in Switzerland when he was fifty, he took daily walks of thirty miles. His wife worried about him only on the day he walked forty-five miles. His body was fine, he said. His illness was in his head—"mental muddiness," he called it.[36] During his bad spells, he couldn't even write a coherent letter. "I cannot remember the beginning of a sentence to the end," he wrote to a friend.[37] But, as much as possible, he continued his correspondence, asking his friends to excuse him because he was forgetting how to spell, and he was forgetting the science matters they used to discuss. To a good friend whom he had been writing for many years, he wrote, "When I want to write to you it seems as if only nonsense would come to mind, and yet it is not nonsense to think of past friendship and dear communions. When I try to write of science, it comes back to me in confusion. . . . After all, though your science is much to me, we are not friends for science sake only, but for something better in a man, something more important in his nature, affection, kindness, good feeling, moral worth; and so, in remembrance of these, I now write to place myself in your presence, and in thought shake hands, tongues, and hearts together."[38]

Faraday was not incoherent or mentally incompetent, but his memory loss was affecting all areas of his life. He turned down the presidency of the Royal Society and of the British Association for the Advancement of Science because he didn't think it proper for him to hold these honors if he couldn't fulfill the duties.

"I cannot remember from day to day the conclusions I come to," he wrote after trying to work in his lab, "and all has to be thought out many times over. To write it down gives no assistance, for what is written down is itself forgotten."[39] When he was sixty-four, he had to stop his own re-searches because he couldn't hold his thoughts together to carry on any type of sustained research. He had noticed that he was repeating experiments that he had done months earlier and had entirely forgotten about it. "This in some degree annoys me," he said. "I do not mean the labour, but the forgetfulness, for, in fact, the labour without memory is of no use."[40]

But even when he couldn't do his laboratory researches, he hated the thought of just resting on his laurels and not doing active work anymore. So he worked on the condensation of gases, because this largely involved technique, and he could rest his mind while he just went about the mechanics of the work.

He went back to consulting work, and for a time, he was able to help others with his advice. He worked on preserving and protecting the art in the National Gallery. The glass that he recommended to put over the paintings was originally a temporary measure, but he was unable to come up with a good protective coating. For many years he had been a consultant for the government lighthouses and he continued this work—helping to perfect electrical lighting and making the lamps more efficient and the light brighter. Even when he was seventy years old, he was still traveling to different lighthouses and going several miles out on the ocean to measure the brightness of the lights.

He accepted his fading memory with poise and grace. "I am at present as well as I think any man at my age has any reason to expect to be," he wrote to his niece, "and in many points I am much better. It is true my memory is much gone, nearly all gone; and the power of recollection is nearly lost, *as to precision*. But then all about me are very kind. My worldly friends remember the times past, and do not want me to give up my posts or pay, yet willingly remit the work; and then He who rules over all is kinder than all . . . and I call to mind that His throne is a throne of grace, where prayer may be made for help and strength in time of need. And He makes my brethren so kind, that there is only one of the number who teases me, and that is myself, and I often think pride and the absence of humility has much to do with that."[41]

He kept lecturing until he was seventy, but it was a strain on him. He carefully wrote his lectures out, but he was still worried that he would embarrass himself and his audience if his memory trouble showed. He finally had to resign all his duties at the Royal Institution. But by far the saddest loss occurred when at age seventy-three, he had to give up his position as elder of his church.

His comfort and trust in the finished work of his Lord

After he resigned from his duties at the Royal Institution, the queen gave the Faradays a house in Hampton Court near the palace. Faraday spent his last nine years there. By now, he had only rare moments of mental clarity, but he never forgot his love for Christ.

"I am, I hope, very thankful that in the withdrawal of the power and things of this life,—the good hope is left with me, which makes the contemplation of death a comfort—not a fear. Such peace is alone in the gift of God, and as it is He who gives it, why shall we be afraid? His unspeakable gift in His beloved Son is the ground of no doubtful hope; and *there* is the rest for those who like you and me are drawing near the latter end of our terms here below," he wrote to a friend.[42]

In a letter to his niece he wrote, "My worldly faculties are slipping away day by day. Happy is it for all of us that the true good lies not in them. As they ebb, may they leave us as little children trusting in the Father of mercies and accepting His unspeakable gift."[43] As he became weaker, he loved to sit in a chair by the window and watch the clouds and the sunset. He said that looking at the sky made him think of heaven.

When he was spending his last days in bed, a victim of creeping paralysis, his niece who was caring for him said that he would sleep often and then wake up and say portions of Scripture. "Between whiles," she said, "he speaks most pleasant words, showing his comfort and trust in the finished work of our Lord."[44]

He was ready to die. He had written to a friend, "I bow before Him who is Lord of all, and hope to be kept waiting patiently for His time and mode of releasing me according to His Divine Word, and the great and precious promises whereby His people are made partakers of the Divine nature."[45] That release came on August 26, 1867.

He could have been honored with a burial in Westminster Abbey if he had wished, but he insisted on a private funeral and wanted everything done in a plain and unpretentious manner. His grave is marked with a simple white gravestone. He was plain Michael Faraday to the end. But since his death, the influence of his work has been widely appreciated. He has been honored with several memorials, including one in Westminster Abbey. The promise that "whatsoever he doeth shall prosper" was fulfilled in Faraday's life in a remarkable manner as his faith, his perseverance, and his genius combined to pursue each piece of research until he had obtained a definitive answer.

---

[1] Joseph Agassi, *Faraday as a Natural Philosopher* (Chicago: Univ. of Chicago Press, 1971) p. 16.

[2] Ibid., p. 17.

[3] Some of Dr. Watts classic hymns are still sung today—"O God, Our Help in Ages Past," "Joy to the World," "When I Survey the Wondrous Cross," and "Jesus Shall Reign Where'er the Sun."

[4] Philip Cane, *Giants of Science* (New York: Pyramid Publications, 1962), p. 160.

[5] L. Pearce Williams, *Michael Faraday: A Biography* (New York: Clarion, 1971), p. 44. See also Dr. Bence Jones, *The Life and Letters of Faraday*, Vol. 1 (London: Longmans, Green, and Co.: 1870), p. 202.

[6] Williams, p. 449.

[7] From "Biographical Introduction" by Sir J. Arthur Thomson, in *The Chemical History of a Candle* by Michael Faraday (Atlanta: Cherokee Publishing Co., 1993), p. xvii.

[8] Silvanus P. Thompson, *The Life of William Thomson: Baron Kelvin of Largs* (London: MacMillan and Co., 1910), p. 945. Faraday was referring to the use of electricity for electroplating as well as for lighthouses.

[9] Williams, p. 196.

[10] Jones, Vol. 1, p. 196.

[11] "Sandemanianism—The theology and church practices of the Glasites. Robert Sandeman (1718-1771) was the son-in-law of John Glas, a Scottish Independent minister of mainly Calvinistic persuasions. Sandemanianism was an attempt to get back to primitive, apostolic Christianity. It was based on a fiercely independent theory of the church." They had a peculiar theory of faith limiting it to its intellectual content. This was probably an overreaction to un- warranted mystical notions of faith. (From the *Dictionary of Theological Terms* by Alan Cairns [Greenville, SC: Ambassador-Emerald, Intl., 1998], p. 327.)

[12] In a Presidential address to the Royal Society of Edinburgh, Sir David Brewster said, "With a judgment thus sound and thus patiently exercised, Faraday had no difficulty in answering the question, 'What is truth?' among the complex laws of the material world, and he had none in answering the question as put by the Roman Governor. Like Newton, the greatest of his predecessors, he was a humble Christian, with the simplicity of apostolic times. Among the grand truths which he had studied and made known, he had found none out of harmony with his faith; and from the very depths of science he had proclaimed to the Sciolists, that there is a wisdom which is not 'foolishness with God.'" (From Margaret Maria Gordon, *The Home Life of Sir David Brewster* [Edinburgh: Edmonston and Douglas, 1870], p. 329.)

When Lord Kelvin spoke at the dedication of a plaque to Faraday in the place where the Sandemanian church used to meet, he said, "In the place it- self you will see a monument of Faraday. These walls tell a story, not of a magnificent cathedral, but of the humble meeting-house of earnest Christian men. Here were carried on the religious services of the Sandemanians in London, a very simple association devoted to faithful and earnest Christian work. Throughout his life Faraday adhered faithfully to this denomination as an officiating elder. . . . I well remember, at meetings of the British Association in Aberdeen and Glasgow, how he sought out the meetings of his denomination, and spent, as a preacher or worshipper there, the Sunday and any time he could spare from the work of the Association. How very interesting it is to think of Faraday's life-long faithfulness to his religious denomination." (From Silvanus P. Thompson, *The Life of William Thomson: Baron Kelvin of Largs* [London: MacMillan and Co., 1910], p. 1192.)

[13] Jones, Vol. 1, p. 285.

[14] His favorite portions of Scripture were the following:

"O Timothy, keep that which is committed to thy trust, avoiding profane and vain babblings, and oppositions of science falsely so called: which some professing have erred concerning the faith" (I Timothy 6:20, 21a).

"Therefore all things whatsoever ye would that men should do to you, do ye even so to them: for this is the law and the prophets" (Matthew 7:12).

"But when thou doest alms, let not thy left hand know what thy right hand doeth" (Matthew 6:3).

"For the invisible things of him from the creation of the world are clearly seen, being understood by the things that are made, even his eternal power and Godhead; so that they are without excuse" (Romans 1:20).

[15] F. W. Boreham, *A Handful of Stars* (London: The Epworth Press, 1930), pp. 181-82.

[16] Williams, p. 6.

[17] Ibid., p. 158.

[18] Ibid., p. 89.

[19] Jones, Vol. 2, p. 387. See also Lewis Campbell and William Garnett, *The Life of James Clerk Maxwell* (London: Macmillan, 1882), p. 145 (page number in the electronic version of the book from Sonnet Software, Inc.)

[20] Faraday gave a lecture on Mental Education in 1854. He began with a word of warning: "Let no one suppose for a moment that the self-education I am about to commend, in respect of the things of this life, extends to any considerations of the hope set before us, as if man by reasoning could find out God." He let his listeners know that the truth about the future life "cannot be brought to his knowledge by any exertion of his mental powers, however exalted they may be; that it is made known to him by other teaching than his own, and is received through simple belief of the testimony given." (Jones, Vol. 1, p. 298) In other words, in matters of religious belief, only the revelation of God in the Scriptures was sufficient. No amount of mental exertion could uncover the salvation that God reveals in His Word.

[21] Williams, p. 465.

[22] Williams, p. 105. (quoting Job 9:20) About his scientific work, Faraday said, "In all kinds of knowledge I perceive that my views are insufficient, and

my judgment imperfect. In experiments I come to conclusions which, if partly right, are sure to be in part wrong; if I correct by other experiments, I advance a step, my old error is in part diminished, but is always left with a tinge of humanity, evidenced by its imperfection." (Williams, p. 105)

[23] Thompson, p. 312.

[24] Cane, p. 158.

[25] It is possible that Joseph Henry in the United States preceded Faraday in his electromagnetic discoveries; but Henry did not record his findings until after Faraday published his.

[26] Agassi, p. 74.

[27] These lines of force are illustrated by strewing iron filings on a piece of paper and placing it near a magnet. These filings will form fibers that indicate the direction of the lines of force.

[28] D. K. C. MacDonald, *Faraday, Maxwell, and Kelvin* (Garden City, NY: Doubleday, 1964), p. 16.

[29] John H. Gladstone, *Michael Faraday* (New York: Harper & Brothers, no date), p. 164.

[30] F. W. Boreham, *A Handful of Stars* (London: The Epworth Press, 1930), p. 179-80, quoting II Timothy 1:12.

[31] Jones, Vol. 1, p. 64.

[32] Michael Faraday, *The Chemical History of a Candle* (Atlanta: Cherokee Publishing Co., 1993), p. 10. Excerpt from Christmas Lecture Number 1.

[33] J.G. Crowther, *Men of Science* (New York: W.W. Norton, 1936), p. 93.

[34] Jones, Vol. 2, p. 344.

[35] Williams, p. 358.

[36] Jones, Vol. 2, p. 375. See also Williams, p. 493.

[37] Williams, p. 359.

[38] Jones, Vol. 2, pp. 433-34.

[39] Jones, Vol. 2, p. 375. See also Williams, p. 493.

[40] Jones, Vol. 2, pp. 245-46. See also Williams, p. 445.

[41] Jones, Vol. 2, p. 461.

[42] Williams, p. 500.

[43] Jones, Vol. 2, p. 425.

[44] Gladstone, p. 79.

[45] Jones, Vol. 2, p. 471.

Samuel F.B. Morse (1791-1872)

SAMUEL F. B. MORSE
(1791-1872)

Inventor and Painter

Seest thou a man diligent in his business? He shall stand before kings.
Proverbs 22:29

Finley Morse glanced over his shoulder to make sure that the teacher was still busy with the older students. He quietly scratched the wood with a pin and smiled as a head took shape. Then he began adding the dress.

School was so boring. He would much rather be drawing, but he couldn't use his school slate for drawing or he would get in trouble. He had found a pin on the ground while he was walking to school that day. A perfect drawing tool, he had thought as he stooped to pick it up. Later that morning when the teacher was busy, he slipped over to the chest of drawers in the corner and began drawing. After a few minutes, he stood back to admire the portrait. "It needs shoes," he thought.

Suddenly he heard his name and looked up to see Old Ma'am Rand motioning to him. At that moment, the schoolmistress didn't see a budding artist. She saw a naughty four-year-old boy, scratching her fine chest of drawers with a pin. "Come here!" she demanded. She was holding the long stick that she used for swatting, and she was ready to use it on him. By now all the students had stopped working, and they watched as Finley walked slowly to the front of the room to confront the teacher.

Old Ma'am Rand was an invalid and couldn't walk, so she had learned to rule the children with her stern voice and her long swatting stick. But she didn't spank Finley. She decided to give him her worst punishment. She pinned him securely to her dress, and he would have to stay beside her the rest of the morning. But Finley struggled away from her, dragging part of her dress across the room with him. The old teacher swung her long stick at the fleeing boy and rapped him smartly on the shoulder.

Samuel Finley Breese Morse often remembered the painful reception of this early attempt at artwork. When he grew up, he studied art professionally and became a noted painter. But he was more than a painter—he was undoubtedly one of the most versatile geniuses the United States has produced. In fact, one of his biographers dubbed him "The American Leonardo da Vinci." He was an artist, an inventor, a college professor, and a writer. More important, though, he was a sincere Christian who pursued his various endeavors to glorify God.

The young artist

Finley Morse came from an impressive heritage, both spiritually and intellectually. He grew up in a parsonage that was bustling with important visitors. His father, Jedidiah Morse, was the town pastor of Charlestown, Massachusetts (now part of Boston). Dr. Morse was a prominent Calvinist who tenaciously fought the rise of Unitarianism. He was an incredibly energetic man, and his motto in life was "Better wear out than rust out."[1] He published religious writings and constantly waded into theological controversies. But Dr. Morse's pursuits were wider than theology. He was the author of the first geography textbooks published in America, *Geography Made Easy*. Morse's geographies were so well known that Jedidiah Morse became a household name, in Europe as well as in the United States.

Mrs. Morse was the granddaughter of Dr. Samuel Finley, president of Princeton College. Her first three boys were born healthy, but her other eight children died in infancy. Mrs. Morse enjoyed reading aloud to her children and to anyone else who happened to be present. She was a wise mother who encouraged her boys to develop their remarkable talents and their inclination for original thinking. Like all mothers, she wanted her boys to excel and be useful to society, but her overriding desire and prayer for her boys was that they would be true followers of Christ. Her prayer was answered. These three sons lived long, productive lives and never wavered from the faith that was instilled in them as children.

As a child, Finley was not noted for his good behavior. When he was seven, his parents tried to improve his conduct by sending him to the preparatory school of Phillips Academy at Andover—a Christian school founded for the purpose of promoting "true piety and virtue."[2] The only records that remain of his scholastic efforts there are those of his demerits—eight in spelling and eighteen for whispering. To encourage better behavior, his parents offered rewards—cakes, pies, books, and vacations from schoolwork. Undoubtedly, though, his parent's insistence on daily prayer and Bible study imposed stability and the much-needed restraint on his waywardness.

As he grew, he developed a godly spirit that stayed with him throughout his life. When he was fourteen, he wrote a letter to his two brothers away at boarding school to inform them that their newest baby brother had died. "Now you have three brothers and three sisters in heaven and I hope you and I will meet them there at our death. It is uncertain when we shall die, but we ought to be prepared for it, and I hope you and I shall."[3]

Years at Yale

The next phase of his education took him to Yale College as a fourteen-year-old. Although most of his classmates at Andover went on to Harvard, that prestigious school had already departed from the fundamentals of the faith on which it had been founded. Yale, however, was still orthodox, and Pastor Morse was concerned that young Finley be instructed in sound doctrine as well as academics. He did not want his son's careful religious instruction undone by a liberal college.

Perhaps the greatest influence on Finley at this time was Timothy Dwight, the grandson of Jonathan Edwards. Dwight was the president of Yale and the professor of divinity at the college. He took a special interest in Finley because he was the son of his good friend Jedidiah. Dwight believed that the study of science was a valuable tool for a Christian because it was a powerful weapon against unbelief. The Christian faith, he said, would be soundly supported, not weakened, by the firm facts of science. So he added science courses to Yale and brought in science professors.

One of these new classes, Professor Jeremiah Day's physics lecture, was Finley's favorite. The electrical demonstrations interested Finley the most. The arcing of a spark gap was presented as evidence that the electrical "fluid" can be seen wherever a break occurs in the circuit. On one memorable occasion the entire class joined hands in a circle while the good professor attached the students to the contacts of a high-voltage generator. All feet left the floor in unison in a chaos of screams and grunts. The scientific purpose of the experiment is somewhat in doubt, but from that day onward young Morse was impressed with electricity's potential.

Around this time Morse was developing his artistic talent. In his spare time he decorated the walls of his dormitory room, and before long one entire side of the room was covered with a mural depicting struggling freshmen "climbing the hill of science."[4]

In his junior year, art became a more serious part of his life. A freshman offered to sit for a portrait. Morse captured his likeness so successfully that other students were soon paying for his services. At this point, he was largely self-taught, but his reputation as a portrait artist spread throughout the city of New Haven, and during the remainder of his stay at Yale, he was generously supplied with commissions.

Art training

Dr. Jedidiah Morse was never wealthy and found it difficult to support his family with his pastoral salary and his writing. Yet, at great personal sacrifice, he managed to give his children the best education that America had to offer. When Finley showed promise as a painter, his parents scrapped the plans they had made for their oldest son and decided to send him to Europe to study painting.

The year after his graduation from Yale, Morse became a pupil of the noted painter and author Washington Allston and accompanied him to England to study for four years. Morse admired Allston's work tremendously, and he quickly became an eager and dedicated student.

Allston would come by his room every day and supervise his painting. He rarely flattered Morse. He would stand in front of the easel, hands behind his back, and shake his head slowly. "Very bad, sir," he would say. "That is not flesh; it is mud, sir; it is painted with brick dust and clay." Then he would show Morse how to mix a lifelike flesh tone.[5] At first Morse's pride was hurt by such blunt criticism. But then he realized that Allston didn't just criticize; he always showed him how to remedy the problems.

Allston then introduced Morse to Benjamin West, who at that time was the most respected person in the world of art. Morse's introduction to the elderly West and the friendship that ensued from the meeting proved to be a vital link in his chain of success. For it was West who administered the mental discipline that Morse needed.

On one occasion Morse appeared at the West mansion to display his latest drawing. He had labored on it for two full weeks, and he was confident that he had produced a creditable piece of work. Somewhat boldly he asked the master for his opinion. Fortunately for Morse, West's fondness for him in no way inhibited his frankness. His comment was simply "Very well, sir, very well; go and finish it."[6] He pointed out the omissions, and Morse dutifully went back to his studio to add the missing ingredients.

A week later he returned only to have the same thing happen again. After enduring this three times, Morse realized that he had been existing in a world of mediocrity. He had yet to learn how to scrutinize and communicate the subtle details in his subject. West skillfully filled in the gaps in his technique and showed him how to mark each muscle, each tendon, each articulation. Before many years had passed, Morse had taken his place alongside West's most gifted pupils—men such as Gilbert Stuart, Rembrandt Peale, and John Trumbull.[7]

Morse's conversion

Morse's mother was constantly concerned about his spiritual welfare while he was traveling abroad. She was stern and unbending in her principles, and her letters were full of maternal advice and scolding. Anxious about his choice of friends, she warned in her letters that most Americans in Europe were "dissipated infidels"[8] and should be shunned. Allston and West, however, she recognized as exceptions to the rule.

To her delight she learned that her Finley had come under the influence of William Wilberforce and his zealous group of evangelical Christians known as the Clapham Sect. Morse was thoroughly impressed with Wilberforce and said afterward, "What I saw of him in private gave me the most exalted opinion of him as a Christian."[9] The witness and testimony of these godly men soon brought Morse himself to follow Christ. The specific time of his conversion

Morse studied painting in Europe.

is not known, but when he returned to the States four years later, he made a public profession of his faith in his own church.

The War of 1812 broke out while Finley was in England, and his letters were often delayed. He longed for a way to let his mother know instantly that he was safe. In one letter he moans, "I only wish you had this letter now to relieve your minds from anxiety, for while I am writing I can imagine mother wishing that she could hear of my arrival, and thinking of thousands of accidents which may have befallen me. I wish that in an instant I could communicate the information: but three thousand miles are not passed over in an instant, and we must wait four long weeks before we can hear from each other."[10] At this point, the telegraph had not yet occurred to Morse. But the longing to communicate instantly over long distances was often in his mind.

Morse's godliness

Growing up in a strict Puritan minister's home, Finley had few opportunities to indulge in blatant sin. Yet, when he was in Europe, without parental supervision, he showed that the lessons of his childhood had stuck. He demonstrated how godly training can restrain and protect a young person, even before he comes to saving faith in Christ. His parents knew that they could not legislate godliness, but their insistence on Biblical morals served as guardrails to keep him safely on a moral highway.

As a young man, Morse recognized that even though he did not sin outwardly, in his thoughts he was perfectly capable of all types of sin. His journals show his preoccupation with his thought life. "Actions proceed from thoughts," he wrote; "we act as we think. Why should we, then, so cautiously guard our actions from impropriety while we give a loose rein to our thoughts, which so certainly, sooner or later, produce their fruits in our actions?" He goes on to say that Christians should carefully guard their hearts from evil thoughts and influences. "The soul is too precious to be thus exposed. Where then is our remedy? In Christ alone. 'Cleanse thou me from secret faults. Search me, O God, and know my thoughts; try me and know my ways and see if there is any wicked way in me, and lead me in the way which is everlasting.'"[11]

As a young Christian, he began a daily routine of self-examination. In his journal he wrote out his answers to questions such as these: "What have I done this day?" "How did I pray; did I ask sincerely for certain blessings, or was there a secret disinclination to have them?" "Did I feel weighed down with sin, or did I pray as the self-righteous Pharisee?" "Have I not received particular blessings this day which I have not been thankful for?"[12] He felt that writing down his answers helped bring his secret thoughts more readily to light.

His painting career and marriage

Back in the States after his study in Europe, he envisioned himself painting grand historical scenes. These impressive scenes required imagination and intelligence, certainly two talents that he possessed. But he quickly discovered that historical works did not sell. Desperate to support himself, he turned to portrait painting.

The next few years found Morse busily engaged in painting portraits up and down the eastern seaboard. During this period of his life he painted such notables as General Lafayette, President Monroe, and Noah Webster (the portrait used as the frontispiece for Webster's Dictionary). Painting President Monroe proved to be a challenge. Morse would get his paint palette ready to begin painting at 10:00 a.m., but the president wouldn't have time to sit until much later in the day. Usually the president could stay for only ten or twenty minutes before he was called back to his work.

While working in Concord, New Hampshire, Morse met his bride-to-be, Lucretia Pickering Walker. Morse had the privilege of pointing her to Christ before they were married. Morse advised her to carefully examine her thoughts and actions each day to know her own sinfulness. "I might flatter you, dear, as some would," he wrote to her. "I might tell you that your amiable disposition, and your correct conduct would certainly recommend you to God, that you need only go on, live correctly, be charitable, and you have nothing to fear; and whilst I thus deceived you, you might love me most sincerely; but think, my dear, what a part I should act; I could see one whom I loved so tenderly resting in false security, (which if I did my duty, ought to be disturbed), and I could live with her through life, and when death separated us, know for an awful truth, that if I was saved, we were separated forever. Could I love you, dear girl, if I could do this?"[13]

Theirs was an especially close marriage, marred only by his protracted absences and the financial problems that often accompany the painting profession. The only thing Morse ever wished to change about her was that she might be less lovely, because he felt there was a danger that he might idolize her and "put her in the place of Him who has said, 'Thou shalt have no other Gods but me.'"[14] Lucretia was sickly and Morse tried to be home with her during her sick spells. But he often had to leave her in the care of his parents and travel to the places where his portrait commissions were.

Other inventions

Even as a painter, Morse showed a decided bent for invention. He invented a marble-carving machine that would make statue carving easier. Another invention, a flexible piston pump that he invented with his brother Sidney, was whimsically named "Morse's Patent Metallic Double-Headed Ocean-Drinker and Deluge-Spouter Valve Pump-Boxes."[15] This water pump was useful for fire engines. He hoped that the income from his inventions would support his art career, but they proved to be financial disappointments.

Morse the scientist was always lurking inside Morse the painter. He devised a theory of color that proved workable, at least to him. He thought artists often had an instinctive feel for color combinations, but he felt they could improve their work significantly if they understood colors scientifically. He experimented with colors with scientific precision and enjoyed mixing his paints with different materials to achieve different effects. On his wife's portrait, he achieved a rich creamy flesh tone by mixing his paints with milk.

The mail moves too slowly

Shortly after the birth of baby Fin, confident that Lucretia was recovering well from the birth, he traveled to Washington. There he began working on the portrait of General Lafeyette, the French general who had helped America win her independence from Britain. During a break in the painting, he eagerly read a letter from his father that had just arrived.

February 8th, 1825

My affectionately beloved Son,

Mysterious are the ways of Providence. My heart is in pain and deeply sorrowful while I announce to you the sudden and unexpected death of your dear and deservedly loved wife. Her disease proved to be an *affection of the heart*—incurable, had it been known. . . . Everything was done that could be done to save her life, but her 'appointed time' had come, and no earthly power or skill could stay the hand of death.

It was the Lord who gave her to you, the chiefest of all your earthly blessings, and it is He that has taken her away, and may you be enabled, my son, from the heart to say: "Blessed be the name of the Lord." . . .The shock to the whole family is far beyond, in point of severity, that of any we have ever before felt, but we are becoming composed, we hope on grounds which will prove solid and lasting.[16]

This devastating news of Lucretia's sudden death was a severe blow. Morse stopped work on the portrait and quickly traveled home. But news traveled so slowly that several days had already passed since her death. By the time he arrived home, the funeral had already taken place.

Morse grieved deeply, yet he had the blessed hope of all who truly believe what the Lord has revealed: "God shall wipe away all tears; . . . there shall be no more death, neither sorrow, nor crying, neither shall there be any more pain: for the former things are passed away" (Revelation 21:4).

He threw himself into his painting, and, thankfully, he finally had enough commissions to keep him constantly busy. But he found that he could not properly take care of his three young children while doing his painting. With great regret, he left his children with his relatives and continued his painting so that he could provide for them. He always took care of his children financially, but he longed to reach a degree of financial stability that would allow him to stay home and bring his family all together again under one roof.

His scientific career begins

As a general rule at that time, Americans were not willing to spend the money on fine art that the Europeans spent. Morse explained to a friend that Europeans were eager to buy paintings and vie with each other to see who could own the best piece of art. Americans, however, were content to buy furniture and compete with each other to see who had the best pieces of furniture. For this reason, it was hard for even an excellent painter like Morse to make a living in the States just by painting.

Morse decided it was time to study in Europe again. This time he wanted to study the great masters of Italy and France. He toured the galleries, studying the great paintings by making copies of them. His great masterpiece of this time, *Gallery of the Louvre*, was a large canvas that included some fifty paintings from the Louvre. He knew that many Americans would never be able to make the trip across the ocean to visit the Louvre, and he thought they would be willing to pay a fee to see his faithful copies of some of the Louvre's great works. This project, too, proved to be a financial disappointment. Americans just weren't enthusiastic about art.

While he was in Paris, he became intrigued with the French semaphore system of communication. In this system, movable crossarms were mounted on towers. Different positions of the crossarms symbolized letters of the alphabet. Visual signals were sent from tower to tower, and in good weather, a message could be carried through the fourteen stations from Paris to the Rhine in six minutes. But the system was useless in the fog.

This semaphore system is much better, Morse thought, *than the mail system back home*. Ever since the delay in hearing about his wife's death, the galling slowness of the mail system had gnawed at him. But the semaphore system was still too slow for Morse. To his friend Habersham he remarked rather cryptically, "The lightning would serve us better."[17]

His vague wish for faster communication was gradually forming into a concrete idea. He would harness electricity to communicate intelligence across distance. It would be a telegraph, meaning literally that it was an instrument that would write or record a message at a distance. Being intimately familiar with the Scriptures, his curiosity may have been piqued by the challenge of Job 38:35—"Canst thou send lightnings that they may go, and say unto thee, Here we are?"

Further discussions followed with his close circle of friends at the home of the novelist James Fenimore Cooper. Their general reaction was that this was rather fanciful thinking for a sober-minded artist such as he was.

During his return voyage to America, a specific idea crystallized in his mind. In fact, this trip actually marked the beginning of his scientific career. Around the dinner table aboard ship, he discussed his dream with several of the travelers in his group—a Boston physician, a Philadelphia lawyer, an American ambassador to France, and the captain of the ship. Their exchange of ideas stimulated his thinking.

Early model of the telegraph key

Morse was no stranger to the world of electricity. He was conversant with Benjamin Franklin's work in electricity. As a teenager, Morse had experimented with voltaic cells under the supervision of Professor Benjamin Silliman at Yale shortly after their invention. Morse had been a close friend of James Dana, an authority on electromagnetism and a pioneer in the use of the horseshoe electromagnet in America. Dana used to spend hours in Morse's studio discussing their favorite subjects, art and electricity.

Now Morse welded these bits and pieces of electrical knowledge with his own imagination. Working late into the nights, he pondered the questions that arose and made sketches in his notebook. When he disembarked from his ship in New York Harbor, his notebook contained sketches of the first crude electric telegraph.

His brothers met him at the wharf, expecting to hear about his painting. Instead, Morse eagerly showed them his sketchbook and explained his invention. What he envisioned was a recording telegraph that would impress dots and dashes on a moving paper tape. An electrical impulse coming from a remote station would energize an electromagnet, pulling down one end of an armature. Being pivoted at its center, the bar end of the armature would move up, causing a pencil to make a mark on a moving tape. When the incoming pulse of energy had ended, a permanent magnet would then restore the armature to its original position, ready to receive the next pulse.

With some minor modifications this mechanism proved to be very beautiful in its simplicity and reliability of operation. The sending device and the code, however, were both to undergo profound changes. He did not realize it at the time, but years of experimentation still lay ahead before the telegraph was perfected. Many trials, heartaches, and disappointments awaited him along the way.

Painting gives way to invention

Providentially, Morse received an appointment as professor of sculpture and painting at the University of the City of New York (later called New York University). He had several private students who paid for lessons, but he did not earn a salary yet. The most attractive part of this job was that it gave him a place to experiment. One corner of his art studio resembled a workshop and laboratory. Here he fashioned his telegraph equipment from scratch, working from models that he whittled out of wood. His art students were dismayed at the amount of time he spent on his invention, and they whispered unhappily about their brilliant teacher's "sad infatuation."[18]

It was hard, lonely work those first few months. There was no one to help him in the early days until his invention first showed unmistakable signs of promise. Morse was still poverty-stricken from his years as a freelance painter. He carried out all testing and development on a shoestring budget. Such lowly items as old clock mechanisms and artists' canvas-stretchers were pressed into service.

Besides the loneliness, Morse had to deal with the misunderstandings and rumors that were circulating. In the public mind the new phenomenon of electromagnetism was something akin to animal magnetism, hypnotism, and the occult.

Morse acquires assistants

Gradually, the unworkable ideas were discarded and replaced. With increasing confidence Morse began to demonstrate his collection of voltaic cells, coils, and wires for his colleagues at the university. Some of them saw it as only an intriguing plaything, lacking any practical value. Others with more vision undoubtedly had some vague inkling of its future. But none could deny that intelligence was being communicated from one side of the room to the other.

Soon Morse found individuals who would make capable assistants. The first to join him was Leonard Gale, a geology professor at the university. Gale, on the basis of what he had learned from Joseph Henry, advised him concerning battery voltages and currents and assisted in determining the number of turns to use on the electromagnets. (Joseph Henry was the head of the Smithsonian Institution and had made valuable contributions to electrical knowledge.)

Next to join the group was Alfred Vail, a recent graduate of the university. Morse took an immediate liking to Vail; they shared the same beliefs and attended the same church. Vail was a clever mechanic and helped Morse perfect the telegraph design. He also provided the financial assistance to set up a model telegraph for demonstration purposes—the system that was to help them in securing a patent.

One of the earliest public demonstrations took place in Vail's hometown, Morristown, New Jersey. The sender and receiver were both at the same location, but the signals were traversing some two miles of coiled wire between the two units. The spectators were enthusiastic and the local newspaper praised Professor Morse and his invention extravagantly.

Developing Morse Code

At first Morse used a very primitive and inefficient number-word code for his tests. A number had been assigned to each commonly used word in the language, and a dictionary had been tediously compiled to help translate from English into numbers and back again. By 1838, however, letters were represented directly by a new system of dots and dashes— Early Morse Code. Still later, additional improvements were incorporated to yield the International Morse Code, used even today by thousands of radio amateurs around the world.

Patenting the telegraph

In 1838 Morse and Vail demonstrated a model at the Franklin Institute in Philadelphia. Again the equipment functioned successfully and a favorable report was issued—the first acclaim to be received from representatives of the scientific world. The next demonstration was in Washington, because they hoped to secure funds from Congress for a trial line between two major cities. Among those witnessing the demonstrations were President Van Buren and several members of his cabinet. Congressman Francis O. J. Smith, chairman of the Committee on Commerce, was so impressed that he immediately wanted to become an associate of Morse and his coworkers. Thus four men were in partnership when the American patent was finally granted in 1840—Morse, Gale, Vail, and Smith.

Little did the partners realize then that several years were to pass before Congress would take action. During that period, the truth of the principle "tribulation worketh patience" became abundantly apparent in the inventor's life. His years as a struggling painter stood him in good stead for the disappointments and delays that were to come.

In the meantime he attempted to secure English and French patents. His failure to impress the British official with his invention was more than offset by his spectacular success in Paris.[19] Such illustrious men of science as Gay-Lussac, Humboldt, and Arago were present when he exhibited the telegraph before the French Academy of Sciences. Those who saw it were warmly enthusiastic, and he experienced little trouble in obtaining a French patent. Parisian newspapers called Morse one of the two greatest inventors of the age, the other being Daguerre who had just perfected the world's first photographic process.

Funding for an intercity telegraph

Unfortunately for Morse and his associates, America was then in a severe depression. In 1841 a congressman informed him that the Treasury and the government were both bankrupt. Congressional appropriations for something so speculative and experimental as a telegraph line would have to wait.

But Morse kept persevering. Late in 1842 he set up a demonstration line between the rooms of the House Committee on Commerce and the Senate Committee on Naval Affairs. Faithfully he remained on duty by his equipment sending sample messages for the legislators and answering their questions. By the end of the year the Committee on Commerce had submitted a favorable report. Representative Ferris, the chairman of the committee, recommended that $30,000 be appropriated to set up an intercity telegraph system.

The resolution came before the House on February 21, 1843. After several facetious remarks linking the telegraph with the occult and with religious fanaticism, the bill was carried eighty-nine to eighty-three, with seventy abstaining. Historians tell us that at least one congressman was defeated in the next election for having supported the bill.

The next hurdle was the Senate. A week and a half went by. When the last day of the session arrived, there were still 140 bills ahead of Morse's. His friends in the Senate became increasingly pessimistic and advised him to prepare for the worst. Evening came and the lamps were lighted in the Senate chamber. Believing the situation to be utterly hopeless, he returned to his hotel room, had his devotions, and retired for the night.

The next morning at breakfast a waiter informed him that he had a visitor in the hotel parlor. It was the daughter of the Commissioner of Patents, Annie Ellsworth. She had come to bring the good news—his bill had passed around midnight without discussion and had been quickly signed by President Tyler.

When he recovered sufficiently from his mingled joy and disbelief, he made her a promise: "When the lines are finally completed from Washington to Baltimore," he said, "you will be allowed to choose the text for the first message."

Laying the telegraph cable

In addition to the $30,000 appropriation for materials, Morse was placed on government salary as superintendent of the project. Gale, Vail, and Professor James Fisher of New York University were hired as assistant superintendents. Smith, untrained as a technician, donated his services as legal adviser. Ezra Cornell, then a little-known plow salesman, was engaged to supervise the details of laying the underground cable. (Later

Locust Grove, Morse's home on the Hudson River

Cornell founded the university in Ithaca, New York, that is named for him.)

The plan was to bury the wire two feet down, insulated in lead pipe. When approximately nine miles of cable had been successfully buried, Vail discovered defects in the insulation. Signals transmitted through the cable would undoubtedly be short-circuited before reaching their destination. The entire project faltered. Fisher was dismissed for incompetence. Gale resigned. And $23,000 of the appropriation had already been spent, seemingly for naught.

Smith suggested that Morse submit dishonest bills to Washington to obtain more funds. Morse flatly refused. "I cannot consistently with any consideration of honor ask the Secretary of Treasury to approve an agreement which violates truth on the face of it," he told Smith.[20] Because Morse was unwilling to compromise in any way, Smith too parted company with the group. Only Morse and Vail now remained, held together by their common bond of Christian faith.

Winter had now come upon them, and nothing further could have been done, even if they had known the next step. During the next few weeks, the two men spent much time searching though libraries for ideas. As a result of his reading, Vail believed that the best solution would be to place the wires on poles. Spacing them every two hundred feet, only twenty-seven poles would be required for each mile. Morse saw the wisdom of this plan. As soon as weather permitted, the cable was dug up and the wires were salvaged from it. The pipes encasing the wires were sold. Several hundred poles were quickly erected, and wires were strung between them using the necks of broken bottles for insulators.

"What hath God wrought!"

It was May 24, 1844. Morse had terminated the Washington end of the line in the Supreme Court chamber of the Capitol Building. As he took his place by the instruments, several dozen distinguished spectators gathered around. Vail was ready in Baltimore. Annie Ellsworth had chosen her message from Numbers 23:23—"What hath God wrought!" Morse transmitted the words slowly and accurately, requiring a full minute to complete the sentence. Almost immediately the identical words came back from Vail in Baltimore and registered on the paper ribbon for all to see. It was a great moment of triumph for the inventor.

He was delighted that appropriate words of Scripture had been chosen for the first intercity demonstration. In a letter to his brother he wrote, "That sentence of Annie Ellsworth's was divinely indited [conceived], for it is in my thoughts day and night. 'What hath God wrought!' It is His work, and He alone could have carried me thus far through all my trials and enabled me to triumph over the obstacles, physical and moral, which opposed me. 'Not unto us, not unto us, but to Thy name, O Lord, be all the praise.'"[21]

We knew it long ago

It has been said that there are three stages in the acceptance of a new scientific idea: (1) It's impossible. (2) What difference does it make? (3) We knew it long ago. Stage three had now arrived. No fewer than sixty-two individuals claimed prior invention. Several of them began pirating Morse's rights and erecting lines of their own.

Frequently he was required to defend his patent rights in court. Although he almost invariably emerged victorious from his legal encounters, there were occasionally times of great anguish. The best remedy for such times of testing, he found, was reading from the Bible, and he derived great comfort from Psalm 37:1—"Fret not thyself because of evildoers, neither be thou envious against the workers of iniquity."[22]

Blessings in later years

In time Morse received all the remuneration and honor that were rightfully his. He was finally able to purchase a home and settle down for the first time in his life. Soon after acquiring his famous Locust Grove property on the Hudson River, he remarried, but not without first seeking divine guidance. Concerning his marriage to Sarah Griswold he wrote to his brother Richard, "You are at least aware that in all my movements especially in relation to so serious a subject, I am in the habit of asking counsel from the source of all wisdom, and the paintings of His hand, and His leadings are so manifest that I have not a lingering doubt that He has at length heard my prayer, and granted me a gift worthy of Himself."[23] Already a grandfather, he became the father of four more children. Once again there were family devotions, and what had been his lonely pilgrimage to church became joyful family occasions.

In his later years he saw his prediction of a transatlantic cable come true. He watched the rapid development of photography, which had stemmed from his introduction of the daguerreotype process in the States. Instead of painting portraits, he now took portraits using the daguerreotype process. And his lasting contribution to the arts, The National Academy of the Arts of Design that he helped establish as a young painter, was still flourishing.

For many years he had been a forceful writer for the cause of orthodoxy and conservatism. He waded into political and religious battles fearlessly, taking after his father in his desire to defend the truth. One of the verses Morse often quoted was "Woe unto you, when all men shall speak well of you!"[24] He did not relish making enemies, but he did not shy away from standing for what he believed to be right.

Now he was able to assist with generous contributions all those organizations that were so dear to his heart—the American Tract Society, the American Bible Society, the City Mission Society in New York, the American and Foreign Christian Union, and many others. Baptist, Presbyterian, and Methodist churches were helped substantially in their building programs, and he assisted in the founding of at least two Christian colleges.

After his two younger brothers died, Morse felt that he was just waiting for his turn to go to heaven. He enjoyed reading his Bible more than ever, and he would say to his friends: "I love to be studying the Guide-Book of the country to which I am going." Shortly before he died of pneumonia at the age of eighty-one, he confidently told his pastor, "The best is yet to come."[25]

Here truly was a man who had labored diligently and had, as the proverb states, stood before kings. He had been decorated by the sovereigns of Austria, Denmark, France, Italy, Portugal, Prussia, Spain, and

Turkey. To demonstrate their appreciation, ten European nations joined in awarding him a gratuity of $60,000.

But Morse never lost sight of eternal matters in the glitter of worldly acclaim. After attending a great banquet at which Napoleon III had shown him special honor, he wrote home to his brother Sidney, "And after all of what account is it, except to confirm the wisdom of Solomon in his utterance of 'All is vanity and vexation of spirit'? I make this reflection not in a cynical, or ascetic spirit, but in view of the better things laid up for those who love God, and whose crowns and treasures are not the perishing temporary baubles of earth."[26]

[1] Carleton Mabee, *The American Leonardo: A Life of Samuel F. B. Morse* (New York: Knopf, 1943), p. 366.

[2] Ibid., p. 12.

[3] Edward Lind Morse, ed., *Samuel F. B. Morse: His Letters and Journals* (New York: Da Capo Press, 1914, reprint 1973), Vol. 1, pp. 5-6.

[4] Mabee, p. 19.

[5] Morse, p. 75.

[6] Mabee, p. 39.

[7] Those who have been privileged to view the Benjamin West religious paintings in the Bob Jones University chapel in Greenville, South Carolina, will appreciate the incredible patience and attention to detail that West was able to marshal in everything he undertook to depict. Many similarities may be detected in Morse's subsequent paintings, such as his famous *Congress Hall*–a remarkable panoramic view of the House of Representatives that includes more than eighty portraits of actual statesmen.

[8] Morse, p. 117.

[9] Ibid., p.140.

[10] Samuel Irenaes Prime, *The Life of Samuel F. B. Morse, LL.D., Inventor of the Electro-Magnetic Recording Telegraph* (New York: D. Appleton and Co., 1875), p. 31.

[11] Morse, pp. 296-98.

[12] Mabee, pp. 58-59.

[13] Ibid., p. 59

[14] Morse, p. 268.

[15] Ibid., p. 211.

[16] Ibid., pp. 265-66.

[17] Ibid., p. 418.

[18] Prime, p. 246.

[19] Germany and England boasted similar inventions that sent intelligence over wires but used different mechanisms. Each of these was invented independently—each inventor was unaware of the work of the other. But Morse's invention worked better and was simpler.

[20] Mabee, pp. 269-70.

[21] Ibid., p. 280.

[22] Ibid., p. 301.

[23] Ibid., p. 305.

[24] Morse, p. 439. (Luke 6:26)

[25] Mabee, pp. 376-77.

[26] Ibid., p. 364.

Matthew Maury (1806-1873)

MATTHEW FONTAINE MAURY
(1806-1873)

Oceanographer

They that go down to the sea in ships, that do business in great waters;
These see the works of the Lord, and his wonders in the deep.
Psalm 107:23-24

The doctor finished examining Matthew and turned to his parents. "He bit his tongue nearly in half, but that will mend," he said. "His back injury is the real problem." He paused for a moment and ran his fingers through his hair. Even after all these years of practice, he didn't know how to break bad news gently. "He will probably be crippled for life," he said, and quickly looked down because he didn't want to see the sadness in Mrs. Maury's eyes.

Matthew closed his eyes tightly, but the tears still slipped out of the corners of his eyes. "Why did I climb so high?" he thought. "I should have come down when Dick told me."

He couldn't remember actually falling out of the tree, but Dick told him how afraid he had been to see Matthew tumbling out of the tree and then lying on the ground unconscious.

In the following weeks, the doctor came often to check on Matthew, but he didn't expect much progress. One day, after checking Matthew's reflexes, he smiled in surprise. He turned to Mr. Maury. "I think your son just may walk again," he said.

Mr. Maury jumped out of his chair. "That's great news!" he said. "We need him in the fields."

"Oh, no!" said the doctor, shaking his head. "I don't mean that he will be able to work. He will be too weak to do his chores. But he will be able to walk, I think."

Matthew was secretly relieved to hear this. He had despised the farm work and wished that he could be studying instead. Mr. Maury couldn't understand why his son so stubbornly insisted on reading and trying to learn more. What was wrong with good old-fashioned farm work? *Mr. Maury thought.* Why couldn't the boy be content with farming like his brothers?

For several years Matthew had been begging to go to Harpeth Academy because his local schoolteacher had run out of things to teach him. But Mr. Maury always answered with the same argument: "I need you on the farm, Matthew. Education doesn't help a farmer. We need strong bodies, not strong minds."

But the accident made Mr. Maury think again about his son's future. After the doctor left that day, Mr. Maury came into Matthew's room and sat on his bed. He cleared his throat to break the silence. "Son," he said, awkwardly patting Matthew's leg, "I've changed my mind about school. You can go to the academy when you are strong enough to ride those six miles on horseback."

Matthew was too surprised to answer. But he smiled and reached for his dad's hand. As they sat there in a comfortable silence, Matthew imagined the books he would find at the academy. Perhaps he could find science and geography books there.

Mr. Maury knew he had made the right decision when he saw his son's happiness. He picked up Matthew's shoe from its place beside the bed and handed it to him. "You'll be using these again, Lord willing," he said.

Matthew nodded and stared at the shoe. He still hadn't had enough time to absorb all the good news that day. It was amazing enough that he would walk again; but on top of that, he could go to the academy. He turned the worn shoe idly and laughed when he saw the sole. "Look Dad," he said, pointing to the little x's and y's that were scratched onto the sole. "Here's where Old Neil practiced on my shoe."

Matthew thought of the happy times he had spent in the old shoe cobbler's workshop, watching him repair shoes. Old Neil used to scratch algebra problems on the soles of the shoes that he repaired. Matthew had always been fascinated by these x's and y's. "I wanna learn math like Old Neil," Matthew told his dad.

"Perhaps you will," Mr. Maury said. "Perhaps you will at the academy."

Growing up in Tennessee

Matthew Fontaine Maury had been born twelve years earlier in 1806 to Richard and Diana Maury. Mrs. Maury was an energetic and intelligent woman. Her godliness and kindness made her an ideal mother. Mr. Maury was never a successful farmer and always struggled to make ends meet. He suffered from poor business judgment, and his relatives thought of him as a failure. But he was a success in the religious training of his children.

For many generations the Maury family had trained Huguenot preachers and strong Christian laymen. The Maury ancestors had left France because of the Huguenot persecution and had immigrated to England and then to Virginia. Matthew's parents appreciated the religious freedom their grandparents had found in America, and they carried on the family tradition of diligently passing on the faith. Each morning and evening, Mr. Maury gathered his nine children to read responsively from a psalter during family devotions. Matthew became so familiar with the book of Psalms that throughout his life he could quote most of them from memory.

When the family financial situation became worse, Matthew's oldest brother, John, joined the United States Navy instead of going to school. The family reasoned that John would receive a good education this way and earn money at the same time. So, at the age of thirteen, John's distinguished naval career began.

John became the family hero for his younger brothers and sisters. Matthew thought the greatest thing in life would be joining the Navy like John and learning about the world. When John came home on leave, he entertained his brothers and sisters with stories of his adventures.

Matthew's favorite adventure, the one he begged John to tell over and over, was the time John and several other men were stranded on the island of Nukahiva during the War of 1812. For two years John Maury and his shipmates lived safely among friendly cannibals. But during raids by an enemy tribe, three of the Americans were killed. John and his friend Baker escaped the attackers and survived by living in a tree house for a year and a half. They were finally rescued; but with his tattered clothes and long beard, John had tremendous difficulty persuading his rescuers that he was actually an officer in the United States Navy.

On a later voyage John died of yellow fever and was buried at sea. John's death was a great shock to the Maury family. Although John had been absent from the family for many years, he was still very much in their thoughts and prayers. They had prayed for him twice a day when they gathered for family devotions. Mr. Maury grieved deeply and became more protective of his remaining sons. He didn't want them entering such a dangerous profession. For Matthew, though, not even his brother's death could dampen his desire to join the Navy.

Joining the Navy

Since Matthew knew he would never get his parent's permission to join the Navy, he decided to go ahead and enlist and then see whether they would change their minds. Like most teenagers, he thought that it was easier to get forgiveness than to get permission. When Matthew told his father that he had received his orders from the Navy, Mr. Maury was furious.

Matthew knew his parents were baffled by his determination. He had never openly defied his father. How could he make his parents understand that this defiance had a purpose? He had privately vowed to make his life "useful." *How can I be useful*, he wondered, *if I'm confined to the family farm?* He knew that his family couldn't afford to send him to college. The only way he could get the education he craved was to join the Navy. He was convinced that the Navy held the key to his future, because they would teach him math, science, and navigation—the tools that he needed to be useful.

But no explanations about usefulness would appease Mr. Maury. He refused to support his son in any way, thinking that if he left Matthew without money, all this foolishness about joining the Navy would stop. But Matthew was still determined to go. He borrowed a horse, collected his money for tutoring the younger students at his school, and traveled alone to Washington, D. C., to report for duty.

Matthew began active duty at once because the Navy had no established academy. After all the years of dreaming about life in the Navy, he finally discovered the unromantic reality of life aboard ship: the work was grueling, the pay was abominably low, the food was monotonous, and the cockroaches multiplied as the voyage progressed. But Matthew ignored these inconveniences. He was fascinated by the changing weather, the new ports, and the different languages and cultures he encountered.

Matthew quickly understood why his parents had so strongly opposed his decision to join the Navy. For all practical purposes he had cut himself off from his family. Communication was so slow that sometimes it would take an entire year for a letter from home to reach him. It was common for a sailor to be out of the States for two or three years at a time. Five years passed before Matthew could get enough leave time to visit home. He loved seeing his brothers and sisters again and eating his mother's cooking. But the happiest part about coming home was hearing his father say that all was forgiven.

During his next voyage, Matthew's ship sailed around the world in a peace mission for the United States. The ship stopped at Nukahiva, the island where John Maury had been stranded. When the friendly king realized that Matthew was John's brother, the king excitedly offered him his scepter and two wives if he would remain on the island. Matthew politely refused. He was flattered, but being a king on a remote island was not his idea of being useful.

Matthew soon discovered that the Navy did not give him the rigorous education that he had imagined. He longed for a structured teaching program, but there was no such thing. Each ship was given a teacher, but many times the teacher had other duties to fulfill, and he didn't have time for his students. When the midshipmen were off duty, they certainly did not want to study. They were busy shouting, singing, and wrestling. On one cruise, Matthew said, the students decided that the Spanish teacher and the subject were boring and gleefully threw the textbook overboard.[1]

If Matthew were to learn anything, he would have to teach himself. And so he began a diligent program of self-education. Whenever he was in port, he would search the bookstores for textbooks that might be useful. He read every book he could lay hands on and kept careful notes of everything he learned. When he had a spare moment, he would dash down to his bunk and read a sentence or two from his books.

Matthew worried about the exams he would have to take when he arrived in America again. If he didn't pass, he wouldn't be promoted. The exams covered Spanish, French, navigation, mathematics, and practical seamanship. The examining board was a panel of elderly seamen who asked whatever questions came to mind. They gave the highest ranking to the men who memorized formulas by rote. They didn't care about the mathematical concepts behind the formulas. Matthew, an enthusiastic mathematician, demonstrated his answers on the chalkboard instead of quoting formulas. The examiners were not impressed. Matthew passed, but he was disappointed with his low ranking. He was even more disappointed when he noticed that several friends he had coached scored higher than he did. Right then he determined to help the young midshipmen who were just starting in the Navy. *They shouldn't have to struggle so much to learn basic navigation and to prepare for their examinations,* Matthew thought.

Where are the charts?

His next assignment was to be the sailing master of the *Falmouth*. Before he sailed, he carefully searched for information on the wind and currents that his ship might encounter. To his amazement he discovered that the data he was searching for did not exist in any printed form. He

The students secretly threw the textbook overboard.

also talked to naval and merchant ship captains and found that each of them had different opinions on the best route to take. Some captains who had discovered time-saving routes were unwilling to share their "secret" with him. This secrecy upset Matthew. He thought that helpful information on shorter routes should be shared with everyone who sailed. He determined that someday, somehow, he would find out these secrets and share them with the other captains.

Marriage and a textbook

When Matthew returned from this voyage, he had completed nine years of sea duty. He decided that it was finally time to get married, even if he had no money saved up. His fiancée, Ann Herndon, agreed that a three-year engagement was long enough. They had met six years earlier at a relative's house, and it was a classic case of love at first sight. The couple decided that waiting really wouldn't make a big difference in Matthew's finances.

His financial situation was worrisome. The pay in the Navy was low, and promotions were infrequent. There were few positions available on board ships, and while the men were waiting on shore for orders, they received half pay. This waiting for the next assignment was the most frustrating part of Navy life. Matthew described his life while awaiting orders as "hanging by his eyelids."[2]

Matthew certainly could have earned more money if he had resigned from the Navy and worked a civilian job. But he never plotted his life course based on money or convenience. He had made up his mind that his life would be more useful in the Navy, and he wasn't going to change his mind now because of financial difficulties.

Soon after the wedding Matthew published a book entitled *A New Theoretical and Practical Treatise on Navigation*. This was his answer to the poor training he had received. He wanted the other midshipmen to have an easier time learning navigation than he did. Everything they needed to know should be found in one thorough textbook, he reasoned.

He received wide recognition within the Navy, and his book soon became the navigation textbook for the midshipmen. President Andrew Jackson suggested that Matthew be promoted and reimbursed for the publication of the book. But the Secretary of the Navy decided that having the book published was enough of a reward, and he didn't carry out the president's wish. This incident was the beginning of a long line of petty jealousies that would plague Maury's career.

His career in jeopardy

Matthew's next orders were to survey Southern harbors. During a leave from this duty, he traveled to Tennessee to arrange for his elderly parents to come live with him. Afterward, he headed back to New York by stagecoach to join his ship and continue the harbor surveying.

Late one night, when all the seats in the coach were full, they stopped for three more passengers. Two of the new passengers climbed on top of the coach where the luggage rested. The other passenger, a young lady, stood in the rain trying to calm her crying baby. *She shouldn't have to sit outside*, Matthew thought. He graciously helped her into his seat and climbed up beside the driver.

A passenger leaned out the window. "Hey," he yelled. "This coach is top heavy. You can't put so much luggage on top—and then men, too!" The agent shrugged his shoulders and told the driver to go ahead.

Matthew leaned back on his uncomfortable perch. A steady drizzle fell in his face, and he couldn't sleep. He listened as the driver talked to the men on the roof. A little after midnight, they came to a section of the road that was being repaired. The driver guided the horses onto the detour and then urged them back to speed. The moon was hidden by clouds, and there were no lanterns on the coach. The driver couldn't see the road ahead, but he didn't seem worried.

"I reckon we're a bit overloaded for this stretch," he said. "This new road's still soft." As soon as he said the words, the wheels sank in the mud. The coach jerked to the right and overturned, throwing Matthew to the ground. A terrific pain shot through his leg when he landed, and he knew immediately that he was seriously injured.

Later the doctor confirmed that Matthew had broken his leg. In fact, it was worse than just a broken leg because the knee joint had been severely damaged. He had fractured his thighbone in two places, dislocated his knee, and torn ligaments. Now Matthew found himself stranded in a remote little town, far from his family, and far from good medical attention. The local doctor set the bone incorrectly, without anesthesia, and it had to be reset later, again without anesthesia.

Maury stayed at a shabby inn in Somerset, Ohio, while he slowly recuperated. Ann tried to come and nurse her husband, but she became ill on the trip and had to turn back. A few weeks later his cousin John came to nurse him and cheer him up.

After three months at the inn, Maury was hobbling about on crutches, anxious to get back to his assignment. It was winter now, and Matthew traveled by sleigh to meet his ship. Blizzards and snowdrifts slowed him down so much that when he finally reached New York, his ship had sailed. Disappointed and discouraged, Maury returned home. He was far from well, but he didn't want to admit just how injured he was. He could not even get out of bed alone or dress himself.

Will I ever be strong enough to go to sea again? he asked himself as he exercised his leg each day. *Is this just a temporary interruption, or is my naval career over?* He often lay awake at night worrying about his future. He comforted himself during these long nights by quoting the psalms that he had memorized as a young boy.

Writing for naval reforms

While Matthew was recuperating, he spent his time writing articles about the problems he saw in the Navy. For fifteen years he had experienced the inefficiency of the Navy firsthand. During those years, he had traveled widely and had observed other nations and their naval defense. He knew that the United States was in grave danger if the Navy were allowed to continue in such a haphazard manner.

Matthew signed his articles with a pseudonym because he didn't want to be thrown out of the Navy if his ideas offended the officials. Most of the time he used the name Harry Bluff. Other times he was Union Jack or Will Watch writing to his old messmate Harry Bluff. He called the articles "Scraps from the Lucky Bag" after the "Lucky Bag" that was on board ship. (This bag functioned as a lost and found and was filled with miscellaneous items. He chose this title so he could write about a wide range of topics.) One of the problems he exposed was the inefficiency and waste in building and repairing ships. He had the figures to prove that repairing a ship cost more than the original building cost. He also complained about the lack of standardized training in the Navy and the poor system of promotion. But he didn't just expose the problems; he gave clear suggestions for solving each problem.

One great service of the articles was that Maury made the general public aware of the desperate need for a naval academy. He asked why the Army had West Point to train their men, while the Navy made do with an ineffective method of teachers on board the ships. He pointed out that building officers was just as important as building ships.[3] These articles helped lay the groundwork for the United States Naval Academy that was established at Annapolis in 1845.

Maury's articles created a stir in the general public, but especially so among his fellow officers. They were grateful that someone had the courage to speak out. When the news of Maury's authorship leaked out in 1841, he instantly became famous. There were suggestions from the public and from within the Navy that Maury should become the new Secretary of the Navy and supervise these changes. But politics disgusted Maury, and he had no intention of having a cabinet position "inflicted" on him. He merely wanted the satisfaction of seeing these changes implemented.

But not everyone was favorably impressed by the articles. Some high-ranking naval officials were angered by the specific attacks that Maury had made. These officials had a long memory and determined to make Maury pay sooner or later for embarrassing the Navy. Maury anticipated the animosity and said he expected to have the "*honor* of a sly cuff from them now and then."[4] However, Maury figured the animosity was worth it. Over the next few years, he had the satisfaction of seeing many of his reforms brought before Congress and adopted.

Directing the United States Naval Observatory

Maury's leg had not mended well, and whenever he requested active sea duty, he was turned down because of his injured leg. Finally, after months of "hanging by his eyelids," he was assigned to shore duty. But this was no ordinary desk job. He was appointed the superintendent of the United States Naval Observatory. (At that time it was still called the Depot of Charts and Instruments.)

In fact, this assignment changed the course of his life. Once again, a painful accident became the turning point in his life. Both his fall out of the tree as a boy and his being thrown from the stagecoach as an adult seemed at the time to be tragedies. But, looking back, he could see how God had used these accidents to change the course of his life. Now, instead of being just a brilliant navigator in the United States Navy, Matthew Maury was in a position to make lasting contributions to mankind.

His department was in charge of the instruments used aboard ships—sextants and quadrants (for determining a ship's position), barometers and thermometers (for determining atmospheric pressure and temperature), and chronometers (for telling the exact time on board ship). His staff purchased the instruments, checked their accuracy, and distributed them to the ships. His department also made observations in astronomy, marine meteorology (the ocean's weather), and hydrography (ocean research).

At the Observatory, Maury continued his program of rigorous self-education that he had begun as a young sailor. He was not college educated, and this fact bothered several of the influential American scientists. They believed that any man who hadn't attended a proper university was a charlatan, and his scientific contributions were not worth noticing. This cliquish attitude of the other scientists plagued Maury throughout his naval career.

In the early days of the Observatory, Maury put in long hours. He did a good deal of the astronomy observations himself until he had enough assistants to help him. When Maury published the Observatory's first edition of astronomical observations, European astronomers were impressed. They concluded that the Naval Observatory belonged in the same rank as the older astronomical institutions of Europe.

Maury fell several years behind in the astronomy work because he didn't have enough mathematicians to make the intricate calculations following the observations. His chief problem was that his trained assistants were continually called out to sea. Soon Maury realized that his department could not effectively cover three areas. He didn't entirely abandon the astronomical work, but he decided to concentrate on the hydrographic (ocean) and meteorological (weather) research because it had more immediate practical value for the United States Navy.

Charting the oceans

As Maury read his Bible, he often paused over a passage in Psalm 8: "Thou madest him to have dominion over the works of thy hands . . . and whatsoever passeth through the paths of the seas." He wondered whether it would be possible to use these paths when sailing.

He also noticed Ecclesiastes 1:6, which says, "The wind goeth toward the south, and turneth about unto the north; it whirleth about continually, and the wind returneth again according to his circuits." From this verse, Maury believed that the winds followed a predictable course and that knowledge of these wind currents would also speed ocean travel. (Maury admired the brevity of this statement and said that the Bible could describe in a single sentence the system of atmospherical circulation, a phenomenon that Maury described at great length in his oceanography textbook.)

Since the time Maury had been the sailing master of the *Falmouth*, he had realized the deplorable lack of information regarding wind and ocean currents. He was embarrassed that United States ships had to obtain charts from the English Admiralty just to sail up the Chesapeake Bay to Washington. Now he was finally in a position to correct this disgrace.

Maury envisioned publishing a chart unlike any that had been made before. He would generalize the experience of many navigators in a condensed, easy-to-understand way. He began his first chart by painstakingly examining hundreds of old logbooks that were stored by the Navy Department. Some of the logs were over one hundred years old! It was slow, tedious work that lasted five years. Based solely on the data from these old logbooks, he published "Wind and Current Chart of the North Atlantic" in 1847.

He discovered that the ships had been fighting nature instead of working with it. Now that he had noticed patterns in the winds and currents, he could show captains how to work with the winds and the currents. His strategy was simple and obvious: wherever possible, use the winds and currents that were moving in the right direction and avoid those that were not. Of course, the idea was not new, but never before had there been accurate charts showing the exact locations of the winds and currents for each month. He carefully plotted the most favorable routes and called these instructions the "Sailing Directions." He showed the captains the best paths to use, and from then on, Maury was known as the "Pathfinder of the Seas."

But Maury was not satisfied with this first chart. He wanted to publish updated charts using present-day information, so he issued blank charts for keeping daily records on naval voyages. The Secretary of the Navy ordered the naval captains to use Maury's log and to forward their observations to the Observatory. Maury also tried to get the merchant ship captains to use the log, but they were not interested. The charting was time consuming, they complained, and it certainly wouldn't have any practical use.

In 1848 Captain Jackson sailed from Virginia to Rio de Janeiro using Maury's charts. The trip took thirty-eight days instead of the usual fifty-five![5] Then he turned around and made the return trip in thirty-seven days. Suddenly ship captains believed Maury. Short passages were not the result of luck; they came from understanding and working with the winds and ocean currents.

With the California Gold Rush of 1849, ship captains wanted to make faster passages to the West Coast. Now they demanded to use Maury's charts. The charts and sailing directions were provided free to any captain who agreed to record his observations on his voyages. By 1852 one thousand ships were observing for Maury. The charts he compiled from this new data included Trade Wind Charts, Thermal Charts, Track Charts, Storm and Rain Charts, Pilot Charts, and Whale Charts.

Maury's sailing directions proved to be valuable time-savers. By 1855, the route from New York to San Francisco was reduced from 187 days to 144 days.[6] Maury also helped shorten the passage from England to Australia. He suggested using the west winds and circling the globe for the return trip.

These shortened passages were also great money savers. In one year Maury's sailing directions and charts saved the British Empire an estimated ten million dollars. And the United States saved over two million dollars a year in trade with the East Indies, China, and South America.[7] The marine insurers were so grateful for the money they were saving with the quicker passages that they gave a generous appreciation gift to Maury.

Maury showed the ship captains how to work with winds and currents.

When the ship captains returned their logbooks, they wrote enthusiastic letters of appreciation to Maury. One grateful captain wrote that ever since he had been forced to do the observing and charting, his eyes had been opened to God's wonders in nature. Before, he had been traveling the ocean blindfolded.

Worldwide observations

Maury imagined a system of worldwide observations that would benefit navigators in all parts of the world. Eventually his dream was realized when ten nations participated in a marine meteorology conference in 1853. During the conference, Maury extended the United States' offer of a free copy of the charts and the sailing directions to every ship that would participate in the observations. The delegates unanimously adopted an observation log that was to be used by the merchant and navy ships of each country. Maury was delighted with the spirit of cooperation among the nations and commented that even though they were enemies in everything else, at least they were friends when it came to the observation project.

Soon other countries who had not attended the conference asked to join the project. With these observations coming in from all over the world, Maury continued to revise his charts and to include larger areas.

Maury had always felt that ordinary seamen were in a unique position to observe God's wonders in nature and that their observations could add tremendously to scientific knowledge. He thought often of verses in Psalm 107: "They that go down to the sea in ships, that do business in great waters; these see the works of the Lord, and his wonders in the deep."

He was deeply proud of his "corps of observers" who made his charting possible.[8] After fifty years, the grand total of logbooks sent to the Observatory was well over twenty-six million![9]

The Atlantic Telegraph Cable

Maury's oceanic research contributed to the laying of the Atlantic Telegraph Cable in a very practical way. When Cyrus Field, an American businessman, decided to finance the project, the first thing he did was to contact Samuel F. B. Morse and Matthew Maury. He asked Mr. Morse if it were possible for a wire to carry a message under water over such a long distance. Mr. Morse assured him that it was possible. Morse had already laid a two-mile underwater cable and shown that his technology would work under water. Unfortunately, the cable had been destroyed by a ship's anchor.

Mr. Field's letter to Maury asked where the cable should be laid. The letter arrived on Maury's desk just as he was completing his report of successful deep-sea soundings. From this new information about the ocean floor, Maury believed that there was a perfect spot in the ocean to lay the cable. Maury named this section of the Atlantic Ocean floor the Telegraphic Plateau. Here he believed a cable could rest without danger.

Maury came to this conclusion after having samples of the ocean floor analyzed. (To the modern mindset, deep-sea soundings and obtaining samples of the ocean floor seem routine-enough procedures. But Maury's staff first had to perfect a technique for accurately measuring the depth of the ocean and then invent the device that collected samples at great depths.) Maury deduced that the floor of the ocean was undisturbed by currents because the samples consisted of unscathed microscopic shells and no sand particles.[10] The absence of sand and the absence of abrasion marks on the shells told Maury that the ocean floor was peaceful. He said the cable would be as safe as if it were in an airtight case.

Mr. Field also asked Maury to decide the best route for the ships and the best time of year to attempt the laying of the cable. Maury consulted his charts and drew upon his own experience as a navigator to answer this question. He was realistic about the obstacles. He reminded Mr. Field that it would be a tremendous challenge to find "a time calm enough, a sea smooth enough, a wire long enough, a ship big enough."[11]

The obstacles were staggering. Even though Maury, of all people, understood how rough and unpredictable the North Atlantic Ocean could be, he fully believed that the transatlantic cable would be laid successfully. It was a huge undertaking involving both the American and British governments. Maury put pressure on the United States government to offer the naval ship *Niagara* as the contribution from the United States. The British government supplied the ship *Agamemnon*. Each ship had to be rebuilt on the inside to accommodate the miles and miles of cable. The holds of the ships needed extra bracing to withstand the pressure of the tons of cable. Dela____ ___nd setbacks hampered each phase of the project. Just winding the c___ ___ ___ hold of the ships took a whole month and had to be done ____

It is hard ____ ____ ____stand just how exciting the prospect of i____ ____ ____ two continents was. At that time, i____ ____ ____ bring messages from London to ____ ____ ____ able would promote internation____ ____ the success of the cable laying. ____ ____ ____oth nations involved the progre____

W____ ____ ____. huge celebration took place in N____ ____ ____mn thanksgiving service. Then the ____ ____ld and a parade and dinner. In th____ ____Maury was given special recogni ____ ____ul laying of the transatlantic cable.

____mous Prussian scientist, declared that ____ ____v branch of science. Humboldt termed ____ ____eography of the Sea.[12] Maury liked the ____ ____r a book he wrote in 1854. Maury's other ____ ____n strictly for sailors and had brought him ____ ____ublisher thought that a chapter of his *Sailing* ____ ____ed for the enjoyment and information of the lay reader.

Maury's writing had a smoothness and readability that appealed to lay readers. He had the ability to make a potentially boring subject fascinating to even the disinterested reader. In this book, Maury made it clear that God is the Author of nature. He boldly stated that "the laws which govern the atmosphere and the laws which govern the ocean are laws which were put in force by the Creator when the foundations of the earth were laid, and that therefore they are laws of order."[13]

The completed *Physical Geography* contained twenty-two chapters covering currents, clouds, winds, rain, fog, monsoons, storms, and other related subjects. He also included charts that helped to explain the text. The Wind Chart was the compilation of 1,159,353 wind observations and over 100,000 barometric readings![14] (Imagine doing this compilation entirely by hand, without the aid of computers!)

Because Maury's book was a pioneering work, some theories are far-fetched; but as new discoveries were made, scientists were able to fine-tune Maury's original hypotheses. Perhaps the greatest tribute to *The Physical Geography's* popularity is the fact that several publishers produced unauthorized versions of the book, and it was eventually translated into six languages. It was used for many years as an oceanography textbook throughout the world. It is still an excellent model for writers of popular science.

Maury's family life

Maury's family provided affection and relaxation and kept him from becoming overly absorbed in his work. Ann Maury proved to be a devoted, submissive wife who taught her children catechism and Bible lessons. Maury frequently mentioned Ann's gentleness, love, and quiet strength. She suffered frequent headaches and had poor stamina, but Matthew was a considerate, protective husband. He did not demand too much of her and took over some of her domestic duties. He frequently took the children on long walks to give Ann a chance to rest.

Matthew enjoyed romping with his children and reading to them in the evenings. He attached affectionate nicknames to his children soon after birth—Betty, Nannie Curly, Tots, Sat Sing, Goggen, Davy Jones, Glum, and Brave. When he called them by their real names—Elizabeth, Diana, Lucy, Eliza, John, Richard, Mary, or Matthew—the children knew he was displeased with them.[15] His two rules for the children were these: no lying and obey without question.

He disapproved of the shallow training his girls were receiving at their girls' school, so he taught them himself. His children remembered the de-

Maury was the superintendent of the United States Naval Observatory.

lightful, energetic lectures he would give at the breakfast table. Sometimes the girls would finish a reading assignment but couldn't explain the text to their father. He would shake his head and say, "Then your head is just like an old gourd stuffed full of newspapers—a great deal of information in it which you can't get out or make use of."[16]

Occasionally he offered prizes for academic achievements and found that these were excellent motivators. In one month Diana won a small telescope by learning how to make an astronomical observation using the big telescope at the Observatory.

Maury frequently dictated his correspondence and other writing to his children because his own handwriting was illegible. Sometimes he dictated to two girls at once. Maury had the enviable ability to concentrate even when his children were playing around him. (He didn't have a study of his own until he was sixty-three years old.) His daughter Diana wrote that sometimes a child would play horse with the ties of Maury's dressing gown while he paced around the room; Maury, however, was "paying not the slightest attention, but dictating gravely."[17] Years before Maury had taught himself to study onboard the noisy ships. Now he could concentrate in the middle of a houseful of lively children.

There was always a full house at the Maurys because Matthew and Ann Maury frequently invited relatives to live with them. The Maurys' definition of family included more than just their own children. They cheerfully parented the extra family members who came under their roof. At different times, Matthew cared for his aging parents, his brother John's widow and two children, and Ann's niece Ellen Herndon. Ellen married Chester Alan Arthur, who became the twenty-first president of the United States.

For such a busy man, Maury spent a remarkable amount of time with his children. That is because he did not separate his family and his work life. He cheerfully jumbled them all together. Maury insisted that the children always be present in the parlor in the evenings. No homework was to be done in the evenings because he wanted the children to benefit from the many interesting people who came through their house. He believed that meeting the guests who came to the home was an important part of their education.

Dignitaries who visited Washington often stopped at the Observatory for dinner and a look through the telescope. On Maury's tight budget, he could not entertain extravagantly. But he supplemented his income by planting fruit trees, a vegetable garden, and a strawberry patch on the Observatory grounds. Visitors enjoyed the excellent conversation and the good Southern cooking around the Maury's table.

His Christian character

Like many children who grow up in Christian homes, Matthew could not point to a specific time when he had accepted Christ. But he heartily accepted the gospel message, even as a child. He regularly attended church from his childhood, but he never partook of the Holy Communion until well into his adult life. This bothered Ann when they were first married, and Maury confessed to her that he did not feel worthy. For many years he couldn't get over this thought until a clergyman convinced him that personal worthiness was certainly not the issue. If a person had to be worthy, his friend assured him, then no one would presume to take the Lord's Supper! It brought Maury great joy to finally take communion.

As a Christian, Maury had an exemplary testimony with his family and peers. When he was twenty-eight, he wrote this to his brother Dick, who had surprised the family by joining another church:

Learn your duties, Dick, from the Bible. There you have them laid down in example, law and precept. I love to see Christians *after* the Bible and according to their own consciences and not according to the opinions of other men. I hope, Dick, whatever persuasion you join that you will be a Christian according to the Bible as you understand it.

[He went on to urge Dick to use his own good sense] and never to adopt a sort of easy religion, a newly devised way of getting to Heaven without the trouble of repenting for, and imploring the divine forgiveness of past sins.[18]

Matthew Maury was never afraid to confess his Christian faith in public and in his writings. During an address at the University of the South in southern Tennessee, he expressed his views on science and the Bible.

I have been blamed by men of science, both in this country and in England, for quoting the Bible in confirmation of the doctrines of physical geography. The Bible, they say, was not written for scientific purposes, and is therefore of no authority in matters of science. I beg pardon: the Bible *is* authority for everything it touches. What would you think of the historian who should refuse to consult the historical records of the Bible because the Bible was not written for the purposes of history? The Bible is true; and science is true . . . they are both true; . . . and when your man of science with vain and hasty conceit announces the discovery of disagreement between them, rely upon it the fault is not with the Witness or His records, but with the "worm" who essays to interpret evidence which he does not understand.[19]

He sprinkled Biblical quotations throughout his writing because it was perfectly natural for him to quote the Book that guided his life and his science.

Praised abroad but mistreated at home

Unfortunately, the United States was slow to recognize Maury's achievements. He received several honorary doctorates and monetary awards for his service; but after thirty years in the Navy, he was still a lieutenant. He was doing the work of three men, but certainly not receiving a fitting salary. The bulk of Maury's recognition came from abroad. He was knighted by several countries, given numerous medals, and made a member of at least twenty foreign societies of learning.

Maury's agitating for reforms had caused hard feelings among fellow naval officers, especially his superiors. The opportunity for his enemies to vent their true feelings occurred when Congress passed a bill authorizing the Naval Retiring Board. This board, composed of fifteen naval officers, was instructed to streamline the Navy by weeding out officers who were "incapable of performing promptly and efficiently all their duty both ashore and afloat."[20]

One day, to Maury's shock, he received a notice from the Secretary of the Navy informing him that he was removed from active duty and placed on leave-of-absence pay because his injured leg prevented him from fulfilling his obligation to sea duty. Ironically, though, he was ordered to continue with his present duties at the Observatory.

This action put Maury in official disgrace and considerably lowered his pay. Yet nearly three years passed before a Court of Inquiry vindicated Maury. At Maury's hearing two doctors declared that he could capably carry on active sea duty if so ordered. His leg had mended to the point that he didn't need crutches, although he still limped. The court ruled to promote Maury to a Commander and put him back on the active list. On the surface, his lameness seemed to be the central issue. But the Naval Retiring Board's actions seemed to have been motivated by personal jealousies and devious ambitions. By removing senior officers, each board member paved the way for his own promotion.

Maury's honor was finally avenged, but the ordeal had been trying and disheartening. During the years that the Naval Retiring Board was deciding Maury's fate, he received several medals from other countries. At least the world recognized his greatness even if his own country didn't!

Maury's role in the American Civil War

When the relations between the North and the South deteriorated, Maury began a personal letter campaign. He urged the Southern leaders to cooperate with arbitration efforts instead of seceding. Yet as committed as he was to the unity of the States, he knew he could never fight against his relatives; if Virginia seceded, Maury would cast his lot with her.

On April 19, 1861, Virginia's secession became public. The following day, Maury finished his work at the Observatory and asked his secretary to write the letter of resignation. The young man refused to write the letter. He realized that Maury's resignation would terminate his illustrious career and ruin his reputation. So Maury himself penned the letter to President Abraham Lincoln. He had spent thirty-six years of his life serving the United States Navy. He had been offered civilian jobs at considerably higher pay, but he always refused because he wanted to serve his country in a practical way. As he walked out of the Observatory for the last time, he didn't even try to hide the tears that rolled down his cheeks.

Maury immediately gave his services to the Confederate Navy. When Robert E. Lee joined the Confederacy, the Lynchburg newspaper wrote that "these two noble men, the very flower of the Army and Navy of the late United States, respond to the call of their glorious old Mother."[21] During the war, Maury's scientific research took a different turn, and he experimented with electrically and manually detonated submarine mines. While Maury was not the first man to experiment with them, he was the first to use them successfully in wartime.[22] He also devised a clever way for operators scattered along a coastline to communicate with each other over telegraph lines. They could collaborate in their decisions as to which mines to detonate and when, and they could test each mine's circuitry daily.[23]

Maury helped establish a strong defense for Richmond by mining the James River. He confessed to his family that he hated the thought of blowing men up in their sleep, especially since they perceived their cause to be as righteous as Maury's.[24] On Maury's first mission, his crew was ready to blow up three ships. This business of war was so hateful to Maury that he was waiting in a small boat ready to pick up the survivors. But the fuse failed and the mines never went off.

Ann Maury was deeply troubled by her husband's involvement in the mine research. This was the first time in their marriage that she had ever opposed him. He explained his reasoning to her this way: If he could make war terrible enough, then perhaps men would stop fighting and sit down to discuss their differences in a civil manner.[25] Maury believed that if the South could prove herself invincible, then the North would certainly give up and accept an offer of peace. Whenever the South won a victory, Maury urged his superiors to make peace overtures to the North. Maury's terms, though, would have been unacceptable to the North: he wanted the Confederacy recognized as a separate nation.

Although many Army and Navy men had left their Union posts to join the Confederate ranks, the northern press singled out Maury for scathing criticism. *How*, they wondered, *could Maury participate in research whose purpose was to undermine and destroy the very Navy he had spent his life serving?* The *Boston Evening Traveller* published a notice that read

> $5,000 reward for the Head of Jeff Davis
> $3,000 for the Head of Gen. Beauregard
> $3,000 for the Head of the Traitor, Lieut. Maury[26]

This criticism hurt Maury deeply because he believed that he was only doing his duty in helping his own people. His rivals in the North were quick to denounce not only his present work with the Confederate Navy but also his entire life's work as well. In 1864 the National Academy of Sciences issued a statement saying that "the volumes entitled *Sailing Directions*, heretofore issued to navigators from the Naval Observatory and the Wind and Current charts which they are designed to illustrate and explain, embrace much which is unsound in philosophy and little that is practically useful, and that therefore these publications ought no longer to be issued in their present form."[27] Unfortunately, this wartime criticism permanently damaged Maury's scientific reputation.

A member of the Confederate Navy

The war was a difficult and frustrating time for Maury. He had given up a prestigious career, a comfortable home, many friends, and his financial security. He invested most of his assets in Confederate bonds, as all good Southern patriots did, and suffered the loss when they became worthless after the war. His wife and children had to live with relatives or in temporary housing. Maury saw them on rare weekends when the fighting permitted his traveling. Otherwise they saw very little of each other.

Working for the Confederate Navy was a severe trial for Maury. There was a fundamental difference in strategy between Maury and his superiors. Maury believed that the South needed to quickly build a fleet of small ships that carried big guns. These "mosquitoes" would be effective because they were highly maneuverable and difficult to hit. But Maury's mosquito fleet never materialized because the naval authorities believed that ironclad ships were more effective. Maury knew that the South did not have the resources to build ironclads. All available iron—fences, railing, plows, and pots—had been melted down just to create the South's only ironclad, the *Monitor*.

Besides the difference in strategy, Maury also suffered from personal conflicts with the other Confederate naval leaders. Unfortunately, several of the Confederate leaders were the very men who had worked against Maury in previous years. In fact, some of them had personally campaigned against Maury's ideas in Congress or served on the Naval Retiring Board (the committee responsible for Maury's demotion). He had made the grave mistake of siding politically with his personal enemies.

Secret Service

In 1862 Maury was reassigned to the Confederate Secret Service to serve in England. Maury turned over his equipment and diagrams to his assistant. Unfortunately, his assistant ran his ship aground on the first mission, and Maury's detailed diagrams were confiscated by the Federals. Maury lamented to a friend that the enemy used his diagrams to construct an electrical mine, sent a ship over it, and, to use their own amusing expression, they "blew her to toothpicks."[28]

Sailing to England was no small feat because Maury's ship had to break through the Federal blockade. Enroute to Bermuda, the captain of the ship became disoriented after a storm. After six days of muddling, the captain finally confided to Maury that he was hopelessly lost. Using the stars and a sextant, Maury guided the ship safely to Bermuda, proving his reputation as an excellent navigator. He even predicted within ten minutes when they would sight land.

Maury's "special duty" assignment in the Secret Service consisted of purchasing arms and ships and acting as a special agent of the Confederacy in England. Although Maury's scientific expertise seemed wasted in this new post, his international reputation served him well as a diplomat. Between writing letters to gain support for the Confederate cause, Maury received the many visitors who came to pay their respects to the great oceanographer.

Maury's official duty was to buy and outfit Confederate ships. His work, though, was difficult to carry out because of the ever-present Federal agents. His thirteen-year-old son, Matthew, Jr., had come along to keep him company. Brave, as his father called him, helped run confidential messages through the city.

Maury's greatest obstacle was the Confederate's insufficient money supply. Maury wrote to a friend that he had "plenty of orders and no money."[29] He was, however, able to purchase and outfit two ships, the *Georgia* and the *Rappahannock*. Unfortunately, Maury's success with the ships and his diplomatic role further increased the North's outrage at him.

The war takes its toll in Maury's family

The greatest difficulty for Maury at this time was the separation from his family. He knew they were living in danger and lacked fresh food and new clothes. Two of Maury's own children, Richard and John, had joined the Confederate Army. He confided to his wife in a letter that he dreamed each night that his family and friends had been killed or hurt. His fears came true one day when he received a sympathy letter consoling him over the loss of his son John. This was the first Maury had heard of John's disappearance that had occurred several months before. His family couldn't figure out how to break the news to him, so they waited, hoping that John would be found. The full story was never known, but it appeared that John had been ambushed while on a scouting mission.

Then Maury received word that Dick, his oldest son, had been shot through the hips and would probably die. A week later, Maury learned that Dick would live, but he would be crippled. Maury's sorrow and shock took their toll physically. His beard and mustache became white within a week, and he could not concentrate on his work. Then he suffered from an intestinal disorder and had two kidney operations.

When the Confederacy began crumbling in 1865, Maury was told to come home at his own discretion. He left England and sailed for Cuba. When Maury landed in Havana, he realized he could not return to the States because he would be imprisoned. After Maury received word of President Johnson's amnesty declaration, he realized how hopeless his situation was. Johnson had listed fourteen categories of people who were ineligible for pardon, and Maury fit into six of those categories! Maury could not, with honor, ask for a pardon. He believed he had followed moral principle and that secession was a constitutional right, not treason to the United States.

The years in exile

Maury was in a desperate situation. He had no job and no income. In fact, he had no country. He decided to live in exile in Mexico where Maximilian, an enthusiastic admirer of Maury's, was ruling. Maury invited other Southerners who had lost their fortunes to start over in Mexico in a colony that he wistfully named "New Virginia." Maury's immigration proposal was not so far-fetched. Other Confederate officers who could not return to the United States were living abroad, some in Canada, Brazil, and England. Maximilian liked the colony idea and named Maury the Imperial Commissioner of Colonization. However, many Americans considered the plan unpatriotic, and few families actually immigrated.

Maury's family was embarrassed by this immigration plan, and Ann did not want to leave her familiar surroundings to live in Mexico. So Maury told her to sail to England and wait for him, and they would decide what to do when they were together again. After three and a half years of separation, Maury was finally reunited with his family in England. When Lucy saw her father, she cried, "This is not my papa! This is an old man with a white beard."[30]

While Maury was in England, Maximilian wrote of the growing hostility to the immigration plan. Maury promptly resigned from his Mexican duties. Once again Matthew Maury was a man without a country or a job.

To support his family at this time, he instructed several nations on the use of mines for defense. He also wrote grade school geography textbooks, drawing on his observations made when he had been in the Navy and had personally traveled around the world. These textbooks were widely used in the South.

When Maury heard of Maximilian's assassination, he realized that, once again, God's special care had been evidenced in his life. If he had not come to England to visit his family, he would have been caught in the collapse of Maximilian's empire. Earlier, if he had not been sent to England on secret service, he would have been imprisoned following the war.

While Maury was in England, Cambridge University presented him with an LL.D. This honor was especially heartening to Maury after enduring such hateful criticism for his actions in the war. The scientist who had never had the opportunity to attend a university was honored by one of the greatest institutions in the world.

Back in the States the sentiment against Maury seemed to be diminishing. Several American universities offered Maury positions as a professor or administrator. After considering the options, Maury decided to accept the Virginia Military Institute's offer to be a physics professor and to supervise the Physical Survey of Virginia.

Coming home at last

After six years abroad Matthew Maury arrived in New York, just twelve days after President Andrew Johnson had pardoned those accused of treason against the United States. Maury had come home to help rebuild Virginia. The Physical Survey of Virginia was to be Maury's chief concern, and he was to lecture when time permitted. His job with the survey was to catalogue Virginia's natural resources and outline ways to capitalize on them so that people would be interested in investing and immigrating to Virginia. He collected this data in the same efficient way that he had collected his data for his hydrography charts. Instead of logbooks, he asked the farmers to fill out a chart that he had designed.

By now, though, the elderly Maury was suffering from poor health and rheumatism in his leg. He had only a few short years left. During a lecture tour, he became ill. When he finally made it home, he told Ann, "My dear, I am come home to die."[31]

He suffered with constant abdominal pain and nausea in his last weeks; but he was thankful that, in spite of the suffering, God gave him a clear mind until the very end. He spent his last days in bed thinking over his life and confessing his sins. He told his family that he had experienced a great sense of God's forgiveness.

Before Maury died on February 1, 1873, he rewrote his will so that he could leave each family member one of the medals or decorations of honor that he had received from foreign countries. Like so many other Confederate patriots, his entire fortune had been lost in the war, and he had nothing to leave his family.

As the developer of a new branch of science, it is obvious that Matthew Maury deserves more fame and attention than he receives. Unfortunately, in Maury's later years, his scientific work was obscured by politics. Because he is relatively unheard of today, it seems that those who sought to damage his reputation were somewhat successful.

But there are still a few memorials to his name. Maury Hall at the United States Naval Academy in Annapolis was named in his honor. And his native state of Virginia has honored him with a magnificent statue in Richmond, Virginia, that sits along Monument Highway. Here Maury sits in a chair holding a compass and sea chart. Above the seated figure is a globe with symbols representing Maury's work in hydrography, meteorology, and geography. A Bible leans against the chair, symbolizing the source of inspiration for his discoveries.

The Bible had always been Maury's guide, in his daily life as well as his scientific pursuits. He believed that God's word revealed in the Bible and God's works revealed in nature were perfectly compatible pursuits for him to study. Studying science was to him a way of furthering his knowledge about God. He said:

> When I, a pioneer in one department of this beautiful science [physical geography], discover the truths of revelation and the truths of science reflecting light one upon the other and each sustaining the others, how can I, as a truth-loving, knowledge-seeking man, fail to point out the beauty, and to rejoice in its discovery? . . . As a student of physical geography, I regard earth, sea, air, and water as parts of a machine, pieces of mechanism, not made with hands, but to which, nevertheless, certain offices have been assigned in the terrestrial economy. It is good and profitable to seek to find out these offices . . . and when, after patient research, I am led to the discovery of any one of them, I feel with the astronomer of old, as though I had "thought one of God's thoughts," —and tremble. Thus as we progress with our science we are permitted now and then to point out here and there in the physical machinery of the earth a design of the Great Architect when He planned it all."[32]

[1] Charles Lee Lewis, *Matthew Fontaine Maury: The Pathfinder of the Seas* (Annapolis: The United States Naval Institute, 1927), p. 19.

[2] Frances Leigh Williams, *Matthew Fontaine Maury: Scientist of the Sea* (New Brunswick, N.J.: Rutgers University Press, 1963), p. 119.

[3] Ibid., p. 131.

[4] Ibid., p. 136.

[5] Ibid., p. 180.

[6] Ibid., p. 190.

[7] Ibid., p. 194.

[8] Ibid., p. 186.

[9] Ibid., p. 221.

[10] Ibid. pp. 230-31.

[11] Jean Lee Latham, *Young Man in a Hurry: The Story of Cyrus W. Field* (New York: Harper and Brothers, 1958), p. 64.

[12] Williams, p. 258.

[13] Matthew Fontaine Maury, *The Physical Geography of the Sea* (Cambridge, Mass.: The Belknap Press of Harvard Univ. Press, 1963), eighth ed., p. 81.

[14] Ibid., p. 424.

[15] He said that Betty grew up so fast that he never had time to give her a funny nickname.

[16] Williams, p. 329.

[17] Lewis, p. 138.

[18] Williams, p. 106.

[19] Ibid., p. 340.

[20] Ibid., p. 273.

[21] Ibid., p. 368.

[22] Ibid., p. 391.

[23] Ibid., p. 417.

[24] Ibid., p. 377. When Lincoln declared surgical instruments and medicines to be contraband of war, Maury abandoned his scruples against using mines. "It is a business, this thing of blowing up men while asleep that I don't glory in, and nothing but the implacability of the enemy would induce me to undertake it. But has not Lincoln sent forth against our women and children the pestilence that walketh in the darkness? Against all rules and usage he has made medicine contraband of war. I strike at their fighting men in their strongholds, he at us all in our sick chambers." Ibid., p. 379.

[25] Ibid., p. 613, endnote 85.

[26] Ibid., p. 370.

[27] Ibid., p. 472.

[28] Ibid., p. 393.

[29] Ibid., p. 410.

[30] Ibid., p. 438.

[31] Ibid., p. 475.

[32] Ibid., p. 340. He also said, "There is no employment more ennobling to man and his intellect than to trace the evidences of design and purpose, which are visible in many parts of the creation." (From Maury, p. 81)

Lord Kelvin (William Thomson) with his mariner's compass (1824-1907)

LORD KELVIN
(WILLIAM THOMSON)
(1824-1907)

Engineer, Mathematician,
Inventor, Physicist

When I consider thy heavens, the work of thy fingers, the moon and
the stars, which thou hast ordained; What is man, that thou art
mindful of him? and the son of man, that thou visitest him?
Psalm 8:3-4

*William hunched over his book, munching on an apple. The light was
poor down here, but he didn't dare read his book upstairs where his father could see him. He had been sneaking down here every day for
several weeks to read this book, Fourier's* Théorie analytique de la chaleur
(Analytical Theory of Heat).

*It was a mathematical treatment of heat conduction, certainly not the
kind of vacation reading you would expect a sixteen-year old to be doing.
But William had been fascinated from the moment he picked it up, and
he couldn't stop reading it.*

*He didn't hear the sound of footsteps coming down the cellar stairs,
and he almost fell off his stool when he looked up and saw his father
standing quietly beside him. William knew he was caught. He hung his
head as his father reached down, picked up the book from his lap, and
flipped through the pages.*

*He knew exactly what his father would say. Why aren't you outside
with your brothers and sisters, visiting with the neighbors? Don't you
know that I brought you children to Germany this summer so that you
could learn German—not spend your time by yourself, reading in French?*

*But Mr. Thomson didn't say any of that. He shook his head as he gave
the book back. "I told you to leave all your schoolwork behind!" he said
with a sigh and headed back up the stairs. But he was inwardly pleased.
Who else had such a brilliant son that would secretly read mathematical
treatises?*

Childhood

James Thomson had always taken the education of his six children seriously. Ever since his wife's death ten years earlier, he had taught the children himself. William, his fourth child, seemed to have the most promise. He had been born in 1824 in Belfast, Northern Ireland, when Mr. Thomson was teaching math there. But the family soon moved to Scotland so that Mr. Thomson could teach at the University of Glasgow.

In Glasgow the family lived right on the university grounds. Here the children played on the college green or sailed their homemade boats in the nearby river. After his lectures were done for the day, Mr. Thomson taught his boys higher mathematics, using the math textbooks he had written himself.

William attended his father's university mathematics lectures when he was eight. Sometimes the students couldn't answer the questions and young William would beg, "Please, papa, please *do* let *me* answer!"[1]

When he was ten, William enrolled in the University of Glasgow. His brother James, who was twelve, also enrolled that year, and the two boys were usually at the top of their class. (Students usually enrolled when they were fourteen.) From his very first year, William won prizes in various classes for being the best student.

He had excellent professors at the university. One of his professors was a cousin of Michael Faraday, and he exposed his students to Faraday's new ideas. At first William disagreed with these odd notions about electricity and magnetism, but he soon realized that Faraday was right and became his admirer.

William did all the work for a degree at Glasgow, but he did not take a formal degree so that he could enter Cambridge University as an undergraduate. He enrolled in St. Peter's College, Cambridge, when he was seventeen. In 1845 he was presented the top award in mathematics from the college "in consideration of his great mind and of his exemplary conduct."[2] He won many other academic honors and awards—in fact, far too many to mention.

Mr. Thomson was not a wealthy man, but he was determined to give his children a good education. He had taken the entire family to Paris when William was fifteen so that the children could work on their French. William's knowledge of French helped him the next year, when he discovered Fourier's monumental work. His fascination with Fourier lasted all through his life.

Jean-Baptiste-Joseph Fourier's work was a mathematical study of heat flow through any solid object, but its implications were far-reaching. William extended the arguments of Fourier to show that there must have been a beginning—an actual time of Creation. In later years he was talking to one of his students about his writings on Fourier, and he said, "All mathematical continuity points to the necessity of a beginning—this is why I stick to atoms . . . and they must have been small—smallness is a necessity of the complexity. They may have all been created as they were, complexity and all, as they are now. But we know they have a past. Trace back the past, and one comes to a beginning—to a time zero, beyond which the values are impossible. It's all in Fourier."[3]

William's first scientific paper was a defense of Fourier's work—published when he was seventeen years old! A year later he published another work based on Fourier. This second paper contained the nucleus of much of Thomson's later work. He was still consulting it years later. The last time he used it was a few months before he died.

A well-rounded student

While studying at Cambridge, William discovered music. He learned to play the cornet and the French horn. He was so excited when he first started playing that he practiced with a friend late into the night. He and his friend were playing tunes in the lowest keys they could manage. It might have been bearable if they had not been beginners and they had been playing in unison, but they were standing in different parts of the room, playing different tunes. William was in the middle of playing "Adeste Fideles" when they were interrupted by a knock on the door. When William opened the door, a man in his nightgown said, "Perhaps you are not aware, gentlemen, how much noise these horns make."[4] They apologized and never made that mistake again.

William didn't mean to spend so much time with his music, but he would see his music open on the mantle and start to play. He often spent evenings practicing instead of studying mathematics. He played second horn in the orchestra and served one year as president of the Cambridge University Musical Society. He was one of the founders of the musical society, along with his friend John Dykes, who was famous for writing hundreds of hymn tunes.[5]

William never lost his great love for music. In the evenings, he frequently attended concerts, enjoying the orchestral music of his favorite composers Beethoven and Weber, the singing of Jenny Lind, or the violin playing of Joachim or Ysaye, two of the greatest violinists of that time.

William was a superb student, at the top of his class in every subject. But he also took time for exercise. He went rowing every day for two hours because he found that it made his mind sharper and gave him more energy. He won the university championship for skulling, using a one-man rowing craft. But he dropped out of competition after that year, much to his father's relief, because he admitted that he became obsessed with the races and could think of nothing else.

Mr. Thomson wrote him often, with the usual parental concern for his habit of spending money too quickly. His letters were full of fatherly advice. "Be most circumspect about your conduct and about what acquaintance you form. You are young: take care you be not led to what is wrong. A false step now, or the acquiring of an improper habit or propensity, might ruin you for life."[6] In another letter he wrote, "Never forget to take every care in your power regarding your health, taking sufficient, but not violent exercise. In 'your walk in life' also, you must take care not only to *do* what is right, but to take equal care always to *appear* to do so."[7]

Accepting the gospel

Mr. Thomson had brought up his children in the Presbyterian Church of Scotland. The preaching that the children heard there was Biblical and practical. At an early age William accepted the gospel message. When he was a teenager, he carefully thought through what he had been taught and confirmed that his childhood faith was true. His brother James, though, rejected the family's Calvinistic faith and became a Unitarian. William tried to reason with him, but he wouldn't listen.

William never wavered from his simple childlike faith and found that as he grew older, his studies in science strengthened his faith in God. He faithfully attended church all his life, but he despised mere ritualistic religion.

After graduation

When he completed his bachelor of arts degree at Cambridge University in 1845, he went to Paris for half a year to work at the Regnault Laboratories. Henri-Victor Regnault was a famous French chemist, called the "master of the art of minute and accurate experiment."[8] Thomson's work here was tedious and mundane, but he had a chance to observe and learn from Regnault.

When he returned from Paris, he received an appointment to the Chair of Natural Philosophy [Physics] at the University of Glasgow—

when he was only twenty-two! At first, it seemed that William's youth was definitely against him and the university leaned towards the older, more experienced candidates. But William's brilliance and original thinking were so evident that he was finally offered the post.

Mr. Thomson was pleased to have him working at the same university where he taught mathematics. He had hoped for several years for his son to fill this post, and he had campaigned to have William accepted. But he enjoyed only two years of working with him. One winter when an epidemic of cholera swept through Glasgow, Mr. Thomson died. It was a huge loss for the close-knit family, especially for William.

William may have been young when he became a physics professor, but he had already made a name for himself. By now he had published over twenty-five scientific papers and had been working as the editor of the *Cambridge and Dublin Mathematical Journal*. He had contributed papers on physics and mathematics to this journal as an undergraduate, but he did it anonymously because some people wondered about the "propriety" of a young undergraduate writing such advanced papers.[9]

His productive years at Glasgow

His years teaching at Glasgow proved to be both enjoyable and fruitful. The university session lasted six months, from November 1 to May 1. This left time for the students to earn a living and gave the professors time to research. During his first years at Glasgow, Thomson returned to Cambridge each summer to study and to renew friendships.

He received his master of arts degree, also from Cambridge University, in 1848. Before he became too busy with his own research, he would come back to Cambridge to play for the May concert of the music society, playing in his usual spot, second horn.

Thomson's light teaching load at Glasgow left him ample time for research, and he was able to turn out literally hundreds of papers covering an unbelievably wide range of subjects. A few of the general areas included in his investigations were heat, light, sound, gravitation, electricity, magnetism, pure mathematics, hydrodynamics, viscosity, telegraphy, elasticity, astronomy, meteorology, geology, navigational aids, tides, mechanical calculators, osmosis, and radioactivity.

In collaboration with James Prescott Joule, Thomson made the discovery that an expanding gas that does not perform work on its surroundings undergoes a slight reduction in temperature. This phenomenon has come to be known as the Joule-Thomson Effect.

Thomson was a great fan of collaboration in scientific work. That is why he so faithfully attended the meetings of the British Association for the Advancement of Science. He felt that scientists would accomplish much more by sharing ideas and working together. He was always carrying on scientific correspondence with a number of friends. He loved to take walks with his friend Sir George Stokes and run ideas by him. Thomson also checked his ideas with his brother James, who was a civil engineer and a genius in mechanics.

When Thomson was a new professor, he met Michael Faraday. He had been following Faraday's ideas from reading his scientific papers and had already developed a great respect for him. But when they met, they developed a deep friendship. Thomson was especially impressed with Faraday as a Christian.

After this meeting, Thomson corresponded with Michael Faraday and often went to London—four hundred miles away—just so he could attend Faraday's lectures. Afterward they would spend time discussing their latest investigations. By now Faraday was a middle-aged man, but the two men had about twenty years to work together. Thomson later said that Faraday was the inspiring influence of his early love for electricity. Faraday's kindness and encouragement were very valuable to Thomson. Thomson often said that the two greatest influences on his scientific thinking were Fourier and Faraday.

The brilliant professor

Thomson began each class with prayer and then launched into his lesson. (It was still the custom in the Scottish universities to open each class with prayer.) In the classroom, he was an enthusiastic lecturer, but he digressed often from his notes and interjected the "immediate workings of his living thought."[10] He might never get back onto his lecture topic once he pursued the side points that occurred to him. Sometimes a discovery would occur to him even as he was talking.

His rapidly moving thoughts were often too profound for the average student to follow. It seemed at times as though he were talking to himself, happily pursuing whatever idea came to mind, and forgetting that he had a class full of students in front of him. If students were lazy, or of average intelligence, the lectures went over their heads. One student complained, "Well, I listened to the lectures on the pendulum for a month, and all I know about the pendulum yet is that it wags."[11]

Thomson had one class of students who were not science students— they were studying law, divinity, or medicine. It would have been wiser

Thomson taught at Glasgow University for over fifty years.

for the university to appoint an assistant to teach them the basics of physics; but they had Thomson teach them. He could not teach basic physics because he kept inserting more advanced concepts that he thought were fascinating.

There were about one hundred students in this class who showed up when attendance was taken, but when Thomson turned to write on the blackboard, students began slipping out the back door. Thomson would lift up his eyeglass that was tied around his neck with a string, look at the back of the room, and comment dryly on the curious decrease of *density* in the back rows.

But no matter how bewildered his average students were, they always enjoyed his classroom demonstrations. For the acoustics lecture each year, he brought his French horn to class and played for them. The class rewarded him with an enthusiastic round of applause after his demonstration. For another demonstration, he brought an old rifle to class. He fired the rifle into the wooden bob of a pendulum to determine the velocity of a bullet. He was at the blackboard scribbling calculations before the smoke cleared.

When they were studying spinning bodies, he would happily spin his gyrostat, an instructive spinning toy. He had spun tops as a young boy, but even then, it was much more than child's play. He never outgrew this fascination with spinning bodies. He would show the class how to tell the difference between boiled and raw eggs by doing spin tests.

Students with a desire to learn science found Thomson absolutely stimulating. Often his lectures were extemporaneous, and he would share his latest research with the students. He frustrated his lecture assistants because they could never predict what demonstration or experiment he would ask them to perform. They learned to prepare for anything because he was always digressing from the planned lecture.

In those days, there was no laboratory apparatus for the students to use, no lab assistant to help them through their experiments, not even the idea of teaching students a laboratory course. So Thomson decided to start a laboratory program of his own and use the students to help him collect accurate data for his own research.

When he had worked in Regnault's laboratory in Paris, he had learned the importance of minute and accurate measurements. He had observed his friend Joule and had taken note of how skillfully and patiently he came up with accurate measurements. Now Thomson needed this same accuracy for his own research because he was finding himself hindered without data.

He set up a rustic laboratory in an unused wine cellar in the basement of the college. It was right next to the coal cellar, and there was always a faint cloud of coal dust in the laboratory. But the half dozen students who volunteered to help Thomson weren't bothered by the primitive conditions. They were infected with his enthusiasm. This was the first physical laboratory for students to use in any of the British universities.

Thomson knew students would be tempted to skip the hard work of laboratory research and try to take a shortcut to scientific discoveries. "Accurate and minute measurement seems to the non-scientific imagination a less lofty and dignified work than looking for something new," he told his students. "But nearly all the grandest discoveries of science have been but the rewards of accurate measurement and patient, long-continued labour in the minute sifting of numerical results."[12]

When Thomson talked about these early days with his volunteer workers, he said that about three-fourths of his students went into the ministry. When he talked to them later as they were working as ministers, they always mentioned the fond memories they had of their work in Thomson's laboratory. They never felt that the time had been wasted. By learning to make accurate and definite measurements, they learned the importance of accuracy and perseverance. And Thomson added, "There is one thing I feel strongly in respect to investigation in physical or chemical laboratories—it leaves no room for shady, doubtful distinctions between truth, half-truth, whole falsehood. In the laboratory everything tested or tried is found either true or not true."[13]

Thomson, the man

The days were never long enough for Thomson. There was so much he wanted to do and never enough time to do it all. He had a tremendous store of energy, and his mind was full of plans. He always timed things down to the last second. He would stay in his laboratory until the last possible minute and then dash out to change for an evening concert. He would come breezing into his classroom as the bell was chiming, still putting on his robe. Even when he had guests to dinner, he wasn't always there on time to receive them. When Thomson came home in the afternoons, his pet parrot, Dr. Redtail, greeted him by saying, "Late again, Sir William! Late again!"[14] And it was usually true.

Thomson was a gentleman at all times. He was quick to praise others, and he played down his own contributions. He carefully acknowledged the help of others in forming his ideas. He was well liked and had many, many friends. Even after he became internationally famous, he was the same modest, courteous man. He seemed always to have a kind word to say about someone, even when he disagreed with him or knew he was wrong. When he criticized a man's theories, he used tame language. He might mention that someone was "wildly adrift" in his ideas, but he was always respectful when disagreeing.

When his assistant wanted to take issue with another man who disagreed with Thomson, Thomson let him. But he said, "Don't hit too hard. *Remember he is four times as old as you.*"[15] For many years, Thomson had been the amazing youngster moving among the older men of science. He read his first paper to the British Association and became a fellow of the Royal Society when he was in his early twenties. But the older men never seemed to resent him. Even those who disagreed with him held him in great esteem. When he found himself as one of the older men, he treated the younger men with great kindness and encouraged them.

He studiously avoided controversy and felt that questions of fact "could and should be discussed without coming within a hundred miles of anything acrimonious" [biting or caustic].[16]

Thomson's work in thermodynamics

It would be difficult to overstate the importance of Thomson's work in the field of thermodynamics. In fact, he was the one who popularized the use of the term *energy*, the most important of all the quantities dealt with in physics. Further, he divided energy into two categories, potential and kinetic.

In the 1840's Mayer, Joule, and Helmholtz published papers establishing the fact of conservation of energy—the principle that energy can be changed from one form to another but cannot be created or destroyed. This has come to be known as the first law of thermodynamics.

The first law tells nothing about the direction in which natural processes occur. Yet some things are observed to happen with ease in nature; other things never happen at all. For instance, heat always flows from a hot body to a cold body, never the reverse, unless energy is supplied, such as in a refrigerator.

A gas tends to expand and occupy a larger volume, never to contract into a smaller volume, unless energy is supplied from the outside to compress it forcibly. It had been observed for some time that there is a definite "one-wayness" in nature—a preferred direction in which natural processes occur spontaneously.

Four men—Carnot, Clapyron, Clausius, and Rankine—had all made important contributions in this general area. There was, however, no general unifying principle to tie together the large number of seemingly unrelated observations. Instead of rejecting or condemning the work of these men as some of the other scientists had done, Thomson suspended judgment and pondered the problem for many months.

Finally, early in 1852, he formulated what is undoubtedly one of the most important generalizations in all of science. In a paper entitled "On a Universal Tendency in Nature to the Dissipation of Mechanical Energy," he set forth three propositions which are today known as the second law of thermodynamics.[17] Though energy is conserved, he said, it is becoming less available. It is, to use his terminology, "irrevocably lost to man, and therefore 'wasted,' though not annihilated."[18]

The implications of the second law are momentous. It indicates that the universe as a whole is running down, that it must have had a definite beginning, and that it will die a "heat death" at some time in the future unless a Power greater than itself intervenes beforehand. It rules out such imagined processes as perpetual motion and spontaneous generation. The second law argues strongly against any theory of evolution that has ever been proposed, either biological or cosmological. If, then, dissipation rather than improvement is the trend of nature, one could hardly expect increasing order and complexity to arise from less organized states of existence.

It is significant that, after all these years since Thomson formulated this law, there have still been no exceptions observed. The second law is remarkably enduring and consistent.[19]

His thoughts on evolution
It was no secret to those who knew him that Thomson stoutly rejected the idea of spontaneous generation of life on the earth:

> Mathematics and dynamics fail us when we contemplate the earth, fitted for life but lifeless, and try to imagine the commencement of life upon it. This certainly did not take place by any action of chemistry, or electricity, or crystalline grouping of molecules under the influence of force, or by any possible kind of fortuitous concourse [lucky combination] of atoms. We must pause, face to face with the mystery and miracle of the creation of living creatures.[20]

One can readily see the sharp contrast between Thomson's clear insight and the philosophy of present-day science, which regards life as but a collection of chemicals.

In his presidential inaugural address before the British Association in 1871, he stated:

> Careful enough scrutiny has in every case up to the present day discovered life as antecedent to life. Dead matter cannot become living without coming under the influence of matter previously alive. This seems to me as sure a teaching of science as the law of gravitation. . . . I am ready to adopt, as an article of scientific faith, true through all space and through all time, that life proceeds from life, and from nothing but life.[21]

To the Bible-believing Christian, nature speaks of God and "sheweth His handiwork." Scripture implies that its Author placed each subtle detail of nature there with a definite purpose. Thomson perceived how the idea of teleology—the fact that purposefulness in nature points to a Designer—was suffering at the hands of the evolutionists. He said that "overpoweringly strong proofs of intelligent and benevolent design lie all around us; and if ever perplexities, whether metaphysical or scientific, turn us away from them for a time, they come back upon us with irresistible force, showing to us, through nature, the influence of a free will, and teaching us that all living beings depend on one ever-acting Creator and Ruler."[22]

In his lectures on optics, he expounded on that "most wonderful of instruments, the eye."[23] Here, he said, was one of the very clearest proofs of design—the fact that an optical device of such amazing complexity had been structured in accordance with all the known physical laws of light.[24]

To illustrate how difficult it is to believe that life can come together on its own, Thomson quoted what his friend Liebig said to him. Once when Thomson was walking in the country with Justus von Liebig, the celebrated organic chemist, he asked Liebig whether he believed that the grass and flowers that surrounded them had come into being by mere chemical forces. "*No,*" Liebig answered emphatically. "No more than I could believe that a book of botany describing them grew by mere chemical forces."[25]

Science and the Bible
Thomson never saw the study of science as being contrary to the Bible or somehow detracting from worship of God. He said that the study of sci-

ence takes us away from atheism. When he gave a lecture on Christian apologetics, he said,

> I do not say that, with regard to the origin of life, science neither affirms nor denies creative power. Science positively affirms creation power. Science makes every one feel a miracle in himself. It is not in dead matter that we live and move and have our being, but in the creating and directive Power which science compels us to accept as an article of belief. . . . Do not be afraid of being free-thinkers. If you think strongly enough you will be forced by science to the belief in God, which is the foundation of all Religion. You will find science not antagonistic, but helpful to Religion.[26]

Thomson said that people should not be so awed with the progress of science that they neglect to consider the impression that the study of nature ought to make on every mind. The more people study the wonderful works of God, he said, the more awe and veneration they should feel for its Author. He continued,

> At a time when astronomy could hardly have been said to exist as a science, the Psalmist exclaimed, "When I consider thy heavens, the work of thy fingers, the moon and the stars which thou hast ordained; What is man that thou art mindful of him, and the son of man that thou visitest him?" . . .

> When we comprehend the vastness of the dimensions of that part of creation of which we know a little, and yet consider what an infinitesimal portion this is of the whole universe, how insignificant a being we must feel that man is, and how grateful ought we to be that God should still be mindful of him and visit him, and for the gifts and the constant care bestowed on him by the Creator of all. By such feelings the earnest student of philosophy must always be impressed; so will he by his studies and successive acquirements be led "through nature up to nature's God."[27]

Marriage

In the summer of 1852, at the age of twenty-eight, Thomson married Margaret Crum, his second cousin. She and William had seen each other often when they were growing up. She noticed the great love that he had for the women in his family—his sisters and his widowed aunt who had taken care of the family after his mother died. He had always held deep affection for these women in his life and faithfully kept in touch with them by letter. Margaret felt that his devotion to his sisters was an excellent indicator of the feelings he would have for his wife. She proved to be right.

Margaret was very talented and deeply spiritual. In spite of her chronic poor health, she was a continual source of blessing for him. She was in poor health from the very first year of their marriage. Her illness was never given a name, but she was often in great pain, and she could not exert herself at all. William often carried her up the stairs or carried her from room to room, putting her on her day couch where she spent her days, running the house and writing poetry or helping him with his correspondence.

His patience with her illness is touching. He went to great lengths to try to find a cure for her. They traveled to Germany many times because the spas there were supposed to be curative. William took advantage of his stays in Germany and met with Hermann von Helmholz, the great German scientist. For many years they continued a warm friendship and scientific correspondence. William read German, but he never learned to speak it well. He said he would have learned it better if he hadn't been reading Fourier in the cellar that summer that his family spent in Germany.

After many years of seeing doctors and trying to improve Margaret's health, Thomson said that they were very skeptical of all cures and had learned to have only "very moderate expectations" whenever she had a few good days.[28]

The limp

One Christmas, when William was thirty-seven, he was playing a game with his friends on a frozen pond. The game, called curling, resembled ice hockey a bit. During the game, he fell hard on the ice and broke his thighbone. It was a very painful break, and it mended slowly. For many weeks he had to lie flat on his back, and he was unable to teach the rest of the session. When he could finally get up, he limped about on crutches.

When the leg healed, it was shorter than the other, and he had a permanent limp. He could still get around, but his sports activity was limited. The leg bothered him off and on over the years. Sometimes it would swell again, and the doctor would order him to bed for several weeks. He fretted over this inactivity because he couldn't go to his laboratory or teach his students. He had his lab assistants come to his house and report to him, and he would direct them from his bed.

During the months that he was confined to bed right after the break, he started using a green notebook to jot down his thoughts—calculations, diagrams, or ideas for experiments and scientific papers. He got into the habit of carrying this little green notebook around with him all the time. His wife had his jackets made with a special pocket to tuck this little book in. Whenever he had a thought, he would pause wherever he was and jot it down. Sometimes he would wake up with a thought and reach over to his nightstand and grab his notebook. Even before he got out of bed, he would jot down what he was thinking, always beginning each entry with the exact date, time, and place.

He might be talking to his guests at dinner when a thought came to him, and he would slip out of the conversation and begin working out a calculation in his notebook. He didn't mind working with life moving around him. He worked wherever he found himself—in a train, in his garden, on his boat. Over one hundred of these green notebooks have been preserved and show the amazing versatility of his genius.

The transatlantic cable

Up until now Thomson's work was mainly in mathematics and pure science—the theory of magnetism, the flow of heat, and his thermodynamic studies. But he was soon pulled into the practical application of science.

When Thomson was in his early thirties, he became a director of the Atlantic Telegraph Company. By this time the use of Morse's invention had spread through much of the world. Land lines hummed with messages on both the North American and European continents. Submarine cables had been successfully laid in short lengths, such as that connecting England with Ireland and England with the continent.

But the feat of spanning the two thousand miles (4000 km) between the two continents on either side of the Atlantic Ocean still posed many formidable problems. The ocean was known to be some three miles (almost 5 km) deep in places, the cost of materials was prohibitive, and there was no ship in existence that could carry the tremendous amount of cable needed. There was also the fear that the great distance involved would retard the signals enough to render the system impractical.

Thomson entered the picture actively when the company's electrician bowed out of the expedition because of poor health. Thomson agreed to help even though there was no salary for him. He had no real authority—he just gave advice, and the company often ignored it. He saw mistakes made, but he was powerless to stop them. In this awkward position, he showed his great patience and an unwillingness to speak unkindly of others—even when they deserved it.

Unfortunately no one had thought to consult Thomson before the cable specifications were drawn up. Several compromises had been made to reduce costs. The contract called for a small gauge of copper and a dangerously small quantity of insulation with no guarantee that it would be applied uniformly.

The cable, such as it was, was delivered in 1200 pieces, each two miles in length, during the summer of 1857. These were then joined into eight sections, each three hundred miles long, with the remaining splices to be made during the actual laying.

It would take two ships to carry the cable—the British battleship *Agamemnon* and the United States frigate *Niagara*. The cable was tied at Valencia Bay in Ireland and the two ships proceeded westward together, each carrying half the cable, hoping to land it in Newfoundland. Thomson, on board the *Agamemnon*, supervised the operations as best he could with the materials and equipment at his disposal.

The gear for paying out the cable had been improvised hastily; they quickly found that it was impossible to control the cable properly, especially in rough water. At a distance of 330 nautical miles out into the Atlantic, the cable broke, and the expedition ground to a halt. The ships returned to Ireland and work was suspended until the following year.

In the meantime Thomson continued to work at some remaining theoretical problems—electrical delay in the cable, the tension in the line as it was leaving the ship, and a host of other details that would never cross the mind of the casual onlooker. During the next few months he delivered several lectures and papers on the general subject of the Atlantic cable. In February of 1858 he patented a special mirror-galvanometer, which he designed to receive the minute currents that would be coming through the cable.

He tested samples from the cable and found that they varied widely in conductivity, depending on the purity of the copper. The cable hadn't even been tested before it was delivered. He feared the project was doomed to failure with such poor quality manufacturing. When he told the directors of the cable company about the serious problem with the cable, they didn't care.

Thomson insisted that any new cable be tested to see whether it met his specifications. He didn't trust the manufacturers to follow the stricter specifications, so he set up a testing center at the factory to make sure they were complying. (This was the first factory testing laboratory ever in use. Before this, engineers had never given any thought to quality control. In a sense, Thomson is the father of the concept of quality control and the standardizing of raw materials.[29])

The Atlantic Telegraph Company purchased seven hundred miles of this new cable to replace what was lost in the ocean, and they resumed work early in the summer of 1858. Thomson again accompanied the party, this time equipped with his mirror-galvanometer, the device that proved to be very valuable for testing the cable as it was being laid. This time they revised the procedure somewhat. The two ships were to travel to the middle of the Atlantic and then proceed in opposite directions, laying the cable between them.

Again difficulties plagued the work. The *Agamemnon*, with Thomson aboard, encountered a violent storm that lasted eight days. A portion of the coiled cable was seriously damaged and tangled, the electrical testing room was flooded, and the coal used to fuel the ship broke loose and injured ten of the crew. It took two days to untangle the one hundred miles of cable that had been damaged in the storm.

Thomson's ship finally made a successful rendezvous with the *Niagara*, and the cable was joined and stretched between the ships. When only six miles of line had been laid, a break occurred at the *Niagara*. They met again, made a new splice, and the ships set out again. This time they were eighty miles apart when a break occurred.

Meeting a third time, they set out again, only to have the cable snap when they were over two hundred miles apart. Returning once again to the starting point, they couldn't find each other because of a heavy fog. Defeated at last, the ships returned to land.

At this point the directors of the company differed on what the next step should be. Several believed the endeavor was hopeless and wanted to dissolve the company. Those who were directly involved in the work— Thomson, Cyrus Field, and Charles Bright—had no doubts about the ultimate success of the undertaking. They decided to try laying the cable again immediately.

They used the same procedure, but this time the cable was paid out by hand, requiring a man on duty day and night on each ship. The anxiety on board ship was intense. Thomson slept in his clothes, ready to be called on deck whenever there was a problem. The extra effort in paying out by hand made the difference, and by August 5, 1858, the cable stretched from Heart's Content, Newfoundland, to Valencia Bay, Ireland.

A buoy marked the spot where the cable split.

Although the two ships had been in telegraphic communication with each other through the cable, the first message to be sent over its entire length made a supremely joyful occasion. There were wild celebrations on both sides of the Atlantic. Many hailed it as the feat of the century. Queen Victoria and President Buchanan exchanged congratulatory messages. The famous message that crossed the Atlantic in August of 1858 read as follows: "Europe and America are united by telegraphic communication. Glory to God in the highest, on earth peace and goodwill towards men."[30]

Now what?

But even while the celebrations were going on, there was trouble with the cable. Often there was an unexplained delay in receiving the signals. Just a few weeks after the cable had been laid, the signals grew fainter. Only Thomson's mirror galvanometer worked now. No other equipment could pick up the faint signals. Finally the cable fell silent. All that effort and investment lay useless at the bottom of the ocean.

It was a huge disappointment to the world, but especially to the men who had worked so hard laying it. The critics said that they knew it would never work anyway. It had just been a gigantic, expensive failure. But Thomson was optimistic. He saw it all as a learning experience. He felt that the failure had taught them many things, especially the importance of using carefully manufactured cable that had no defects in the insulation. The insulation of the cable had been imperfect, as Thomson had warned, and it had deteriorated rapidly. Now the manufacturers would have to be more cautious and pay strict attention to cable specifications.

The chance to lay a new cable came in 1865 when enough money had once again been raised. This time Thomson sailed on the *Great Eastern*. This ship could carry the entire cable and a staff and crew of nearly five hundred. The laying went well, and they even fixed a fault that was discovered after the cable was on the ocean floor. They rolled the cable back up into the ship and repaired it.

But when a second fault was discovered and they tried to roll the cable back up, it snapped. The cable fell to the ocean floor, two miles down. They used a grappling iron to hook the lost cable, and three times they actually lifted the cable part way, but then they lost it.

The cable layers had to return to land, once again under the cloud of failure. But Thomson continued to be optimistic. He spent the next year perfecting new instruments for the cable and rushing to London to test the cable as it was being manufactured. Many times Thomson's secretary ran to the Glasgow railway station to stop the train before it started to London. He told the stationmaster to hold the train until Thomson, who had been held up working with his instrument maker, could come. And, surprisingly, each time the stationmaster obeyed. Thomson by now was held in great honor, and his cable work was considered of national importance.

In 1866, the *Great Eastern* sailed again, with Thomson and his newest equipment on board. This time the cable laying was accomplished with no complications, save for a temporary tangle. They landed the cable safely at Newfoundland and then returned to the spot where the cable had split the year before to try to retrieve it. It took two weeks of grappling, but they were finally able to raise it. They spliced it with new cable they were carrying, and it still worked. They landed the 1865 cable in Newfoundland, and then there were two cables working! The engineers temporarily joined the two cables to prove that they could send a signal through 3,700 miles of cable.

Scotland quickly claimed the praise for the achievement. They glowed because Thomson was one of their own, a Glasgow man. And Captain Anderson, who piloted the *Great Eastern*, and Mr. James White, who manufactured the instruments for Thomson, were also from Scotland.

Thomson had been home only a few months when Queen Victoria knighted him for his work on the transatlantic cable. Now, at thirty-four, he was called Sir William. But, with all the fame and recognition that poured in on him, he said with his characteristic humility that "no greater reward could befall the scientific investigator than when his secret and silent labours resulted in some discovery of immediate practical benefit to the world."[31]

Siphon recorder

Now many underwater cables were laid successfully. Thomson became a partner in a telegraphic cable company and traveled with many cable expeditions. They wanted him on board ship with his equipment to help solve the problems that arose.

His mirror galvanometer was a brilliant invention, but he wasn't satisfied with it. He didn't want just to see the signals coming in; he wanted to record them. He knew that it would take the strain off the operators if they didn't have to watch the galvanometer all the time to see whether a signal was coming in. It would be much better to have a permanent record that could be read at leisure. Thomson worked for several years on this problem and came up with his siphon recorder. It was a beautiful invention with a moving paper tape and a fine stream of ink that spurted out and recorded the signals on the tape.

His cable inventions now brought him considerable financial gain. For more than a decade he had worked on the cable problems on his own time and at his own expense, and it was fitting that he should finally be remunerated for all his work.

From his first royalty check for the siphon recorder, he donated a large sum of money to Glasgow College, telling them that their facilities and the training he received there had contributed so much to his success. They used his money to set up scholarships for needy students. In later years, Thomson continued to contribute quietly to the college.

Geological controversy

A most interesting chapter of Thomson's life concerns the controversy he waged with the geologists of his day. No stranger to the field of geology, he had written a magnificent mathematical treatise on the shape of the earth while he was still a teenager. This had included a discussion of its internal structure and rigidity as well as its geometric form.[32]

As the years passed, Thomson became more and more suspicious of the uniformitarian assumptions of the geologists. The uniformitarians said that the processes that are observed today are the same processes that were at work in the past, shaping the earth's features; there is no room for supernatural, miraculous, or globally catastrophic events. They proposed enormous amounts of time to account for such slow processes, and they implied that the earth might not have had a fixed beginning. From several lines of reasoning Thomson knew that the history of the earth could not extend back into time indefinitely. In fact there were very definite limits set by the slowing of the earth's rotation, heat conduction in the earth's crust, and reduction of the sun's fuel reserve.

Thomson had been thinking about this problem for many years. When he was twenty-two years old, just beginning his teaching at Glasgow University, his inaugural address dealt with the earth's heat. He said that the enormous ages that the biologists and geologists claimed were untenable. The earth's heat gave a decisive limitation to the earth's age. [33]

In 1865, when he was forty-one, Thomson read a paper before the Royal Society of Edinburgh entitled "The Doctrine of Uniformity in Geology Briefly Refuted." It was forcefully worded, and it included the calculations on which his conclusions were based. Three years later he lectured to the Geological Society of Glasgow on "Geological Time," stating that "a great reform in geological speculation seems now to have become necessary."[34] He said, "It is quite certain that a great mistake has been made—that British popular geology at the present time is in direct opposition to the principles of natural philosophy [physics]. . . . There cannot be uniformity."[35]

The geologists took up the challenge and fought back. They resented the fact that an "outsider" was intruding into their cherished domain. They did not appreciate any restrictions on their time scale. Thomas H. Huxley, president of the Geological Society of London, became the major spokesman for the opposition.

In an address in 1869, Huxley attempted to justify the uniformitarian position by alleging that Thomson's data were too loose to permit any kind of calculations to be made. Huxley attacked the position of catastrophism—the belief that global disasters helped shape the world's features—pointing out that it involves believing in processes that no man can observe at the present time. His masterful oratory easily swayed the vast majority of his listeners.

Thomson's reply came later the same year in an address, again before the Geological Society of Glasgow. He chided the geologists for being so indifferent to the principles of physics that underlie their field of study. Since so many geologists had not cared about physics, he said, British popular geology was now in direct opposition to the principles of physics.

He pointed out that his calculations had merely set limits rather than establish an exact figure. He showed how Lyell and Hutton, founders of the uniformitarian philosophy, had ignored the implications of thermodynamics. Hutton had gone so far as to claim, "We find no vestige of a beginning, no prospect of an end."[36] Yet Thomson had clearly shown from several angles that there must have been a beginning.

The other scientists were surprised at Thomson's tenacity. He would not budge on this geological issue and brought it up several more times. But even more remarkable than his tenacity was his courtesy. Two years after their encounter, when Huxley was the outgoing president of the British Association and he was introducing Thomson, the incoming president, he mentioned the obvious accomplishments of Thomson, especially his work on the cables. Then he mentioned that he had found out personally what a courteous gentleman Thomson was.[37]

In spite of Thomson's protests, however, uniformitarianism in a somewhat less extreme form persisted and still persists to this very day. It is, in fact, the keystone of modern geology. Despite its great popularity, this position has recently been challenged again by an impressive body of fresh research findings.[38] Thomson's philosophical descendants are still fighting the same battle over a hundred years later!

A great loss

The Thomsons never had children of their own, but they were very close to their nieces and nephews. One of his nephews lived with them and worked as his lab assistant. He could even fill in for Thomson when he couldn't be at his lectures. Another nephew became a skillful electrician and helped lay cables. When his boat went down off the coast of South America, William felt as though he had lost his son.

Even in her poor health, Lady Thomson brought her husband great happiness. She was very bright, and everyone who knew her spoke highly of her, saying that she understood the truly important things in life.

The Thomsons dreaded separations, but the winters in Glasgow were too hard on Margaret, and she often had to go to Italy for the winter while William taught the winter session in Glasgow. She had wanted to accompany him on the *Great Eastern*, but no women were allowed on that voyage. The company allowed the Thomsons to use the cable for their personal messages, and that made the separation bearable.

When Lady Thomson's health was so poor that she could no longer travel, William rented a house for them on the coast so that she could be out of the smoke and pollution of Glasgow. He was fully prepared to resign his professorship to take care of her, but the college granted him a leave of absence that winter to nurse her. Her health became worse that spring, and she died in the summer of 1870 after extreme suffering.

Sir William was devastated. He knew she was happy and out of pain, and he had "the firmest hope of a transcendently happy meeting to come," but that couldn't diminish the bitterness of his present grief. He knew that only God could soften his grief.[39]

Lalla Rookh

After his wife died, he found that the best medicine was sheer hard work. He bought a yacht that he named the *Lalla Rookh* and immersed himself in the problems of navigation.[40] He installed electrical lighting on her and carefully fixed her cabins so that he could have guests. He hired a crew of sailors and a captain, but he did a lot of the navigation himself.

He became a first-rate navigator and often said that he was a sailor at heart. He was a favorite with the other mariners, but they thought he was too daring, going out in bad weather or late in the season. "You will not rest," his captain complained, "till you have your boat at the bottom."[41]

172 Christian Men of Science

He often invited former students or other scientists along on his little trips so that they could study and discuss their research. (After he had the public disagreement with T.H. Huxley over the geological controversy, he still invited him on his yacht.)

He found that he did his best work on his yacht because he didn't have to deal with the interruptions of normal life. "I can only get math work done in the yacht," he said. When the school session was over, he spent a good part of his six-month vacation on the *Lalla Rookh*, coming to shore to visit his lab once a week and usually spending Sunday on land so that he could go to church.

He usually took a quick swim in the ocean before breakfast. Then he would pace the deck thinking through a problem and scribbling in his green notebook. He enjoyed the solitude of the ocean, but he enjoyed being on his yacht more if he had some of his family along, especially his nieces and nephews. He usually brought along his laboratory assistant who also served as his secretary and would take dictation.

A surprise
Thomson traveled often because of his work with the submarine cables. By now a special ship, the *Hooper*, had been built especially for cable laying. On one cable-laying trip, Thomson found himself on the island of Madeira, off of the coast of Portugal. A fault had been discovered in the cable, and the problem was causing a frustrating delay. They had to uncoil four hundred miles of cable to reach the problem spot, splice the pieces, and recoil the cable.

Meanwhile, Thomson had to spend two weeks on the island. As he walked about, he was particularly impressed with the flora and fauna of that region. He found it impossible to keep Darwin's natural selection out of his thinking and made this observation: "Although Madeira gave Darwin some of his most notable and ingenious illustrations and *proofs* (!) we find at every turn something to show (if anything were needed to show) the utter futility of his philosophy." (Kelvin's punctuation)[42]

One of the prominent residents of Madeira, Charles Blandy, welcomed Sir William at his villa. Sir William taught the three Blandy daughters Morse code and was surprised that on the very first evening, they could send and read long telegrams. To pass the time, he taught them other forms of sending dot and dash signals—with lamps and with a flag. The cable was finally fixed, and Sir William headed back to Glasgow. As his ship sailed away, someone from the Blandy's house signaled with a white cloth, "G-o-o-d-b-y-e-S-i-r-W-i-l-l-i-a-m-T-h-o-m-s-o-n."

Lord Kelvin's home was one of the first houses to have electricity.

The next summer he sailed back to Madeira on the *Lalla Rookh* on a different mission, totally unrelated to cable laying. He asked Frances Anna Blandy to marry him. She accepted, and they were married a few weeks later. He often told his friends how his present happiness was due to a fault in the cable, and that certainly it was not chance that had stranded him at Madeira for two weeks. It was God working for his happiness. "I thank God always that I was brought here," he wrote to his sister when he announced his engagement.[43] He had not even considered re-marriage, thinking he would never again find the happiness that he had had with Margaret.

But Fanny proved to be as devoted to him as Margaret was. (He called her Fanny, but to the rest of the world she was known as Lady Kelvin.) One friend commented that Fanny's evident mission in life was to take care of the precious piece of humanity that was entrusted to her care.

Sir William built a house for them by the sea at Largs, Scotland. He named the house Netherhall. This was one of the first houses to have electricity.[44] He also installed a telephone line between their house and his lab so that Fanny could call him for lunch or tea. When he was in his lab, he completely lost track of time.

Lady Kelvin enjoyed having company and was famous as a gracious hostess. They frequently had visitors for tea and dinner, and often they had a dozen or more house guests.

By now Sir William was fifty and just as active as always. He served as president of his local division of the National Bible Society of Scotland and campaigned for Bible instruction in the schools of Scotland. He thought that even though a certain catechism or religion could not be taught in the schools, this restriction should not apply to the Bible.

Honors

Again in 1892 the queen honored Sir William; she conferred a barony on him, and his official title became Baron Kelvin of Largs. This meant that William was now part of the House of Lords, and he cheerfully took part in his duties. He got to pick his new name, and he chose the name Kelvin because of the River Kelvin that flowed near the University of Glasgow. Changing his name was a traditional part of becoming a Lord, but it was confusing to foreigners. *Who is this Lord Kelvin who invented the siphon recorder?* they wondered. *Everyone knows that Sir William did that!*

The total list of distinctions that he earned grew to an imposing length and included twenty-one honorary doctorates from universities through-

out Europe and America. It has been said that Thomson had the most letters after his name of any man who has ever lived.

Contributions

Lord Kelvin's name is probably best known because of his absolute
temperature scale. From his studies in thermodynamics, he suggested
using zero for the lowest possible temperature that is theoretically attain-
able. This would be 273 degrees below zero on the Celsius scale—when
molecules stop moving. This scale eliminates potentially confusing negative numbers—an integral part of the Fahrenheit and Celsius scales.[45]

It is impossible to list all the contributions that Lord Kelvin made. To
an unusual degree he combined the qualities of theoretical physicist and
engineer, covering the entire spectrum of ability from mathematician to
inventor. As a mathematician, he made significant contributions to the
science of thermodynamics; as an inventor, he held over seventy patents
for inventions.

His theoretical work helped lay the foundation for modern physics.
But he thought of himself as a failure in the realm of theory because he
did not succeed in fulfilling his life's dream—coming up with a unified
theory of matter.

But Lord Kelvin's work was more than just theoretical. His science
was immensely practical. "The life and soul of science is its practical application," he would say.[46] His interest in navigation led him to invent a
mariner's compass that was soon adopted by the British Navy to use on
all their ships. The earlier compasses were often inaccurate because of the
rolling of the sea, the firing of guns on the ship, or the iron used in ship
construction. But Lord Kelvin's design was very stable even in the most violent storms and was not disturbed by the iron in the hulls of the ships.

He also invented a sounding machine that could take "flying soundings"—meaning that the ship did not have to stop to do the soundings. He
found that steel piano wire worked much better than the hemp ropes that
sailors had been using. He was always upset to learn of ships that met
with disaster because they didn't take frequent soundings. He often said
that more ships were lost by poor logic than by poor seamanship.

He also invented instruments to measure electric currents precisely,
and he worked with his brother James on mathematical machines, which
were really the first analog computers. Using a calculating machine that
his brother James invented, Thomson invented a tide gauge and a tide pre-
dictor. It could calculate the tide for any hour, past or future. Thomson
also suggested improvements for lighthouses and believed that each light-

house should have a distinctive signal, perhaps a letter of Morse code that it flashed out that would distinguish it from the other lighthouses. His navigational aids ended up saving many lives and millions of pounds of property. Officials in the British Navy used to say that Thomson had done more than any other man to advance navigation.

Thomson and Tait

One of Thomson's most important achievements was the development of a physics textbook, co-authored with Professor Peter Guthrie Tait of Edinburgh. Thomson and Tait (as the textbook is frequently called), a volume of 727 pages, was recognized as the unchallenged leader in its field for many years.

There were physics textbooks in French and German, but there was nothing comprehensive in English that they could give their students. Thomson and Tait spent eighteen years working on this textbook but finished only one volume. They had originally planned four volumes, but they realized sadly that it would never get done because both of them were busy with other research. Throughout the book they used two sizes of type—large type for the portions that were nonmathematical and intended for general readers and small type for the mathematical portions. This made the book accessible to more people.

They did a lot of their communication by mail, jotting a quick question on a post card and sending it off. When the postman came, he would chuckle as he unwrapped their little postcards from his handkerchief where he had tied them so he wouldn't lose them.

Thomson and Tait worked well together. Tait had studied at Cambridge a few years after Thomson. They had different styles and temperaments, but they esteemed each other's work highly. When disagreements arose, they didn't agree to disagree; they always fought it out because they had great fun arguing. They were both full of humor and would make remarks at the other's expense.

In this book, Thomson often had to coin new names to express the new ideas he was explaining. He often complained that math was so inarticulate, that in the past mathematicians had hidden their ideas behind formulas and had not used diagrams or words to express physical ideas. He thought that Faraday was a great reformer in that area with his descriptive language.

Thomson thought the study of mathematics should be practical and deal with the real world. He had no words of praise for people who devoted their skill to abstruse pieces of algebra, which might possibly interest four people in the whole world, and possibly only the person who was working the equation. He always stressed to his students that mathematical analysis was an aid, not an end in itself. He always told his students to keep in mind the meaning of the mathematical processes. Sir William did have the unique gift of translating real facts into mathematical equations, and when he worked with the equations, he never lost sight of the physical reality behind the equations.

Jubilee

When Lord Kelvin finished his fiftieth session as professor of physics, the University of Glasgow staged a magnificent three-day celebration in honor of his jubilee year. Delegates came from all over to honor him, the man that they called the "greatest living scientist." There were 2500 guests, and three cable companies set up siphon recorders with their cables to receive all the congratulatory telegrams that came in from those who couldn't attend. Many of the telegrams were from former students who were now scattered all over the world. The admiration and affection of his students was touching. He had inspired love and reverence in everyone who worked with him.

Cambridge University had tried to lure him away several times, but he always refused because he was comfortable in Glasgow and felt that he did his best work at the university. He thought of himself as a child of the university because he had lived there or worked there since he was eight years old.

Closing years

Lord Kelvin made up his mind to retire from his teaching post when he was seventy-five so that he could make room for younger men. He insisted, though, that the university keep his name on the register as a "research student." He still thought of himself as a student even after all these years.

He still kept up with his normal routine of writing and research, but as the years went by, his leg bothered him more and he suffered from a debilitating facial neuralgia. Sometimes the pain in his face would leave him unable to work for several days. It was hard for him to slow down. He had always had tremendous stamina and could keep three secretaries busy with his dictation.

Lord Kelvin lived several years into the twentieth century, witnessing the advent of the quantum theory, relativity, the automobile, the airplane, and the first voice transmissions by radio. He lived to the age of eighty-three, enjoying the blessings of good health and a keen mind until a month or two before his death. He was still taking out patents the year he died.

As his eyesight and hearing became less acute, he knew that his long life was coming to an end. He told a friend that this would be "Anno Domini," the year that he would see the Lord. That winter he caught a cold from the stormy weather and never recovered. A fever set in and he died on December 17, 1907.

Lord Kelvin was honored with a magnificent funeral and burial in Westminster Abbey, attended by a grand congregation of scientists and dignitaries from England and Scotland. He is buried next to Sir Isaac Newton. There is an impressive Gothic stained-glass window in Westminster Abbey dedicated to Lord Kelvin.

He had lived an unusually full life. He had derived a wonderful sense of fulfillment from his life's work, counting the privilege of scientific investigation as one of the Creator's greatest gifts to mankind. He said, "The power of investigating the laws established by the Creator for maintaining the harmony and permanence of His works is the noblest privilege which He has granted to our intellectual state."[47]

---

[1] D. K. C. MacDonald, *Faraday, Maxwell, and Kelvin* (Garden City, NY: Doubleday, 1964), p. 106.

[2] Silvanus P. Thompson, *Life of Lord Kelvin* (London: Macmillan and Co., 1910), p. 107, footnote.

[3] Ibid., pp. 111-12. Each session William began his course in Natural Philosophy with the same introductory lecture. He said, the "theory of heat and mechanical effect . . . shows that the inanimate world must have had a beginning, and that all motion except that of heat must have an end, unless it please God to restore by an act of new creative power the dissipation of mechanical effect which always goes on." (Thompson, p. 241, footnote 1)

[4] Ibid., p. 50.

[5] We still sing John Dykes's hymns. Two of the better known ones are "Jesus, the Very Thought of Thee" and "Holy, Holy, Holy."

[6] Thompson, p. 37.

[7] Ibid., p. 53.

[8] Ibid., p. 123.

[9] Ibid., p. 38.

[10] Ibid., p. 192.

[11] Ibid., p. 193, footnote 1.

[12] Ibid., p. 600.

[13] Ibid., p. 298.

[14] Ibid., p. 631. See also Sir John Ambrose Fleming, *Memories of a Scientific Life* (London: Morrison and Gibb, Ltd., 1934), p. 95.

[15] Thompson, p. 1108.

[16] Ibid., p. 864.

[17] "1. There is at present in the material world a universal tendency to the dissipation of mechanical energy.

  2. Any *restoration* of mechanical energy, without more than an equivalent of dissipation, is impossible in inanimate material processes, and is probably never effected by means of organised matter, either endowed with vegetable life or subjected to the will of an animated creature.

  3. Within a finite period of time past the earth must have been, and within a finite period of time to come the earth must again be, unfit for the habitation of man as at present constituted, unless operations have been or are to be performed which are impossible under the laws to which the known operations going on at present in the material world are subject." (Thompson, p. 290-91)

[18] Ibid., p. 288.

[19] George L. Mulfinger, "History of Thermodynamics," in *Thermodynamics and the Development of Order,* Emmett L. Williams, ed. (Norcross, Georgia: Creation Research Society Books, 1981), pp. 7-8.

[20] Dagobert D. Runes, ed., *Treasury of World Science*, (Paterson, N.J.: Littlefield, Adams and Co., 1962), p. 545.

[21] Thompson, pp. 604-5. He also said "If a probable solution, consistent with the ordinary course of nature, can be found, we must not invoke an abnormal act of Creative Power." (p. 605)

[22] Ibid., pp. 608-9.

[23] Ibid., p. 244.

[24] Today we comprehend this truth all the more clearly as we contrast the human eye with the finest products modern optical technology can offer. We are still unable to construct a lens of variable refractivity such as that found in the eye. We stand in awe as we consider that the human optical system affords its user automatic aiming, focusing, and aperture adjustment, plus the luxury of stereoscopic color vision with a development time of only a fraction of a second. It will take our best scientific minds some time before this level of performance can even be approached; yet evolutionists teach that such an astonishing mechanism developed by lucky chance.

[25] Thompson, pp. 1099-1100.

[26] Ibid., pp. 1098-99.

[27] Ibid., pp. 250-51.

[28] Ibid., p. 322.

[29] J. G. Crowther, *Men of Science* (New York: W.W. Norton & Co., 1936), p. 237.

[30] Thompson, p. 982.

[31] Ibid., p. 502.

[32] He wrote this prize-winning essay, called "On the Figure of the Earth," when he was sixteen!

[33] Thompson, p. 186.

[34] Ibid., pp. 540-41.

[35] Ibid., p. 543.

[36] Ibid., p. 548.

[37] His biographer said that Thomson "crossed swords with knightly courtesy indeed, but with deadly earnest." (Thompson, p. 599)

[38] The interested reader will find many scholarly papers in the publications of the Creation Research Society, the Institute for Creation Research, and Answers in Genesis (among others) presenting the scientific evidence for creation and a worldwide flood.

[39] Thompson, pp. 534, 655.

[40] *Lalla Rookh* was the name of an Indian princess who was the heroine of a poem written by Thomas Moore in 1817. (MacDonald, p. 135, footnote 6)

[41] Thompson, p. 595.

[42] Ibid., p. 637.

[43] Ibid., p. 645.

[44] Crowther, p. 251.

[45] George Mulfinger and Emmett L. Williams, *Physical Science for Christian Schools* (Greenville, S.C.: Bob Jones Univ. Press, 1974), p. 122.

[46] Thompson, p. 793.

[47] Ibid., p. 246.

James Clerk Maxwell (1831-1879)

JAMES CLERK MAXWELL
(1831-1879)

Physicist

The works of the Lord are great, sought out of all them
that have pleasure therein.
Psalm 111:2

*"Look, Maggy," Jamesie said to his nanny. He stood by the window
and pointed to the place where the reflection from his tin plate hit the
bedroom wall. The spot danced around the room as he moved the plate.
"Go for Papa and Mamma," the two-year old said.*

*When Maggy brought his parents into the room, he moved the sun's
reflection so that it shone in their eyes. Mr. Maxwell laughed and put his
hand up to shield his eyes. "What are you doing, my boy?"*

"It is the sun, Papa," Jamesie said. "I got it in with the tin plate."

*"Yes, Son. And when you are older, I will let you see the moon and
the stars."*

Childhood

James Clerk Maxwell was no ordinary toddler. He was investigating
even before he was three. He didn't need toys to play with—he was too
busy trying to understand how things in the house worked. He locked and
unlocked doors, trying to figure out how keys worked.

He kept his parents busy answering his questions. "Show me how it
doos," he would say. "What's the go o' that? What does it do?" And he
wanted specific answers. If his parents didn't give a detailed explanation,
he kept pestering them. "But what's the *particular* go of it?"

He often stood in the kitchen to watch the servants' bells. High on the
wall, his father had installed a collection of bells that were connected by
wire to each room. Pulling the wire would ring the bell in the kitchen and
summon the servants. James would drag his father around the house, trac-
ing the bell wires and showing him the holes that he had discovered in
the walls. James liked to stand watch in the kitchen while his nanny
pulled the wires. Or he would run around the house pulling the wires,
making the servants shout which bell had rung. James kept the bells

ringing, and it was often hard to tell when it was a real summons for the servants or when it was just James. "These bells will never rust," his mother commented.

Mrs. Maxwell was a gifted lady, and she quickly noticed her son's extraordinary mind. Her first child, Elizabeth, had died shortly after birth, and now she had only James. He had been born in Edinburgh, Scotland, in 1831. Shortly after his birth, the family moved to their country home, two days' journey by carriage from Edinburgh.

Mrs. Maxwell devoted herself to teaching her only child. She let him explore the fields around their country home in Scotland, and when he came home from his walks with a collection of pebbles, sticks, and plants, she answered his questions about each one. But James wasn't always satisfied with her answers. When she commented on a blue stone he brought home, he asked, "But how d'ye know it's blue?"

He spent a lot of time at the little duck pond that his father had built near the house. He caught tadpoles and watched them grow into frogs. He liked to startle his friends by sticking a frog in his mouth and letting it jump out. His friends gasped and said that the frog was *dirty*. "It's clean dirt," he would say.

He had a special way with animals. He was never afraid of animals, and they didn't seem to be afraid of him. He understood animals better than he understood people. He taught Toby, his mustard-colored terrier, to do many tricks, and he enjoyed having Toby perform these tricks for his friends.

When his friends got bored, he entertained them with his favorite toy, the magic disk. This was an arrangement of drawings on a disk that gave the illusion of continuous motion when the disk was spun. He devised clever drawings for his disk—the cow jumping over a waxing and waning moon, a tadpole wriggling from an egg and changing into a frog, and a dog pursuing a rat in and out of its hole.

When James wasn't asking questions or entertaining his friends, he was busy making things. He would weave baskets, making the servants drop their work and help him. He had learned to knit by watching his mother knit, but his knitting projects were even more elaborate than hers.

Mrs. Maxwell was entirely in charge of his education during these years, and she had a clear purpose when she encouraged James to study nature. She always told him to "look up through Nature to Nature's God." She read to him from the Bible, and soon he could recognize quotations

James escaped from the abusive tutor.

from any of the 150 psalms and tell where each was found. Before he was eight years old, he could quote all of Psalm 119 from memory.

But his happy childhood collapsed when he was eight. His mother died of cancer that year after suffering great pain. Mr. Maxwell pulled James aside one morning and gently told him that his mother was in heaven. "Oh, I'm so glad!" James said. "Now she'll have no more pain." It was just like him to think of another's comfort before his own.

Mr. Maxwell hired a tutor to take care of James's education. The tutor reported that James was slow and unmotivated. It turned out, though, that the fault was mainly with the tutor. He was unkind and drilled harshly. James was a quiet child and not openly rebellious, but he knew how to dig in his heels and be uncooperative. One morning he escaped from his tutor and got into a washtub and paddled to the middle of the duck pond. The tutor grabbed a garden rake and tried to bring him back in. But James managed to stay just out of reach.

Sometimes the tutor would get so frustrated that he would hit James on the head with a ruler or pull his ears until they bled. James quietly put up with this abuse. For two years Mr. Maxwell was blind to this unhappy arrangement until an aunt came to visit and told him just how inept the tutor was. His aunt quickly put a stop to the abuse and begged Mr. Maxwell to enroll James in school.[1]

Edinburgh Academy

James went to live with his aunt when he was ten so that he could attend Edinburgh Academy. The academy was a respected preparatory school with a reputation for a good classical education. It emphasized Latin, Greek, and mathematics.

During his first day at school, the boys had descended on him like bees and made fun of his clothes. "Who made those shoes?" they asked.

James looked down at his square-toed shoes. No one had laughed at him at home for wearing them. He looked back at the crowd of boys pressing around him, but he didn't want to give them a straight answer— that his father had designed his shoes so that his toes would have room to breathe. Instead he answered them with an unintelligible riddle.

The boys pulled at his collar and laughed. They had never seen anyone dress so completely out of step with fashion. Mr. Maxwell had designed these clothes, thinking about warmth and practicality; but he had given no thought to the styles here in the city.

So before the first day of school was over, James had already been branded as a misfit. He came home with his clothes torn, laughing about his new nickname. The boys called him Dafty because of his funny country accent and his bizarre outfit. James didn't do anything to change his nickname. He was different from the other boys, and he knew it. They made fun of him on the playground and made him do his frog imitation— squatting and leaping—over and over until he was exhausted.[2]

His sense of humor also branded him as different. It centered on witty word plays and obscure rhymes that he made up on the spot. The other boys were too slow-witted to appreciate his humor and wrote him off as an oddball. He usually took the abuse of his classmates good-naturedly;

but he was no sissy, and on one occasion, he turned on his tormentors in a wild fury and taught several of them respect.

James stood up slowly as the headmaster called his name. He hated this part of the day when he was asked to recite his lesson. If he had been asked to memorize something exciting like poetry or inspiring like Scripture, he would have had no trouble.

But the rote memory drills here at the academy were so dull. He didn't mind when the boys made fun of him for his odd humor, but he hated being teased for not remembering his lessons.

As he stood, he stared at the window and slowly began his recitation. He was relieved to find that his idea had worked. The night before, he had sketched a picture of the window on his paper and copied his lesson inside the window. Now as he stared at the window, the words all came back. He finished the lesson and sat down quickly. Now if he could just see the window every day and his seat wasn't moved, he would survive.

James found his class work so uninspiring. For the first few years, the curriculum centered on rote memory. By the fifth year, the boys could conjugate eight hundred irregular Greek verbs.[3] James was much happier when they were actually reading the classics and not just learning grammar rules. (But he said later in life that learning Greek and Latin had not been a waste. He thought it was an excellent way to train the mind.)

He would much rather concentrate on his own research projects than on his assigned work. He studied geometry before it was taught in school and even constructed cardboard polyhedrons without knowing the names. "I have made a tetrahedron, a dodecahedron, and two other hedrons, whose names I don't know," he wrote to his father.[4]

On Saturdays his father would travel from the family estate of Glenlair to visit James. This was always the high spot of their week. They would take walks and see the local sights—rock formations, excavations for a railroad, or local factories. Mr. Maxwell's idea of a good time was to tour manufacturers and see the "works." He carefully answered his son's questions. In a few years, the tables would be turned, with James answering questions for his father and explaining the "go" of things.

When James was twelve, his father started taking him to meetings of the Edinburgh Royal Society. If James was sick and couldn't attend, he made his father bring him a full report. He had already shown a decided bent towards science, just like his father. James was fascinated with magnetism and the polarization of light even before he was a teenager.

Mr. Maxwell was a lawyer by profession, but he could afford to spend most of his time managing his country estate. He was skilled in architecture and had planned and supervised the building of the family home and the barn.[5] He also dabbled in science and technology and had designed an automatic-feed printing press.[6]

James and his father enjoyed a special friendship, especially after Mrs. Maxwell died. Mr. Maxwell acted more like a loving older brother than a stern father. James understood how lonely his father felt when he was studying in Edinburgh, and he tried to cheer him up with his funny letters. He would tell him the news and then draw pictures, write silly poems, or invent a code that Mr. Maxwell had to decipher.

James was not an outstanding student when he first came to the academy to study. He was often sick and had to stay home from classes. But halfway through his schooling he seemed to come to life. When he finished at the age of sixteen, he was first in math and English and close to first in Latin.

Too young

At one of the meetings of the Edinburgh Royal Society, Professor Forbes stood at the podium, reading a research paper. The paper he read described a method for drawing complex ovals using threads and pins. The method was remarkable for its simplicity and its originality.

After the meeting, the men gathered around fourteen-year old James, shaking his hand and patting him on the back. James was the author of this paper, but he had not been allowed to present it. The men considered it undignified for such a young boy to personally address the Society!

He wrote several more papers as a teenager, and when he was eighteen, he was finally allowed to read his own paper to the Society.

The young scientist

In the summers, James came home to Glenlair with his father. His home was in the rugged countryside of Scotland near the Urr river. James was happiest here at Glenlair, playing with the friends he grew up with—the servant's children. He had figured out how to make the washtub float without its spinning around, and he often explored the river in his washtub. He went swimming every day in the summer and worked on his "aquatic experiments." He studied how sound traveled underwater and told his father, "I can understand how fishes can be stunned by knocking a stone."[7]

Now as a teenager, he had found new ways to occupy himself. The meetings of the Edinburgh Royal Society had given him ideas, and he wanted to work on them. He spent many hours working in his crude laboratory, figuring out how to electroplate things, covering them with a layer of copper.

His laboratory was full of his "experimental litter"—his jars of water, clay, salt, soda, sulfuric acid, and a few other chemicals; and scrap pieces of wire, iron, and glass. He had set an old door on two barrels and called it his workbench. Spiders, beetles, and wood lice would accidentally fall into his jars and poison themselves.

He didn't need expensive equipment. He could make do with the simplest apparatus. He constructed a homemade set of polarizing prisms after visiting the scientist James Nicol and seeing his polarizing prisms. When Maxwell looked through the prisms, he saw fascinating designs. He made exact watercolor pictures of these designs and sent a few of these watercolors to Nicol. Nicol was so impressed that he sent James a real set of Nicol prisms.

Edinburgh University

When James enrolled at Edinburgh University when he was sixteen, his course load was light. He had time to pursue his own creative research using his professor's laboratory. He investigated polarized light, galvanism, rolling curves, the stereoscope, and compression of solids.

Mr. Maxwell had assumed that James would follow him into a legal career and keep up science as a hobby, just as he had done all these years. But James was not interested in practicing law. His interest in science was much more than a hobby. It was now a passion, and he wanted to pursue it seriously.

Mr. Maxwell finally agreed to let his son study science, but he soon realized that James lacked the mathematical discipline to seriously pursue his scientific interests. Mr. Maxwell knew that Cambridge University had the reputation for some of the best math training of the day. But there were several reasons for not sending his son there. One was that it was too far away for him to take care of James when he was ill.

But his most serious objection was that the English universities had a reputation for turning out infidels. A staunch Presbyterian like Mr. Maxwell worried that the unwholesome influences might tempt his son to give up his faith. But after several professors mentioned that James should develop his amazing gift for science, Mr. Maxwell finally gave in and let him go to Cambridge University.

Cambridge University

It was a little after 2:00 a.m. and James was running laps through his college roominghouse. Down the steps, through the hall, and then back up the steps, making a circle. At first the other students ignored the thumping, but finally their patience wore out. As James started another lap around his "track," the other students pelted him with boots and hairbrushes. James decided that this experiment with his sleeping habits would have to wait until he was in a more hospitable environment.

In this experiment, he had tried sleeping in the early evening, studying from 10:00 p.m. to 2:00 a.m., exercising from 2:00 a.m. to 2:30 a.m., and then sleeping again until 7:00 a.m. He learned not to jog in the middle of the night because of the negative feedback, but he continued to juggle his sleep habits to determine whether he could find a more productive schedule.

His other extracurricular experimenting was lighthearted and had dubious scientific value. He studied how a sheet of paper fell and how quickly cats could land on their feet when dropped upside down. The rumor mill accused him of throwing cats out the window for this experiment, but Maxwell patiently explained that the point is to drop the cats from as low as possible, not as high as possible. He dropped the cats onto his bed and found that from the height of two inches, a cat could twist and still land on its feet.

Cambridge was a stimulating environment for James. Up until now, he had made few friends. Most of the other boys had considered him shy and dull. But finally, at Cambridge, he had a troop of friends. Here were other bright young men who understood James and his humor.

His aunt had been worried about him because he seemed so different from other boys. He took after his father and thought and acted in original ways that made him seem unconventional and odd, even a bit eccentric. He had adopted his father's method of dressing for practicality, and he would never wear any adornment—no starch, studs, or collars.

His aunt tried to draw him out and help him act more like other boys. She often got exasperated when he was off in his own world thinking through a math problem. At dinner he would rather watch the light playing off the drinking glasses than talk to her. But when he was alone with his father or a friend who could follow his thoughts, he wouldn't stop talking. These friends were amazed that he could converse knowledgeably on any subject that came up and knew curious, out-of-the-way facts.

His professors at Cambridge were amazed at his immense mass of knowledge, but they said it was in an appalling state of disorder. It was already obvious to the other students and the professors that James was in a class by himself—a genius, complete with the eccentricities.

James did excellent work in all his subjects, but he did not have to spend all his time studying. His friends were aggravated that he could sit and visit and then at the last minute run off to do his class work. And he always arrived at class just as prepared as the rest. He took time for exercise, but he didn't play team sports. He preferred to walk, row, or swim. He would start his swim with a belly flop, swim to the other side, get on the bank, and then fall flat on his back into the water. "Stirs up the circulation," he said.

Christianity

During a school break, James went to visit a friend's family. As an only child, he was fascinated by the workings of this large family. As his visit drew to a close and he was packing to return to school the next day, he began to feel ill. He went to bed early and made up his mind to recover; but by morning he was worse. He was perfectly useless, and if he sat up, he fainted. The doctor came and pronounced it a "brain fever" (a popular Victorian diagnosis), apparently caused by the strain of studying for the upcoming exams.

This family nursed him as their own son. The man of the house, Rev. Tayler, carried James when he was too weak to walk. He often came to sit by James's bed and talk to him about the things of God. James was deeply touched by their kindness to him. This experience taught him much about the love of God and helped strengthen his beliefs.

After this illness, he had a new awareness of his own sinfulness. "I maintain that all the evil influences that I can trace have been internal and not external," he said. "You know what I mean—that I have the capacity of being more wicked than any example that man could set me."[8]

During his college years, Maxwell carefully reexamined his faith. He had been brought up in a Christian home with regular church attendance and daily Bible reading. He had never doubted the truth of what his parents and church had taught him. But now he questioned everything he had believed—no ground was too holy to walk on and reexamine. And he found that it was all true. In his opinion, Christianity is the only faith robust enough to be completely open to scrutiny.

Thomson's encouragement

As soon as Maxwell graduated from Cambridge, he wrote to William Thomson (later called Lord Kelvin) asking his advice on the best way to study electricity. Maxwell ended his letter by saying, "I do not know the Game laws and Patent laws in science. Perhaps the Association may do something to fix them, but I certainly intend to poach among your electrical images; and as for hints you have dropped about the 'higher electricity,' I intend to take them."[9]

Thomson wrote back and told him to read Faraday's writings and Thomson's own writings in chronological order. Then read Ampère and the German physicists. James later told his father that Thomson "is very glad that I should poach on his electrical preserves."[10]

Thomson and Maxwell became good friends, carrying on a delightful correspondence. Thomson's own ideas stimulated Maxwell's thinking and he often carried the ideas further. Maxwell always thought of Thomson as his mentor and frequently acknowledged Thomson's contribution to his thinking.

A great loss

Maxwell finished at Cambridge with the highest honor in math. He stayed for another year and completed a fellowship at Cambridge. But he didn't want to stay in England. He wanted to be near his father, who was in poor health.

James applied for a job teaching at Marischal College in Aberdeen, Scotland. He came home to nurse his father while he waited for the new session to begin. Mr. Maxwell seemed to improve under James's care. James hoped it was a passing illness, but it was ominous that his father carefully set his affairs in order and talked to James about what to do after he died.

Mr. Maxwell died a few weeks later, just a short while before James began teaching. This was a devastating loss for him. He had lost his best friend and his greatest fan, just when he was beginning his career.

He now inherited the family estate of Glenlair, and his first thought was for the servants. He liked the fact that his father had read the Bible to the servants in the evening. But he wanted to combine the family prayers with the servants' prayers; he didn't want them to be separated. He had always felt that the servants were his family. When he was at school, he had often written home telling them what books they should be reading.

Professor Maxwell

As a teacher, Maxwell appealed to the brighter students and tended to lose the slower ones. His lectures were carefully written out, almost nice enough to print. The students often asked to copy straight from his lecture notes because these were so clear. Unfortunately, though, his lecturing was muddy.

He usually began by reading the manuscript; but invariably he would stop and interject explanations and new ideas that flashed across his mind. "Perhaps I might explain this," he would say, and he would start thinking aloud, covering the blackboard with figures. His rapidly moving thoughts were hard for the students to follow. He was obviously a genius, but he had difficulty communicating his ideas to others.[11]

Yet, if his public lecturing was lacking, he compensated for it in his private dealings with his students. He had the habit of staying after class for hours to answer questions and to demonstrate his latest invention for the serious students. Professor Maxwell frequently borrowed library books for his students because their use of the library was so limited. They could have only two books at a time. His use of the library was unlimited, and university policy allowed him to borrow books for friends. When he was scolded for borrowing books for the students, he said, "But the students *are* my friends."

Marriage and King's College

While he was at Marischal College, Maxwell married Katherine Mary Dewar, the daughter of the principal of the college. During their courtship they began studying the Bible together, and they continued this practice throughout their marriage. She was seven years older than he was, and he worried about the reaction in his family. When he wrote to his aunt announcing his engagement, he said, "Don't be afraid; she is not mathematical; but there are other things besides that, and she certainly won't stop the mathematics."[12]

He taught at Marischal College in Scotland for four years and then moved to King's College in London. Maxwell's years at King's College were impressively productive. The nucleus of his gas theory and his electromagnetic theory were hashed out during this period.

Besides his normal lecturing duties, he served on a committee to standardize electrical measurements. He also found time to give evening lectures to working men and tried to get better working conditions for them. He found that he enjoyed teaching these men more than he enjoyed teaching his university students because they were more eager to learn.

In London he had the opportunity to attend Michael Faraday's famous Friday evening lectures. Faraday was impressed with Maxwell's ability and often encouraged him. Faraday was in his sixties by now, and Maxwell was in his twenties, but they held a mutual esteem for each other's work.

Maxwell's church life

Growing up, James had attended the Presbyterian church with his father, but after he went to live with his aunt, she took him to the Episcopalian church. These two influences were blended in his early training. The backbone of his belief was Scottish Calvinism, but he was never attached to any particular denomination.

Maxwell had always paid close attention in church, even as a teenager, and days later could retell the sermon as though he had memorized it. When he was twenty, he said, "I believe, with the Westminster Divines and their predecessors *ad Infinitum* that 'Man's chief end is to glorify God and to enjoy Him forever.'"[13]

When choosing which church to attend in the cities where he worked, his primary concern was whether the Word of God was preached clearly and correctly. After he was married, he attended a Baptist church when he lived in London because, in his opinion, the preacher there "knows his Bible, and preaches as near it as he can, and does what he can to let the statements in the Bible be understood by his hearers."[14]

Maxwell believed in keeping Christianity pure and the gospel message clear. He opposed any effort to ignore differences and merge everyone indiscriminately into a fuzzy mass-Christianity. He strongly disliked indefiniteness and despised the type of preaching that was empty morality without the gospel remedy. He used to complain about the style of preaching that "dings ye wi' mere morality."[15]

Maxwell's private life evidenced his deep unaffected piety. Each evening he would call the servants together to participate in the evening devotions. He knew the Bible practically by heart and was very familiar with the writings of John Owen and Jonathan Edwards. Sundays after church, he studied the theological works of the past. He had nothing against the more current theological writings, but he felt there were great treasures in the old works.

One of his classmates at Cambridge said, "He had an innate reverence for sacred things, which I do not think was ever much disturbed by the scepticism fashionable among shallow scientific men. . . . If shortly described, he might be said to combine a grand intellect with childlike simplicity of trust. He was too deep a thinker to be sceptical, but too well read not to feel for others' difficulties. All his experiments led him to greater reverence for the Great First Cause, heartily agreeing with Young's *Night Thoughts*, 'An undevout astronomer is mad.'"[16]

Maxwell served as an elder in the Corsock Church near his home, a church which had been founded and built through his spiritual leadership and financial assistance. It was his custom to visit sick individuals in the community and to read and pray with them if they desired. He maintained an enviable balance between work, family, friends, and church duties.

Science and the Bible

Maxwell wholeheartedly accepted the Genesis account of Creation and had no use for theories of evolution—chemical, cosmic, biological, or otherwise. In an address to the British Association in 1873 he said,

> No theory of evolution can be formed to account for the similarity of molecules, for evolution necessarily implies continuous change. . . . [T]he exact equality of each molecule to all others of the same kind gives it, as Sir John Herschel has well said, the essential character of a manufactured article, and precludes the idea of its being eternal and self-existent."[17]

In Maxwell's discourse "On the Telephone," written the year before he died, he took special pains to refute the evolutionary speculations of Herbert Spencer (1820-1903), an English philosopher who popularized Darwin's theory of evolution.

Maxwell believed that the study of science helped man subdue the earth as God had commanded. A prayer found in his papers after he died reveals his view.

> Almighty God, who hast created man in Thine own image, and made him a living soul that he might seek after Thee and have dominion over Thy creatures, teach us to study the works of Thy hands that we may subdue the earth to our use, and strengthen our reason for Thy service; and so to receive Thy blessed Word, that we may believe on Him whom Thou has sent to give us the knowledge of salvation and the remission of our sins. All which we ask in the name of the same Jesus Christ our Lord.[18]

Maxwell cautioned against tying scientific theories to Scripture. The rate of change of scientific hypothesis is too great. If theories were tied to Scripture, he said, it would prevent their being discarded fast enough.

Maxwell's personality

Maxwell was a kind, gentle man. His kindness was first revealed in his treatment of animals. He could never bring himself to hurt any animal, not even the insects that he would catch as a child. He literally couldn't hurt a fly. He never liked hunting and fishing. He would much rather study the animals than kill them.

When he was in college, one of his friends hurt his eyes doing experiments with light. Maxwell would often find him in his room, moaning about his eyes, wondering how he would prepare for his classes the next day. Maxwell would stop what he was doing and read to him for an hour and help him catch up on his work.

Throughout his life Maxwell showed an exceptional kindness to those who were sick. He never forgot the kindness of the Tayler family when they nursed him through his illness in college, and he learned from them how to make a sick person comfortable. Maxwell helped nurse Katherine's brother, Donald, back to health. He had come to stay with them when he was recuperating from an operation. Donald's face would light up when Maxwell came home from his day of teaching. "I shall be comfortable now," he would say. "James is home."[19]

Maxwell was also generous. He lived simply and economically so that he could distribute to the needy. Sometimes he was criticized for his simple style of entertaining—he had simple tastes and never drank or served wine. But people didn't realize that the money he "saved" by not entertaining lavishly was given to needy folks. He gave generously to the construction of the church and manse near his home and even offered funds for building an elementary school; but he died before the school plans could be carried out.

Maxwell was shy and awkward, except with his close friends. (His closest friends were ministers, not scientists.[20]) He had a witty sense of humor that deepened with age. But his word play and puns were not always easy to catch. "No jokes of any kind are understood here," he complained at one teaching post. "I have not made one for two months, and if I feel one coming I shall bite my tongue."[21]

Even in his lectures, he would insert his subtle humor. During his last lecture, he spoke about the telephone. He remarked that the great beauty of Professor Bell's invention was the symmetry: "The perfect symmetry of the whole apparatus—the wire in the middle, the two telephones at the ends of the wire, and the two gossips at the ends of the telephones, may be very fascinating to a mere mathematician."[22]

He also enjoyed innocent practical jokes. He once cleaned out a boiler in his laboratory and noticed the large calcium deposits. He sent a specimen to a geology professor asking him to identify it, giving the impression that he had found it outside. The geology professor correctly identified the deposit. If he hadn't, Maxwell would have never let him forget it.

When he returned to Cambridge as a physics professor in his later years, it was customary for the new professors to give an inaugural lecture that was vaguely related to their discipline. Maxwell somehow announced this lecture in such a way that few people attended. When he gave his first lecture to the freshman class, the Cambridge deans and administrators attended en masse, assuming that this was his inaugural address. With a twinkle in his eye, Maxwell soberly lectured on the relationship between the Kelvin and Celsius scales.

His peers considered him a bit eccentric in his speech habits and mannerisms. He spoke in sudden gushes, with long pauses in between. If he was nervous or his mind was jumping too fast, nobody could understand him. His written communication was clear, but his verbal communication often stumped his listeners. He never seemed to get over this difficulty, which his biographer attributed to his traumatic years with the abusive tutor.

Maxwell enjoyed all types of reading—novels, classical English, philosophy. He analyzed and criticized each work that he read, and his literary opinion was considered as sound as his scientific opinion. His verbal brilliance is evident in the poetry he translated from Greek; he often wrote poem parodies using the same meter as the original.

He also wrote original poetry, using it as an emotional outlet. Instead of saying what he was thinking, he often would hand a friend a poem he had written. Most of his poetry was humorous, written to amuse his friends. Some of his poems became well known where he taught, especially a silly ditty he wrote to lament the silence of the transatlantic cable. The memorable lines from that poem are "Under the sea, under the sea / No little signals are coming to me" and "Under the sea, under the sea / Fishes are whispering. What can it be?"[23]

Retirement from teaching

Maxwell retired from teaching after five years at King's College. He gave up teaching because he needed more time to devote to his research and writing. He was thirty-three and just getting warmed up in his scientific work. With the estate and the money he had inherited from his father, he really didn't need to work. He would rather live at Glenlair and finish the construction plans that his father had laid out for the estate. Here at Glenlair, Maxwell had time to do his most brilliant work. He wrote his *Treatise on Electricity and Magnetism* and sixteen scientific papers. Each paper was a brilliant opus, usually seventy to eighty pages long.

After spending the morning in his laboratory, Maxwell took his dogs for their daily run and checked his mail. He was the only resident in the district with his own mailbox. There was always mail waiting for him—proofs from the printer, articles from other scientists for him to read, and his own personal correspondence.

He frequently got post cards from William Thomson or P.G. Tait, his old friend from the academy. They wrote each other so often that they started using post cards instead of letters because the postage was cheaper. These three scientists scrawled their latest research problems to each other on half-penny post cards and

Maxwell's zoetrope gave the illusion of moving cartoon figures.

signed them with their scientific nicknames: T for Thomson, T' for Tait, and dp/dt for Maxwell. Maxwell's nickname, dp/dt, came from the thermodynamic equation dp/dt = JCM. The letters JCM, of course, are James Clerk Maxwell's initials. (It was only a coincidence that these initials had been chosen for that equation.)

Each afternoon he took Katherine riding. The doctor had said that the fresh air was good for her, so he made sure to take her out every day. She rode her pony named Charlie, and he rode his horse, Darling. In the evenings after supper, he read out loud to Katherine—usually Chaucer, Milton, or Shakespeare. Then they called in the servants and finished the day with devotions.

Family life
Even when the Maxwells were sick, they didn't interrupt their devotions. When Maxwell contracted a dangerous smallpox infection, he insisted that Katherine read the Bible to him each evening, even though he was so feverish that he could hardly concentrate on the words. He had gone to a fair to buy her pony, Charlie, and he had caught smallpox. Mrs. Maxwell stayed alone with him all throughout that illness because the servants weren't allowed in the room. He often said that she saved his life with her careful nursing.[24]

Five years later, he cut his head on a branch when he was riding a strange horse. The cut became infected, and he contracted erysipelas, a dangerous bacterial infection. Once again, Katherine nursed him back to health.

The Maxwells didn't have any children, and this drew them closer together. Maxwell took his role as a husband very seriously and was devoted to Katherine. The poems he wrote to his wife are touching and show how seriously he regarded marriage. Yet she was an unpopular figure with Maxwell's colleagues and students. They called her "a difficult woman" and thought she detracted from his scientific work.

She probably did not mean to detract from his work, but she was sickly, and Maxwell often had to nurse her. At one point, he spent his nights in a chair by her bedside for three weeks, but he somehow managed to give his lectures and go to work each day at the laboratory. Once he came into the room to give her medicine, and her little dog took momentary leave of his senses, jumped up, and bit Maxwell on the nose. He didn't want to disturb her, so he quietly carried the dog out—still attached to his nose!

He didn't travel much and was seldom away from home, but on the rare occasions when he had to attend a meeting in another city, he wrote her chatty letters full of the little details that would interest a woman—who said what, who wore what. These were very much like the letters he used to write to his father. Then he would end with a short thought on the passage of Scripture they had decided to read while apart.

One of his letters to her said, "I am always with you in spirit, but there is One who is nearer to you and to me than we ever can be to each other, and it is only through Him and in Him that we can ever really get to know each other. Let us try to realise the great mystery in Ephesians v., and then we shall be in our right position with respect to the world outside, the men and women whom Christ came to save from their sins."[25]

Cavendish Laboratory

In 1871, when Maxwell was forty, Cambridge University convinced him to come out of retirement and become their first professor of Experimental Physics. Cambridge had tried to persuade William Thomson to come, but he didn't want to leave Glasgow University. Maxwell really didn't want to leave Glenlair, but they appealed to his sense of duty and finally convinced him.

Besides being the first Professor of Experimental Physics, his duties also included supervising the construction of a laboratory, called the Cavendish Laboratory. To get ideas for this project, Maxwell visited William Thomson's laboratory in Glasgow and the laboratory at Oxford. But many ideas for this laboratory originated with Maxwell.

Maxwell had learned basic architecture from his father, and he carefully supervised the construction details—from building plans down to instrument design. He was a stickler for detail. He designed a room that contained no iron so that accurate magnetic measurements could be made. He also had tables suspended from the roof beams by wires so that they wouldn't vibrate sensitive equipment. He even spent his own money on instruments and donated his personal equipment.[26]

Thus the Cavendish Laboratory was built and stands as a monument to Maxwell's brilliant planning. Inscribed on the entrance to this famous laboratory at Cambridge is Psalm 111:2—"The works of the Lord are great, sought out of all them that have pleasure therein."

Maxwell had a special talent for guiding research students. In his typically modest way, Maxwell was prouder of his students' work than of his own work. When he first started teaching back in Scotland, his idea of letting students do their own research projects was novel. Usually the students just observed experiments that the professors carefully staged.

Maxwell's contribution at Cambridge was summarized by William Thomson, who said, "The influence of Maxwell at Cambridge had undoubtedly a great effect in directing mathematical studies into more fruitful channels than those in which they had been running for many years. His published scientific papers and books, his action as an examiner at Cambridge, and his professorial lectures, all contributed to this effect; but above all, his work in planning and carrying out the arrangements of the Cavendish Laboratory. There is, indeed, nothing short of a revival of Physical Science at Cambridge within the last fifteen years, and this is largely due to Maxwell's influence."[27]

During these years at Cambridge, Maxwell also worked as the scientific editor of the *Encyclopedia Britannica* and edited *The Electrical Researches of the Hon. Henry Cavendish*. Henry Cavendish was a scientist who had lived a hundred years before Maxwell, and his work had laid the groundwork for the electrical discoveries of Maxwell's era. His fortune provided the funds for the Cavendish Laboratory.

Most of Cavendish's work was unpublished. He had left twenty packages of manuscripts describing his electrical researches. In those days, he did not have instruments to compare the electrical resistances of substances, and he had to use himself and his valet, Richard, as human shock meters! Maxwell repeated and verified almost all of the experiments described by Cavendish, using the latest electrical measuring devices. He did much of this manuscript editing during the nights when he sat by Katherine's bed watching over her.

Other scientists thought that this editing was a waste of his effort and that his time would be better spent in his own original research. But Maxwell felt this was a noble task. In the end, his careful work established Cavendish's rightful reputation as a master of experiments in electricity.

When he proudly showed the Cavendish manuscript to a friend, his friend asked what had happened to Maxwell's own research. "I have to give up so many things," Maxwell said sadly.[28] Already he was feeling an ominous abdominal pain. But he hadn't told anyone yet, not even his wife, because he didn't want to worry her.

Scientific contributions

Maxwell's name has been memorialized in science in several ways. The bell-shaped curve of modern statistics, called Maxwellian distribution, was a direct outcome of his work in molecular physics. Those who have done reading in the field of thermodynamics may be familiar with "Maxwell's demon," an imaginary being who is supposed to operate a trap door between two containers of gas, allowing fast-moving molecules of the gas to pass through but closing the door on the slower ones. And scientists also use his name when they refer to the maxwell, a measure of magnetic flux.

James Clerk Maxwell was undoubtedly one of the greatest geniuses in the history of science. Other scientists would have been content to make even one contribution equivalent to Maxwell's; yet he made major contributions to astronomy, gas theory, color theory, electromagnetic theory, thermodynamics, and molecular theory. Some of his other contributions to science include experiments in color vision and optics, investigations on elastic solids, a mathematical analysis of Saturn's rings, and original extensions of pure geometry, mechanics, and molecular physics.

One of his significant achievements was his mathematical refutation of Laplace's Nebular Hypothesis, an atheistic scheme to explain the origin of the solar system apart from a Creator. The French mathematician Pierre Simon Marquis de Laplace (1749-1827), an avowed atheist, felt that the "laws of nature" were sufficient to account for the world as we know it, with no need for a directing intelligence behind it. (He failed to reveal, however, where the laws themselves came from.)

In his Nebular Hypothesis, he envisioned a hot, slowly rotating cloud that cooled, contracted, and increased in rotational speed. (He neglected to explain how the cloud got there in the first place, but he assured his followers that no Creator was needed to account for it.) Eventually it assumed the form of a rapidly rotating disk with a thin rim of material on the edge moving too fast to be held by gravitational attraction. After being ejected from the cloud, this material coalesced to form the outermost planet of the solar system. Further contraction and ejection of rings formed planets having orbits of diminishing size, while the material remaining in the center became the sun.

Maxwell found two major defects in Laplace's scheme. First, the sun is rotating much too slowly to have been formed by a cloud that was continually contracting and speeding up. Second, the gaseous rings would have broken up and dispersed into space rather than condensing into planets. Clouds, by their very nature, do not naturally condense into large solid bodies. Thus the earth could never have assembled itself from the microscopic particles of the cloud. What Laplace had attempted to establish using mathematics, Maxwell tore down using better mathematics.

of electromagnetic waves that traveled at a speed equal to the speed of light. These equations predicted the existence of radio waves twenty-three years before they were discovered! This was an astounding feat of mathematical prophecy. Thus he united electromagnetism and optics into one field of study. When he realized the unity of the two fields, he wrote to his cousin, "I have also a paper afloat, with an electromagnetic theory of light, which, till I am convinced of the contrary, I hold to be great guns."[31]

During Maxwell's research on electromagnetism, he corresponded with Faraday, sending him his latest ideas. After reading one of Maxwell's papers concerning the "lines of force," Faraday wrote the amusing comment, "I was at first almost frightened when I saw such mathematical force made to bear upon the subject, and then wondered to see that the subject stood it so well."[32]

When Maxwell's ideas were published, they were not fully appreciated. But in hindsight, it is apparent that the electromagnetic theory was actually a turning point in science and had a profound impact on technology, paving the way for television, radio, and radar. In fact, Maxwell's ideas are the foundation for the special theory of relativity and quantum mechanics.

Methods of working

Maxwell walked briskly to the Cavendish Laboratory, lost in thought, mulling over his latest research problem. He looked behind him and realized that his dog, Toby, was dawdling. He called to him and continued walking. He greeted his students in the lab and went to the corner where he did his own work. Toby leaped to the stool beside him.

The students were talking loudly, carrying on a boisterous conversation about which student would excel in the coming exams. But Maxwell was not listening. He was deeply absorbed in his own experiment. He could tune out all the noise around him and concentrate fully on his work. He whistled softly as he worked, no tune in particular, just a running accompaniment to his thoughts. As his experiment progressed, he talked softly to Toby, explaining what he was doing.

After two hours, he sat back, satisfied with his results. He pulled his notebook out of his breast pocket and wrote down the results he had obtained. He kept this notebook with him all the time to jot down his research problems and his poems that he composed. He tucked the notebook away, patted Toby, and turned to the students. Now he could join in the conversation.

Maxwell was a brilliant combination of practical experimenter and theoretical physicist. He was a visual thinker. He liked to develop his theories with models, diagrams, and analogies. He visualized new concepts by using phenomena that were already familiar. To visualize the behavior of electricity, he employed (at different times) fluids, elastic solids, and spinning vortices with idle wheels. But he cautioned against taking the analogies too seriously and locking one's mind into a fixed idea. His analogies were intended to be an aid to the imagination and not an explanation.

He analyzed his own work carefully and quickly discarded his own theories when evidence went against them. Occasionally he even discarded hypotheses and models that were perfectly workable for fear that he would miss further insight if he locked his mind into one model. He didn't hang on to his own ideas with sentimental attachment, as some scientists are prone to do. Maxwell was a true gentleman and conscientiously acknowledged the other scientists who had stimulated his thoughts by their own writing or lectures. Usually his scientific papers opened with such an acknowledgment.

He had the persistence and endurance to work on a problem for years. He would write a paper on a subject and then several years later he would write another paper, answering the questions he had introduced in the first. He never seemed to consider a topic closed, even when he had published remarkable papers that could be considered the definitive word. Thus his electromagnetic ideas spanned five major papers and twelve shorter ones, and he was in the process of revising his *Treatise on Electricity and Magnetism* when he died.

Last days

James Clerk Maxwell first noticed symptoms of his terminal sickness when he was forty-six. He had trouble with his digestion and suffered severe heartburn. He found that if he went to his laboratory after lunch and drank a bit of sodium bicarbonate dissolved in a beaker of water, the pain would calm down. But he didn't complain about this pain because he was more worried about his wife's health than his own. She had gotten worse in the last few years, and he didn't want to worry her. Besides, he figured it was just a passing illness.

Two years later, though, the symptoms became worse. He soon noticed that he was always tired, and he could barely fulfill his lecture duties and make appearances at the laboratory. His students noticed how slowly he and Toby walked to the lab. Then his concentration left, and he found himself falling asleep over his reading. "I have been so seedy," he wrote to his friend Tait, "that I could not read anything however profound without going to sleep over it."[33]

In October of 1879, Maxwell was diagnosed with abdominal cancer, the same illness that had taken his mother's life when she was also forty-eight. He was given one month to live. In that last month, he lived in constant pain. Yet, even in his weakened condition, he maintained a gracious Christian spirit, quietly accepting the Lord's will. His only anxiety was for his wife. He had always taken care of her during their twenty-one years of marriage, and now he wondered what would happen to her.

During his illness, his doctors and ministers mentioned his amazing testimony. His minister said, "Maxwell welcomed me warmly whenever I visited him, joined fervently in all acts of prayer, listened with a most intelligent interest to all I read, either out of the Bible (which he knew well-nigh by heart) or out of any of our great devotional writers in prose or poetry; [he] was especially fond of any new hymns, and frequently capped such by reciting from his wonderful memory some parallel passages of his favourite old authors, specially George Herbert. . . . He was calmly and serenely resigned to the will of God. . . . His one and only care was for his wife. It was a grand sight to see him day by day girding himself calmly and resolutely for the last struggle, and he passed through it undismayed."[34]

He was too weak now to think about science or to read, but his memory was still perfectly clear. He often quoted poems and verses and made brief comments on them.

Before he died Maxwell said to his cousin, "I have looked into most philosophical systems, and I have seen that none will work without a God." Later he told him, "Old chap, I have read up many queer religions: there is nothing like the old thing after all."[35]

James Clerk Maxwell died on November 5, 1879. After he died, the local minister said that "his illness drew out the whole heart and soul and spirit of the man: his firm and undoubting faith in the Incarnation and all its results; in the full sufficing of the Atonement; in the work of the Holy Spirit. He had gauged and fathomed all the schemes and systems of philosophy, and had found them utterly empty and unsatisfying— "unworkable" was his own word about them—and he turned with simple faith to the Gospel of the Saviour."[36]

For those closest to Maxwell, his Christian testimony outshone even his splendid scientific contributions. His doctor said, "I must say he is one of the best men I have ever met, and a greater merit than his scientific attainments is his being, so far as human judgment can discern, a most perfect example of a Christian gentleman."[37]

Shortly before Maxwell died, he said, "The only desire which I can have is like David to serve my own generation by the will of God, and then fall asleep."[38] He certainly served more than just his own generation. We are still reaping the benefits of his outstanding scientific contributions.

The motivation for his life's work is summed up in the last two verses of his poem "A Student's Evening Hymn":

> Teach me so Thy works to read
> That my faith, new strength accruing,
> May from world to world proceed,
> Wisdom's fruitful search pursuing;
> Till, thy truth my mind imbuing,
> I proclaim the Eternal Creed,
> Oft the glorious theme renewing
> God our Lord is God indeed.
>
> Give me love aright to trace
> *Thine* to everything created,
> Preaching to a ransomed race
> By Thy mercy renovated,
> Till with all thy fullness sated
> I behold thee face to face
> And with Ardour unabated
> Sing the glories of thy grace.[39]

---

[1] Lewis Campbell and William Garnett, *The Life of James Clerk Maxwell* (London: Macmillan, 1882), pp. 11-21 covers these incidents from his childhood. The page numbers in these footnotes were taken from the digital preservation of this book done by James Rautio. This electronic version is available from Sonnet Software, Inc.

[2] Martin Goldman, *The Demon in the Aether: The Story of James Clerk Maxwell* (Edinburgh: Paul Harris Publishing, 1983), p. 34.

[3] Ivan Tolstoy, *James Clerk Maxwell: A Biography* (Edinburgh: Canongate, 1981), p. 17.

[4] Campbell and Garnett, p. 27.

[5] James's father was originally named John Clerk (pronounced "Clark"), but because of a complicated legal stipulation, he was required to adopt the name Maxwell when he inherited his estate. So the family name is really a

double last name, "Clerk Maxwell."

[6] C.W.F. Everitt, *James Clerk Maxwell: Physicist and Natural Philosopher* (New York: Charles Scribner's Sons, 1975), p. 38.

[7] Campbell and Garnett, p. 70.

[8] Ibid., p. 100.

[9] Silvanus P. Thompson, *The Life of William Thomson, Baron Kelvin of Largs* (London: Macmillan and Co., 1910), p. 311.

[10] Campbell and Garnett., p. 113.

[11] Goldman, p. 76.

[12] Campbell and Garnett, p. 151.

[13] Ibid., p. 87.

[14] Ibid., p. 170.

[15] Ibid., p. 160.

[16] Ibid., pp. 89-90.

[17] Ibid., p. 176.

[18] Ibid., p. 160.

[19] Ibid., pp. 158-59.

[20] His best friend from his academy days was the Rev. Lewis Campbell. He became the Professor of Greek at the University of St. Andrews. He wrote Maxwell's biography along with William Garnett, Maxwell's lab demonstrator at Cambridge. This biography has delightful personal information about Maxwell, especially from his younger years. But the discussion of his research demonstrates that the impact of his scientific work had not yet been realized. The later biographies are better at covering his scientific contributions; but, unfortunately, they are often written by non-Christians who are mystified by Maxwell's beliefs and often gloss over his Christian testimony. A discussion of his beliefs can be found at http://silas.psfc.mit.edu/Maxwell/maxwell.html. The title of this article is "James Clerk Maxwell and the Christian Proposition" by Ian Hutchinson.

[21] Campbell and Garnett, p. 148.

[22] Ibid., p. 177.

[23] Ibid., pp. 140-41. A sampling of Maxwell's poetry is included at the end of his official biography, *The Life of James Clerk Maxwell*, written by Lewis Campbell and William Garnett.

[24] One biographer has said that this was Mrs. Maxwell's greatest contribution to science—saving Maxwell's life when he had smallpox.

[25] Campbell and Garnett, p. 188.

[26] Everitt, p. 177.

[27] Campbell and Garnett, pp. 175-76.

[28] Ibid., p. 183.

[29] Ibid., pp. 139, 142.

[30] Ibid., p. 109.

[31] Tolstoy, p. 126.

[32] Goldman, p. 143.

[33] Tolstoy, p. 167.
[34] Campbell and Garnett, p. 200.
[35] Ibid., p. 205.
[36] Ibid., p. 201.
[37] Ibid., p. 199, footnote.
[38] Ibid., p. 203.
[39] Ibid., p. 296.

Dr. Howard Kelly with his Christian rose (1858-1943)

HOWARD ATWOOD KELLY, M.D.
(1858-1943)

Surgeon and Gynecologist

I was sick, and ye visited me. . . . Inasmuch as ye have done it unto
one of the least of these my brethren, ye have done it unto me.
Matthew 25:36-40

"This is my best treasure yet," Howard thought, *as he brushed the
plants aside and knelt down. Hiding in the underbrush was an entire family of turtles. "What a perfect way to end the day!" He had walked in the
woods all afternoon, and it was almost time to rush home before dark. His
pockets were stuffed with the specimens that he had collected—several
interesting rocks, a rhinoceros beetle that he planned to dissect, a mush-
room, and two plants that he wanted to look up in his botany book.*

*He whistled happily as he picked up one of the turtles and studied its
markings. "How can I carry them home?" he wondered. His pockets were
already full, and he didn't want just the two that he could carry in his
hands—he wanted them all.*

*As he stroked the turtle's shell, he had a brilliant idea. "If I just buckle
my knickers very tightly right here below my knees," he thought, "then I
will have two large pockets." He set the turtle down and pulled the
knicker straps tighter. Then he gently picked up the turtles and deposited
them in his deep "pockets." He waddled home, a bit slower than usual,
the turtles knocking each other with each step.*

*At home, his mother helped him make a little home for the turtles in
an empty crate. Howard went to bed reluctantly that night. He wanted to
stay up longer to admire his turtles.*

*The next morning, Howard felt miserable. He itched all over and had
a strange rash. Alarmed, he called for his mother. "What happened?" she
asked, touching his swollen face. Then she remembered the turtles.
"Where were the turtles when you found them, Howard?"*

*Howard stopped his scratching and thought a moment. "They were
hiding under some plants that had three leaves on each stem. I brought*

one home in my pocket to show you." He pulled his knickers off the peg on the wall and dug the wilted plant out of his pocket.

"Oh dear!" cried Mrs. Kelly. "That was poison ivy!"

Howard did have a severe case of poison ivy. It took days for the itching and swelling to go away. But as soon as he got better, he insisted on salvaging the turtles. He built a hothouse for them behind the house and spent many hours there, lying beside his turtles and reading.

Howard often told his mother that when he grew up, he wanted to study "bugology" and discover some new species in the "bug" kingdom. His greatest worry was that all the bugs might be found and described before he grew up!

But this young "bugologist" did not become a naturalist; instead, he became Dr. Howard Kelly, a world leader in gynecology, the branch of medicine that deals with women's special medical problems. Dr. Kelly was also a dedicated Christian who maintained a vibrant testimony throughout his life. Being a Christian did not hinder Dr. Kelly's medical career; instead, if motivated him to develop innovations in gynecology to help suffering women.

Early years

When Howard was a very young boy, his father fought in the Civil War on the Union side. During the lonely months while Henry Kelly was in battle and later in prison, Louisa Kelly devoted herself to her three children. Mrs. Kelly was the daughter of a godly pastor, and she carefully trained her children in God's Word. Even before Howard could read, he stood at his mother's knee and listened as she read him the Bible. As he grew older, she taught him to sound out words from the Bible. Once he could read, he devoured books about nature.

Mrs. Kelly encouraged her son's interest in nature and let him keep the critters that he brought home. But sometimes he tried her patience. While a group of ladies was having tea at the Kelly home, one of Howard's pet snakes escaped from his box under the sofa and slithered across the floor in plain sight. The ladies completely forgot their dignity as they fled from the room screaming.

Another time, Mrs. Kelly waited up all night for her son. He had been observing a surgeon perform an autopsy, and he was so enthralled that he forgot to come home until early morning.

Mr. Kelly returned safely from the war and soon realized that his oldest son was brilliant. He knew this potential must be developed, so he enrolled Howard in a prestigious classical institute when he was nine. Howard enjoyed his school days there. They were filled with pranks and the normal boyhood fights. Howard did his share of fighting, but he also knew how to avoid a fight when he was outnumbered. After two boys threatened him, he brought a hatchet to school in his satchel. When he smugly brandished the weapon, the boys immediately backed down.

But in spite of his boyishness, Howard showed genuine spiritual sensitivity. When he was eleven years old, he began carrying a little New Testament with him or a portion of Scripture that he had written on a card and tucked into his vest pocket. During the day he often pulled out the card and meditated on the verse he had written down. He said this helped him memorize Scripture and guarded him from temptation. At the age of thirteen, Howard made a public profession of his faith in Christ.

When Howard was a teenager, he became a member of the Academy of Natural Sciences in Philadelphia, a group that studied nature. Howard's special love was herpetology, the study of snakes. As a young boy he had taught himself about snakes by reading books and observing the snakes he caught. He studied the scale count, the markings, and the shapes of the pupils. But at the Academy of Natural Sciences, he studied snakes with an expert, Professor Edward Cope. As Howard studied herpetology, he dreamed of becoming a naturalist.

Howard stashed the turtles in his knickers.

College education

When Howard Kelly was fifteen, he began his studies at the University of Pennsylvania. His diligence coupled with his natural brilliance made him an outstanding student. He carried a full load of classes but always wanted to study more than the required load. In his free time, he wrote for the local newspaper, studied five languages, taught himself astronomy and architecture, and practiced piano and flute. He enjoyed outdoor sports, and in warm weather he always found time to hike or swim. He thought nothing of a twenty-eight mile hike or a mile-long swim.

As Howard neared graduation, his father discouraged him from becoming a naturalist. Mr. Kelly was a practical man and knew that his son would not earn a stable income studying his beloved snakes. Howard reluctantly agreed with his father and chose to go into medicine since it seemed closely related to the natural sciences.

Medical school

In 1877, Howard enrolled in the University of Pennsylvania's medical school. The university boasted an exceptional medical faculty, and, at that time, it was considered the best place for medical instruction in America. Many of Howard's professors were Christians who promoted a healthy spiritual atmosphere for the students. Howard quickly distinguished himself as the best student in his anatomy class. After all, he had been practicing for years by observing and dissecting his specimens.

Howard's studies and extracurricular activities kept him busy, but he still attended church and prayer meeting regularly. He made time to study the Bible every day, usually with his mother.

During Howard's second and third years in medical school, he developed a persistent insomnia and a ringing in his ears. His parents decided he was suffering from exhaustion, so they sent him to Colorado for a year to regain his health. There he found a job working on a ranch as a cowboy. The manual labor was good for his health, and he gradually regained his ability to sleep. In the country Howard practiced medicine of sorts because he knew more than anybody else around. One night he helped a lady in labor and delivered her little boy. (He often spoke proudly of "his first baby," and he was thrilled to meet him years later when he was a grown man.)

He felt very lonely without any Christian friends on the ranch. Most of the cowboys were aggressive atheists. They spent many hours discussing "religion" with Howard. These discussions helped Howard grow spiritually because he was forced to study his Bible and reason with his atheistic friends.

Howard returned to medical school the following year and graduated when he was twenty-four. The evening of commencement he wrote in his diary, "I dedicate myself—my time—my capabilities—my ambition—everything to Him. Blessed Lord, sanctify me to Thy uses. Give me no worldly success which may not lead me nearer to my Savior."[1]

Medical practice

Dr. Kelly began his residency a few days later at the Episcopal Hospital in Kensington, Pennsylvania. Sometimes he would see eighty patients in one day. He said, "Here at last my real medical education began. . . . Hospital experiences drew me into intimate touch with the problems of suffering humanity and revealed the priceless gratitude of the poor when treated with affectionate consideration; this was the final touch necessary to convert all my interests to my profession, no longer merely a means of livelihood, but a shining path of service replete with rich spiritual rewards."[2]

Howard trained in general surgery, but he found himself attracted to gynecology because he saw such a desperate need for skilled care in dealing with women's medical problems. Actually, gynecology as a specialty was in its infant stages. In the past, abdominal surgery had been so risky that there was little that could be done for women; now, though, the abdomen could be invaded with relative safety.

For many years, women had been too modest to discuss their physical ailments, at least with male physicians. They preferred to suffer in silence. But the price of their modesty was often unnecessary discomfort and sometimes death. Gradually, though, women became willing to harmonize modesty and health in order to be treated by male doctors.

When Dr. Kelly completed his residency, his father arranged for him to open his first office in his home. Mr. Kelly spent a good deal of money renovating a room in the house and buying the latest equipment for his son. This arrangement disappointed Howard because he felt drawn to the mill workers that he had treated at the Episcopal Hospital. He didn't want to seem ungrateful for his father's help, so he compromised by maintaining office hours at home and traveling five miles to his office among the mill workers in Kensington.

Howard's mill practice grew much faster than his practice at home, and he finally had to move out to the mill district. After an exhausting day of operating and seeing patients, he slept on the waiting room sofa. Each

Howard worked as a cowboy in Colorado for a year.

night before he went to sleep, he tied one end of a string around his big toe and left the other end hanging out the window. Whenever anyone needed the doctor during the night, he would pull the string to wake him.

Dr. Kelly's family took a great interest in his work with the mill people. His sister Esther eventually moved to the mill district and worked as a missionary. Through the mission work she started here, called the Lighthouse, she presented the gospel message while meeting the physical needs of the people.

Sterilization improvements

When Dr. Kelly began practicing medicine, physicians didn't care about sterilization techniques. Dr. Kelly, like the majority of traditional medical men, was skeptical about the need for strict sanitary measures. Unfortunately, doctors themselves were the chief culprits in spreading disease. They went from autopsies to operations and then to childbirth— all without washing their hands. The most tragic result of this practice was "childbed fever" that occasionally wiped out entire maternity wards.[3] But, through the efforts of Louis Pasteur and Joseph Lister, the medical profession gradually understood the need for antiseptics.

Dr. Kelly soon realized that these sterilization techniques would benefit his surgery, and he incorporated his own sanitary measures. Because the Episcopal Hospital did not welcome gynecological cases, Dr. Kelly had to operate in the patients' homes. His crude operating table was usually the patient's kitchen table. Before the operation, he insisted that the family scrub the walls, floors, and table. He always brought his own tap water that he had boiled for an hour and his own copper boiler to sterilize his instruments.

Dr. Kelly continued his sterilization improvements throughout his surgical practice. He was always looking for more effective antiseptic techniques and ways to improve surgical dressings. He came to the conclusion that surgeons overused antiseptic solutions, and he stressed the need for asepsis instead of antisepsis—in other words, keeping the surgical field free of germs rather than trying to kill them after they had entered the wound.

Dr. Kelly trained his own nurse, Mrs. Helen Woods, because at this point in time, there were no trained nurses. He desperately needed a place to provide adequate post-operative care for his patients, so he bought a house to serve his needs. The little hospital moved twice, finally arriving at a large building that was incorporated as the Kensington Hospital for Women. Dr. Kelly's own mother did most of the fundraising for this hospital.

Dr. Kelly kept current with contemporary trends in medicine by traveling to Europe to observe operations and attend university lectures. His fluency in French and German came in handy on these trips. During a trip to Germany, Dr. Kelly met Laetitia Bredow, the daughter of a German physician. The following year, Dr. Kelly returned to Germany and married Laetitia. This union was a happy one that resulted in four daughters and five sons.

Johns Hopkins Medical School

As Dr. Kelly's reputation grew, so did his opportunities. He taught obstetrics at the University of Pennsylvania for a year; but by this time, he had determined that this branch of medicine that deals with childbirth would not be the focus of his practice.

Then came a spectacular offer. Dr. Kelly was invited to Baltimore, Maryland, to help open the Johns Hopkins Hospital and Medical School. William Osler, the famous Canadian pathologist, was responsible for this invitation. Osler thought that Kelly was the most skilled abdominal surgeon he had ever seen, and he wanted Dr. Kelly to head the department of gynecology. Osler himself was to head the department of medicine; William Welch, the department of pathology; and William Halsted, general surgery.

These four doctors, called "The Big Four," were destined to become a medical legend and to make the Hopkins Medical School and Hospital a renowned medical center.[4] All were young and ambitious. Dr. Kelly, at thirty-one, was the youngest. He put up with a lot of teasing from the other doctors about his youthfulness. Often patients expressed surprise that "this boy" was their surgeon. "I'm sorry," Dr. Kelly would say. "My youth is a fault that I'm outgrowing."

The four doctors worked well together, and Dr. Kelly observed that there was a noticeable lack of jealousy because they shared a mutual esteem and enthusiasm for each other's work. Dr. Kelly talked frequently to his colleagues about his Christian faith during their lunches together. But although they respected him and grew fond of him, they thought it a bit odd that such a brilliant man should take his faith so seriously.

For four years the young doctors labored in the Hopkins Hospital, each establishing his own department with freedom. Because of lack of funds, the School of Medicine did not open at the same time as the hospital. The Johns Hopkins Medical School finally opened in 1894 when four Baltimore ladies raised the needed funds. However, the patrons stipulated that, in this medical school, women should be accepted equally with men. They also required all applicants to have the equivalent of a college degree and to know German, French, and several premedical subjects. These stip-

ulations were more rigorous than the standard medical school requirements of the day. Some medical schools had merely required that the
applicants be able to read and write. During this controversy, Dr. Osler
said to Dr. Welch, "Welch, we are lucky to get in as professors, for I am
sure that neither you nor I could ever get in as students!"[5]

Teaching methods

Dr. Kelly was a brilliant teacher who was loved and respected by his
students. He taught his students using demonstrations and clinical examinations because he despised the dry lectures that were standard in his
student days. He did not expect many of his students to specialize in gynecology, so he tailored his teaching to emphasize the minor operations
that any doctor might be called upon to perform frequently.

Dr. Kelly did not like to operate in a large amphitheater but preferred
to have a few students assisting who could also watch the operation. He
began each operation by carefully scrubbing his hands and arms and
soaking them in two solutions. Then he discussed the patient's history and
his intended procedure. Before he picked up the scalpel, Dr Kelly prayed
for God's guidance to restore the health of his patient. Then he announced
the exact time and began the operation. As he operated, he talked incessantly, describing what he found and the procedures he was using. When
he finished, he announced the time again. Then he would sketch the procedure on the blackboard using both hands. He was a very gifted
illustrator and could use both hands equally well. He advised his students
to cultivate ambidexterity because it was a great asset to a surgeon.

He always noticed the time in his operations because he believed that
speed was important to diminish the shock to the patient. He urged his
students to study their movements and to eliminate wasted motions.
Surgeons who operated with Dr. Kelly marveled at his speed. One surgeon said he handed Dr. Kelly the scalpel and turned to thread a needle.
When he turned around again, the abdomen was already open! Most surgeons took ten minutes just to open the abdomen.

Contributions to gynecology

Dr. Kelly studied gynecology when it was merely an insignificant
branch of obstetrics. But when he retired from the field, he left gynecology as a respected specialty. Previously, physicians performed only a few
surgical procedures successfully.[6] But with Dr. Kelly's contributions, the
list of successful procedures grew impressively.

Dr. Kelly wrote more than five hundred medical papers and ten textbooks. He wrote his first gynecology textbook shortly after coming to the Hopkins Hospital. This textbook, *Operative Gynecology*, confirmed Dr. Kelly's leadership in gynecology. But it was most remarkable for its illustrations. Dr. Kelly was tired of the same old woodcuts that illustrated previous textbooks. He needed more detail in his pictures, pictures that would show more than a photograph could. He found the medical illustrator Max Broedel and brought him over from Germany to join the Hopkins staff. Kelly and Broedel worked closely on the illustrations—Broedel expanding the sketches that Kelly outlined. These illustrations completely revolutionized medical illustrating. Later the Hopkins Medical School established a Department of Art as Applied to Medicine and Max Broedel trained other artists in this new field.

Dr. Kelly also published his *Stereo Clinic*, a collection of clear photographs that show every important step in an operation. The text explained each step as though he were talking to his students. He thought this was even better than being the first assistant in an operation. Often, in real life, the students couldn't see directly into the operating field and couldn't follow all the steps, nor did they have the luxury to pause and study a step at length. Dr. Kelly wrote his last textbook when he was in his seventies, and he could reminisce about the great changes that had taken place in gynecology in his generation.

Dr. Kelly modified and invented many surgical techniques that were adopted worldwide. At first he followed the normal procedures, but he was quick to innovate when the traditional methods proved ineffective.[7] When Dr. Kelly began practicing medicine, Caesareans (delivering a baby by surgery) were very risky. In fact, few women survived the procedure. *What a tragedy*, Dr. Kelly thought, *to lose both the mother and the baby because we don't have a good technique.* After a visit to Germany where he observed the technique of the Germans, he performed a successful C-section. The last successful C-section in Baltimore had been performed fifty years earlier. Since then, no ladies had survived the operation. Most of his colleagues praised this success, but his former gynecology professor complained that Dr. Kelly was getting too bold.

Whenever Dr. Kelly saw a need for a certain tool in his practice, he would invent a suitable device. He invented the electric portable droplight and the Kelly clamp that is still used in surgery. Many of his instruments became standard equipment in gynecology clinics.

But these impressive innovations were not his real claim to fame. Dr. Kelly was best known for the men he trained. One doctor said of Kelly, "If he had never written a line and had never performed an operation, he would still be classed as one of the great men of our day for the men he has made."[8] These residents who trained under Dr. Kelly became distinguished gynecologists who were constantly in demand throughout the country. The President of Johns Hopkins declared that Kelly was "a born teacher, as is shown by the fact that he gathered around him year after year his group of distinguished interns and residents whose names are almost as well known now in this country as his own, and whose achievements are second only to their master's."[9]

Fees

As Dr. Kelly's reputation grew internationally, he was referred to as America's "most rapid and brilliant" surgeon and the "greatest surgical technician of his time."[10] He charged large fees to those who could afford his expertise, because the money enabled him to treat the poor patients who could not pay. Yet he never charged exorbitant rates. He said, "A great temptation and a danger in a physician's life is that he may be tempted to wear spectacles with dollar marks on them."[11]

Still, he was criticized because his rates were higher than his colleagues. But he estimated that he treated seventy-five percent of his patients without charging them for his services. He even paid for a private nurse to care for his patients who could not afford it.

To him, the greatest remuneration for his services was the life-long affection he received from his patients. His files bulged with thank-you notes from his grateful patients. Years later they would still write to their beloved doctor, reminding him how his skill had relieved their suffering. They were grateful for his exceptional skill, but they also mentioned his kindness and his gentle manner. He had great compassion for his patients, especially the older ones. He made a point to learn their names from their charts, but he usually called his older patients Mother and his younger patients Daughter.

He never discussed his patients with others, not even his family. But sometimes news of his international patients leaked out. The Emperor of Japan and G. Campbell Morgan, the famous English preacher, both brought their wives to be treated by Dr. Kelly.

Howard A. Kelly Hospital

Dr. Kelly bought four houses on the same street as his own house and used these as his private hospital. From the outside they still looked like houses, but inside he installed the finest instruments and equipment in the world—many of them his own innovations. He did his work at his hospital in the early mornings and late afternoons and spent his days teaching and operating at the Hopkins Hospital.

Dr. Kelly was one of the first Americans to use radium for the treatment of cancer. His hospital became a noted center for radiation treatment. He bought a mine in Colorado that supplied him with the radium, and soon he owned the largest amount of radium in the United States. His clinic was far ahead of its time, and he was using electrosurgery and diagnostic x-rays years before other doctors were using them.

When the famous Dionne quintuplets were born in Canada, Dr. Kelly was consulted about a growth on little Marie's leg. Dr. Kelly and his son, Edmund, who was a radiologist, traveled to her home and successfully treated her growth with radiation.[12]

Many contemporary medical persons thought his work with radiation was quackery. This criticism deeply disturbed Dr. Kelly after his years of careful research. He never claimed it was a cure-all for cancer, but he believed that it held promise. He hoped that a combination of surgery and radiation would bring a cure. As the years passed, Dr. Kelly became known as "the cancer specialist."[13]

The Authority of the Bible

But while Dr. Kelly was enjoying the outward success of his early efforts at the Hopkins Medical School, he was experiencing acute spiritual distress. His soul was not being nourished because he doubted the authority of the Bible. These doubts were provoked by higher criticism, a process of thinking imported from Germany that questioned the authenticity of the Bible. These critics dismissed the Bible as being myths of a nomadic people, and they questioned the authorship of many parts of the Bible. Dr. Kelly noticed that this attitude emanated from intelligent men who were highly trained linguistic scholars. *Certainly,* he thought, *these educated men must know what they are talking about.* Since he did not know Hebrew or archeology, he did not know how to refute the critics.

He also faced the stigma of being called unscientific or narrow if he accepted the Bible as the inspired Word of God. (Years later he observed that young people still dread being called unscientific or narrow and that these two phobias still survive on our college campuses.) These doubts seriously affected his spiritual life. For several years, he "floundered on," as he put it, still trying to use the Bible but feeling that a great prop had been knocked out from under him.

Dr. Kelly began his journey to faith by questioning the critics. He wondered why these critics assumed that statements from the Bible may contain errors, but declarations in other ancient works are all accepted as correct and authoritative—authoritative enough to prove the inaccuracy of the Bible. Kelly realized that whenever he needed information on any subject, he consulted a textbook, assuming it to be reliable and accurate. And if he didn't fully understand a textbook, that didn't diminish its reliability. If, for instance, he happened to pick up a mathematics textbook and did not understand all the equations and symbols, he wouldn't declare it a "piece of blessed foolishness" just because he failed to understand it all.[14]

So he approached his problem as an honest scientist and treated the Bible the same way he would treat botany or geology or astronomy. Using the Bible as his textbook in religion, he discovered exactly what the Word of God said about itself. He found roughly a thousand references to "word" and over five hundred references to "the Lord spake." He looked up every reference and found that the Bible claims to be God's literal word to men—God stooping down from heaven to speak to men.

Then he tested what he read by believing it and applying it. He observed from personal experience that the Bible is true and that God uses it to work in a practical way in the lives of men. From then on, he thought of himself as a Christian pragmatist, meaning that he, like the pragmatists, believed that the true test of any doctrine was whether it works well and what the practical consequences are. *Where else*, he wondered, *can we find a book that can completely transform a man's nature and change a lifetime of sinful habits?*

Dr. Kelly called his method crude, but it was effective. Only later did he find out about the archeological discoveries that confirmed the Bible's accuracy. But he was glad that he had used only God's Word, the sword of the Spirit, to defeat his enemy, just as Pilgrim in *Pilgrim's Progress* had defeated Apollyon with the sword of the Spirit.

Later he wrote a tract about his experience with doubt and his journey to faith in the Bible's authority. He wrote, "Perhaps one of my strongest reasons for believing the Bible is that it reveals to me, as no other book in the world could do, that which appeals to me as a physician, a diagnosis of my spiritual condition. It shows me clearly what I am by nature—one lost in sin and alienated from the life that is in God. I find in it a consistent and wonderful revelation, from Genesis to Revelation, of the character of God, a God far removed from any of my natural imaginings."[15]

Dr. Kelly was an authority on snakes.

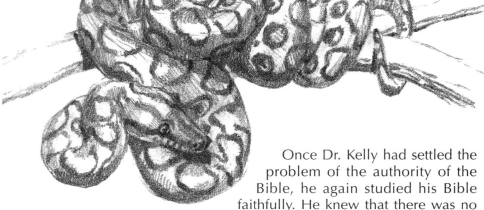

Once Dr. Kelly had settled the problem of the authority of the Bible, he again studied his Bible faithfully. He knew that there was no shortcut to growth in holiness—it came from deep study of God's word. He wrote, "He who enters the Christian life and hopes to grow must work; and no living man may delegate his life's service to priest, minister, or other emissary."[16]

His generosity and good works

Dr. Kelly was now an energetic man in his thirties. His first instinct now that his doubts about the Bible were settled was to attack the social evils in Baltimore. As a doctor, he saw the devastation that alcohol and prostitution brought. His agitation about legalized prostitution helped close these immoral houses. But he knew that lasting benefit would be seen only when Christians were willing "to serve this class as our Lord himself served."[17] With his own money he rented a house so that women of the street could live free of charge until they found another job.

It grieved Dr. Kelly that Christians were so slow to get involved in social problems. He wanted Christians to wake up—to fight vice and feed the poor. "Nothing so dampens zeal in a great cause," he said, "as the refusal of good people to be roused and stirred up to take and maintain a strong stand for right."[18]

Dr. Kelly was blessed with a good measure of wealth, but he did not hoard his money. His generous streak first showed up in the way he treated his assistants. He set up a fund for those students who were having difficulty paying for medical school and helped several of them study abroad. He often invited the students to his home for dinner or to accompany him on his long bicycle treks. During vacations, he invited his residents to relax at his summer home in Canada.

His generosity also showed towards the Hopkins school in the early years. He donated several thousand of his personal books and periodicals to the Hopkins library. When the medical school needed special equipment or new additions, Dr. Kelly helped finance them. Over a fourteen-year period, he donated his entire salary plus $50,000 more to the Hopkins school.

Dr. Kelly found many ways to help the poor. When he heard of Christians who were too sick to support themselves, he would send them monthly checks. He also paid rent and gas for families who could not afford these necessities. He often helped save family farms by paying off the loans. It was heartening for Dr. Kelly to see these families get back on their feet and then in turn help other families in need.

Dr. Kelly set up scholarships for worthy students and helped start schools in underprivileged areas. During the depression, Dr. Kelly helped the children who were coming to school sick and hungry. He sent hundreds of pounds of cereal to the schools so that the children could have a free breakfast. He heard that many of the children didn't have shoes, so he set up a personal account with a shoe store. Any child with a permission slip signed by a principal could buy a pair of shoes and charge it to Dr. Kelly's account. For years after the depression, Dr. Kelly continued meeting with the principals of the area schools to discuss the needs of the school children and to have a time of prayer.

Dr. Kelly set an example for all believers in his unselfish giving to Christian causes. He designated twenty percent of his income every month to give to charities, but by the time he met the demand, he spent closer to thirty percent. He preferred to give to individuals that he knew personally. He helped Christian workers all over the world establish orphanages, hospitals, and schools. He was not concerned with denominational ties, as long as he was convinced of their sound theological stand. (He had grown up in the Episcopalian church, spent time with the Plymouth Brethren, and attended a Presbyterian church with his children.) He was especially fond of medical missionaries and helped them buy state-of-the-art equipment. One of the missionaries he helped was the famous Dr. Hudson Taylor, who was a personal friend.

At home in America he was very interested in missionary efforts to the American Indians. He also helped Christian camps for boys. He had a special love for these ministries because, during his college days, he had started the very first camp for boys in America.

Sometimes his friends raised their eyebrows at his good works. They couldn't understand why he would bother being kind to thieves. On one occasion when his neighbor's property was burglarized, he corresponded with the imprisoned men and took care of their families. When they were released, Dr. Kelly helped them get reestablished. When his own property was burglarized, he sent food, clothing, and guitars to the men in prison. On another occasion, he paid the bail to release a man who had assaulted him while he was poll watching on Election Day. He refused to press charges in this incident.

Witnessing

Dr. Kelly soon became convinced that he needed to redirect his energy. He believed that the social reforms he supported were necessary and good, but he wanted to devote the remainder of his life and energy to drawing Christians into a closer walk with Christ. He said, "While many good works are excellent, the supreme opportunity of life is to know Christ . . . 'in whom are hid all the treasures of wisdom and knowledge.'"[19] Knowing Christ could come only through a deeper knowledge of God's Word. So for many years, he formed Bible classes to train Bible teachers.

He was an active layman in his church, teaching Sunday school and sometimes even preaching. Once a month he traveled around Maryland with a friend and spoke in the different churches as part of the Lord's Day Alliance, urging Christians to keep the Sabbath holy. It was not unusual for the entire medical community to show up when they heard that Dr. Kelly would be speaking at a church.

After the *Sunday School Times* asked Dr. Kelly to write his personal testimony, he wrote a series of articles discussing his doctrinal beliefs. When these articles were first announced, subscriptions to the paper rose by 30,000. These articles were later published as a book, *A Scientific Man and the Bible*.[20]

Dr. Kelly exercised every opportunity to witness, saying, "The only excuse I have for insisting on breaking through the reserves of every man I meet is that Jesus Christ died for him as well as for me, and I want him to know it."[21] He boldly witnessed to the famous people who crossed his path and to the common people he met every day. He even rode in taxicabs for the express purpose of witnessing to the cab drivers. As the cab paused at a traffic light, Dr. Kelly would say, "Cabby, I hope when you and I come to the gates of heaven, the light will be green." Then he would witness briefly and leave a passage of Scripture and a liberal tip.[22]

Dr. Kelly usually wore a small blue button on his left lapel. The button said nothing; it had only a question mark on it. When people who met Dr. Kelly asked him the significance of the question mark, he would say, "That asks, 'What is the most important thing in life?'" The individual would guess something like wealth or happiness. "Oh, no, none of those," Dr. Kelly would answer. "The most important question is 'What think ye of Christ? Whose Son is He?'" And then Dr. Kelly would talk about Christ.[23]

Each day Dr. Kelly put a fresh pink rose in the buttonhole of his jacket. He inserted the stem of the rose in a small vial of water to keep it fresh and tucked the vial behind the jacket. When someone would comment on the freshness of the rose, Kelly would say, "This is a Christian rose, with hidden sources of grace and life," and he would reveal the vial of water underneath his jacket. He used this method to present the gospel to many people.[24]

Occasionally Dr. Kelly's friends chided him for the exorbitant amount of time he spent witnessing. But he would reply, "The only way you can keep your Christian faith is perpetually to give it away."[25]

Dr. Kelly began and ended every day studying the Bible and praying for an hour. He went to bed early, usually by 9:00 p.m. He woke up early, before 4:00 a.m., and began operating by 6:00 a.m.

After breakfast and dinner Dr. Kelly led his family in devotions. He read and taught from a selection in the Bible and then followed with prayer. Dr. Kelly believed that family devotions were crucial to the development of godly children. He wrote, "Fellow Christians, you who have families, hold family prayers daily and read and discuss some Scripture in the family at least twice a day, for the reward is a rich one."[26] Three times a week he also had a time of prayer with the family servants and the nurses in his hospital.

Dr. Kelly was a man of prayer and frequently retired to his bedroom to pray. His family often noticed the elbow marks on his bed where he had knelt to pray. All during the day he would pray silently. Before beginning any task—even writing a letter—he would pause to pray.

Family life
Dr. Kelly took full charge of the spiritual training of his nine children, unlike some men who do not help their wives with this duty. His children

remembered him as a devoted, loving, and generous father. They knew that he enforced his strict rules at all times; but he made their life so enjoyable that they gladly obeyed him.

Each summer he took the children to Lake Ahmic in Canada, where he had built several log cabins. He had discovered this beautiful spot in Ontario years earlier when he was hiking with a friend. The vacation at camp was the high point of the year for the children. They didn't even mind the required swim at 7:00 a.m. They knew they wouldn't get breakfast until they finished their morning swim. The sleeping cabins were built right at the waterfront with porches that hung over the water. They could jump into the water right from the porch.

Dr. Kelly invited his friends to camp and let his children invite their friends. He wished that he could leave his work completely behind, but he brought his writing and continued his work at the camp. Often he sat up on his cabin roof, reading and enjoying the breathtaking view of Lake Ahmic. In the afternoons, he always took time for a swim with the children and often took them on canoe trips. Whenever Dr. Kelly was at his camp, the village pastor took a rest and Dr. Kelly preached for him.

Dr. Kelly guided his children's reading and taught them to love books. On Sunday no secular reading was allowed in the Kelly household. In the summer when the children had more free time, he required them to read for two hours each day. The children built their own libraries, and once they were married, they were allowed to take any books they wanted from their father's library.

Other interests

Dr. Kelly was brilliant. Yet at the same time, he was genuinely modest. He gave all the credit for his accomplishments to his heavenly Father. When the impressive list of his professional honors was mentioned, he would say that his highest honor was his degree of B.A.—"Born Again."

The book publisher Doubleday sent two men to talk to Dr. Kelly about writing his biography. He was completely uninterested and dismissed them with the curt comment that he was not interested in anything about himself. He never sought the limelight, but reporters dogged him. He often came home from his rounds to find reporters waiting for him in the hallway.

Dr. Kelly maintained many interests in nonmedical fields. Besides his numerous works on gynecology, he published works in biography, medical history, and nature.[27] He never lost his childhood interest in nature, and he continued to collect specimens throughout his life. He was a respected botanist and coauthored a book on fungi. He was also an authority on snakes and published a book entitled *Snakes of Maryland*.

He had a friend who traveled to South America to collect snakes for him. It was an exciting event for the entire family when the snake man came. He would dump the snakes out of his bag right onto the living room floor while the family stood around to admire them.

Dr. Kelly often used snakes as object lessons in his speeches. At first the audience responded nervously when Dr. Kelly introduced the snake. Some people sat on the edge of their chairs, ready to bolt if the snake got loose. During one speech, when Dr. Kelly put a poisonous snake back in his bag, it bit him through the bag! The crowd gasped in horror. Dr. Kelly, though, just sucked his finger and calmly finished the lecture. He wasn't concerned because he knew that the snake had been milked of its poisonous venom before the lecture. But, to add a bit of suspense and excitement, he didn't let the audience know that.

During one train ride, a snake he was transporting wiggled out of a breathing hole and got loose in the middle of the night. A porter discovered the snake, and his screams woke everyone up—everyone, that is, except Dr. Kelly. He slept through the pandemonium until the conductor woke him up and demanded that he find the snake and deposit it in the baggage car. The train company was not pleased and tried to prevent Dr. Kelly from traveling with his snakes. He told them to show him the law that specifically prohibited snakes on trains; of course, there was no such law, so he was allowed to transport his snakes, but only in a very secure cage.

He was bitten only once by a poisonous snake. When he was collecting snakes in Florida one spring, a cottonmouth bit him. He quickly applied a tourniquet, made incisions, and sucked his finger. He felt ill for several days, but he was thankful to get off with just a slight loss of sensation in the finger.

Library

Behind Dr. Kelly's home, a three-story building housed his personal library and study. It resembled a museum. Stuffed birds and snake skins hung around the room. In one corner he had a marvelous collection of wax replicas of fungi. On a table sat massive portfolios of botanical drawings and reptile paintings.

Dr. Kelly's snakes lived on the first floor of the library in their cages, but they often got loose. Visitors to the library occasionally encountered snakes on the steps, and sometimes his house guests would discover a snake peeking out of the bathroom drain! When the cook discovered a kingsnake in the pantry, she threatened to quit on the spot. Dr. Kelly used all his powers of persuasion and convinced her to stay.

Dr. Kelly enjoyed collecting rare books during his travels abroad. He considered his books to be dear personal friends. He said, "The books which we assemble lay bare a personality. After all, they are the friends we have chosen as companions—silent friends patiently waiting to speak to us, each questioning when you will let them talk with you. There they are on all sides, ready to advise or control your course. To rob a man of his books would be almost like taking away his life."[28] Nothing gave him greater delight than to give away a favorite book, hoping that it would bring the new owner the same pleasure it had brought to him.

One visitor in his study marveled that one man could own so many books. Dr. Kelly smiled and said, "This is not my library. You have been looking at the books I have accumulated on the Bible."[29] These several thousand theological books in his study were just a small portion of his collection. His entire collection numbered 100,000 volumes—all catalogued. His mycological library (books about fungi) contained over 10,000 books and was considered the best collection in the whole world.

Dr. Kelly hosted afternoon tea in front of the fireplace in the library. He received all kinds of guests—medical students who wanted to find out what it was like to be a doctor and a Christian, businessmen and politicians, and doctors from around the world who had come to see the great surgeon. He also hosted school groups who had come to admire his two-hundred-pound meteorite and his collections of Indian artifacts, old coins, minerals, and shells. During the afternoon, he noticed if his visitors admired a particular book. Often at the end of the tea time, he would give them the book they had admired.

Retirement

After thirty years of teaching at the Hopkins Medical School, Dr. Kelly retired. He had thought of resigning earlier; but the students had sent petitions begging him to stay, and he had complied. Finally, though, he resigned from his teaching duties, but he still operated at the Hopkins Hospital. He wanted to devote more time to his private war against cancer.

Now he also had more time to spend in his library. After his morning operations, he came to his library and worked on his immense correspondence. In the afternoon, after his nap, he worked on his writing and the speeches that he was scheduled to give around the country and abroad.

Dr. Kelly enjoyed reading in his roof chair at Lake Ahmic

Dr. Kelly never lost his youthful vigor or his sense of humor. When he was sixty-five, he was asked to contribute to a book about elderly people. The author asked Dr. Kelly to write down his thoughts about his old age. "I am sorry I can't give you my thoughts as an old man," he wrote back. "I am still far too young for that classification. However, I will write to my mother and father; perhaps they can help you."[30]

His beloved parents died when he was sixty-eight. He was always especially close to his mother because she had taught him to love the Bible. All during his life he had made a point to visit her, taking the train from Baltimore to Philadelphia once a week to spend the afternoon with her. When he lost her, he felt that he had lost his best friend. From then on, his thoughts were always on the Celestial City, and he felt like Pilgrim, running and crying, "Life, life, eternal life."[31]

A year later, he injured his back seriously in a diving accident at the lake in Canada. His children had often scolded him and told him that he was too old to be diving from the twenty-four-foot diving platform. But he wouldn't listen. For many years he had been doing his somersaults and fancy dives without harm. But one day, he dove too deeply and hit the bottom violently. His shoulder took the brunt of the blow and saved him from breaking his neck.

After this accident, he still kept up with his full schedule, but the pain forced him to slow down a bit. He stopped jumping up the stairs two steps at a time and walking briskly down the street with his coattails flapping. Slowing down was an uncomfortable novelty for Dr. Kelly. He told his secretary that the accident had bumped him right into old age.

Dr. Kelly stopped operating when he turned eighty. It was not a matter of physical inability—his hands were still steady and his judgment was sound—but he decided the pressure and responsibility were too much of a strain. He became weaker and took to bed occasionally. Shortly before his eighty-fifth birthday, he was hospitalized. His wife, who was also ill, was in a room beside him. Even in his feeble condition, Dr. Kelly wanted to read his Bible. His last words were "Nurse, my Bible."

On January 12, 1943, Dr. and Mrs. Kelly both died, only a few hours apart. After a joint funeral service, they were buried together in Woodlawn Cemetery in Baltimore, Maryland.

Dr. Kelly once said, "Jesus's first recorded words are 'Wist ye not that I must be about my Father's business?' and His last words are, 'It is finished.' Christianity is a business, a work lasting all through life. God needs three talents: a will given over to Him; willing service; [and] persistence in service in spite of failure."[32] Dr. Kelly abundantly exemplified these three talents. His numerous medical contributions were merely an outworking of his life-long desire to serve Christ.

¹ Audrey W. Davis, *Dr. Kelly of Hopkins: Surgeon, Scientist, Christian* (Baltimore: The John Hopkins Press, 1959), p. 37.

² Howard Kelly, *A Scientific Man and the Bible: A Personal Testimony* (New York: Harper & Brothers, 1925), pp. 24-25.

³ Richard W. Wertz and Dorothy C. Wertz, *Lying-In: A History of Childbirth in America* (New York: The Free Press, 1977), pp. 119-20.

⁴ In the Great Hall of the Welch Medical Library at Johns Hopkins Medical School hangs the famous portrait called "The Four Physicians" painted by John Singer Sargent in 1905. The four doctors traveled to London to sit for this portrait.

⁵ Davis, p. 72.

⁶ The few techniques that physicians had performed successfully were ovariotomies for ovarian tumors, removal of fibroid uterine tumors, and basic plastic surgery to repair the tears resulting from childbirth trauma.

⁷ Among the most important procedures he perfected were a technique for suspension of the retroverted uterus (although later in his career, he decided that surgical intervention was not appropriate), radical surgery for uterine cancer, the "apron method" for treating complete rectal tears, the "scratch mark" method for discovering ureteral stones that did not show up on X-rays, the treatment of fistulas that resulted from traumatic childbirth, and a technique that reduced hemorrhaging during hysterectomies. (Many hysterectomies resulted in death because of hemorrhage.) He also developed catheterization techniques and thought that his contributions to the care of the urinary tract were his most important. (Davis, p. 79)

⁸ Davis, p. 90.

⁹ Ibid., p. 223.

¹⁰ Ibid., pp. 81-82.

¹¹ Ibid., p. 81.

¹² Edmund was the only child who went into medicine. The other children were Olga, Henry, Esther, Fritz, Howard, Boulton, Margaret, and Laetitia.

¹³ Davis p. 134.

¹⁴ Kelly, *A Scientific Man and the Bible*, p. 44.

¹⁵ Dr. Howard A. Kelly, "I Believe," tract printed by the Maryland Tract Society, Baltimore, Maryland, no date.

¹⁶ Kelly, *A Scientific Man and the Bible*, p. 34.

¹⁷ Ibid., p. 35.

¹⁸ Davis, p. 150.

¹⁹ Kelly, *A Scientific Man and the Bible*, p. 38.

²⁰ This was republished in 1996 by Messengers of Hope, Inc.

²¹ Davis, p. 173.

²² Ibid.

²³ Ibid.

²⁴ Ibid., p. 174.

²⁵ Ibid.

[26] Kelly, *A Scientific Man and the Bible*, p. 38.

[27] He wrote *Walter Reed and Yellow Fever* (1906), *Some American Medical Botanists* (1913), and over sixty articles in *Cyclopedia of American Medical Biography* (1912 and 1920) and *Dictionary of American Medical Biography* (1928). He loved to study medical history and biography. He said, "No group should ever neglect to honor the work of forebears, upon which their own contributions are based. This is particularly true in medicine. Great is the loss to anyone who neglects to study the lives of those whom he follows." (Davis, pp. 118-19)

[28] Davis, p. 175.

[29] Ibid., p. 182.

[30] Ibid., p. 220.

[31] Ibid., p. 221.

[32] Ibid., p. 142.

Dr. Henry Morris (1918-   )

DR. HENRY MORRIS
(1918 -   )

Hydraulic Engineer
Father of the Modern Creationist Movement

Ah Lord God! Behold, thou hast made the heaven and the
earth by thy great power and stretched out arm, and
there is nothing too hard for thee.
Jeremiah 32:17

*Henry opened his Bible and tried to read as the bus bounced through
downtown Corpus Christi. A few people smiled at the serious young boy
who was traveling all alone, carrying just a Bible. He had been riding
across town by himself all week to attend Billy Sunday's evangelistic campaign, and he was looking forward to the closing meeting tonight. His
mother was working and couldn't accompany him, and the rest of his
family wasn't interested. But Henry was thrilled with the preaching and
singing. He was just ten years old, but even at this young age, he was interested in the things of God.*

Henry's family

Henry Madison Morris was born in Texas in 1918, during the First
World War. His father worked as a realtor, and the family moved several
times before finally settling in Houston, Texas. Henry grew up in a nominally Christian family that attended a Southern Baptist Church. His father
dropped the family off at church on Sunday morning, but he never went
to church himself. Mr. Morris had grown up with a Christian mother, but
he often said to her, "As soon as I get out of this house, I'm going to stop
going to church." And he did.

Grandmother Morris talked to little Henry whenever he came to her
house, and she planted the seed of the gospel in his heart. The women of
Henry's family, his mother and grandmothers, had a Christian influence
on the children. But the men, his father and grandfathers, were not interested in spiritual things.

Henry was a bookworm and spent many hours at the library. He read
only fiction, but when he was eight years old, his mother gave him his

own Bible. He was thrilled with his new Bible and began reading at the first page with Genesis 1:1.

Soon after Henry started junior high school in Corpus Christi, Texas, his brother was hospitalized with appendicitis. Henry and his youngest brother were sent to Houston to live with an aunt and uncle because Mrs. Morris was spending all her time at the hospital. This emergency visit to his relatives turned out to be a permanent arrangement. Henry's maternal grandmother also lived in this house, and she took care of him for the next few years. A little while later, his parents divorced. This was during the Depression years, and family finances were so bad that his mother and two brothers also moved in with his aunt and uncle. They had to live in the attic, an uncomfortable arrangement for everyone.

High school

During high school, Henry had the reputation of being shy and studious. He enjoyed sports and played tennis, basketball, and softball. He collected baseball cards and invented a game with them in which he had to keep track of the batting and pitching averages. This helped him develop his ability in mental arithmetic. But his real passion was writing about sports. He wrote for the school newspaper and won several contests in sports writing.

Finances were always a struggle for his family. His mother and grandmother finally moved out of the attic rooms in the uncle's house and rented an apartment. There were no welfare programs or food stamps at that time, and everyone in the family had to work to make ends meet. His mother worked as a secretary and as a pianist for a radio station. And his grandmother found work in a florist shop. Henry worked at different times selling newspapers, bagging groceries, pumping gas, and working in a laundry. With their combined incomes, they scraped by. But there was never any extra money. For many years, they didn't have their own car, and Henry had to walk everywhere.

College

When it came time for him to go to college, he had his heart set on going to the University of Texas and studying journalism. But these were the Depression years, and his family simply could not afford the tuition. If he studied at the local Rice Institute (now called Rice University), he could get free tuition. He had read in the newspaper that all the engineering graduates from Rice had been able to get jobs. Since good jobs were so hard to get, he decided to study civil engineering even though he didn't know much about it.

At the time, he didn't even pray about this decision. He simply made a choice based on logic and expediency. But, even though Henry wasn't actively seeking God's will at this time, God was working in the circumstances. In hindsight, it is evident that his training in engineering opened the door for his great contributions to the creation movement.

Henry was an outstanding student at Rice, but he was not a vibrant Christian at this time. He still attended church, but he had stopped reading the Bible for the most part. On Sundays he read the assigned Sunday school lesson, but that was all.

While studying at Rice, he had been swayed by the strong evolution influence. The first chairman of the Biology Department at Rice University was Sir Julian Huxley, one of the most famous evolutionists of the twentieth century.[1] He bragged that he had started a "frame of mind" at Rice. And Henry found that to be very true. The prevailing frame of mind at Rice was evolutionary humanism. Since everyone else believed evolution, Henry absorbed the teaching and became a theistic evolutionist. He reasoned that God must have used the process of evolution to create the world. He hadn't bothered to study the evidence; he just accepted it, he said, "more by osmosis than by persuasion."[2]

In the summers, he worked as a surveyor with the Texas Highway Department. The field engineering experience he received on this summer job was valuable for him as a future engineer, but he picked up the vulgar language of the rest of the crew. This habit of profane speech became very difficult for him to break. Even as he was speaking it, he knew it was wrong. He prayed very hard about this, and the Lord finally delivered him from this besetting sin. (He was thankful that he never got to the point of taking the Lord's name in vain.)

He graduated from Rice with the highest honors possible, but he thought it had more to do with hard work than brilliance. "I believe excellence in anything," he said, "is normally attained much more because of hard work than because of natural talent, and this is as true in scholastic achievements as in anything else."

Marriage

After graduating, Henry took his first job as an assistant hydraulic engineer. He moved to El Paso, Texas, on the Rio Grande River and worked with the problems of river control. In college, he had not been interested in hydraulics or hydrology, the sciences involving water. But as he worked with dam designs and irrigation questions, he found it fascinating to study the problems associated with water. He developed new computation techniques that analyzed the effect of various combinations of dams on the flow of the Rio Grande and its tributaries. The technical study that he wrote about this project was his first publication.

He had left his fiancée back in Houston, and he needed something to fill up the lonely evening hours, so he began reading his Bible. Back home, his evenings had been filled with studying or with dating, but now he had time to fill. He knew the Bible fairly well because he had read it often as a young boy. But the secular college influence had been damaging, and he had stopped reading the Bible. He had never questioned the Bible as a child; but in college, after absorbing the influence of the evolutionists, he had decided that the stories of the flood and creation couldn't be taken literally. It seemed that there were too many legendary embellishments in the stories of Genesis.

While he was working in El Paso, he attended a church that faithfully preached the Bible. He also attended the young people's meetings and was impressed by the warmth and depth of these young Christians. With these influences, Henry felt it was time to reexamine his beliefs and seriously examine his responsibility to Christ. His Bible reading during those evenings led him to the firm conclusion that the Bible is absolutely true.

After three months in El Paso, he married Mary Louise Beach, whom he had met years before in sixth grade. When his brother was hospitalized and he had moved to his uncle's house, he had to change schools in the middle of the year. Mary Louise had been in his new sixth grade class.

Coming from a broken home, he often longed for the stability of a complete family built on love. But he was so shy with girls that it seemed unlikely that he would ever get to the point of marrying one. He finally resorted to listing all the girls he knew who might make a good wife and who possessed the qualities he admired. Then he would call them and ask for a date. When he called Mary Louise, she accepted, and from the first date, he knew that she was the one for him.

They had both come from nominally Christian families and had attended church all their lives, but they had not had good Bible training. Now as a new couple, they wanted to be more than just Christians in name. They wanted to follow Christ in everything. They got under the teaching of a good pastor, and they both began to grow spiritually. Some of the first sermons they heard at that church emphasized the second coming of Christ, and this truth of the Lord's imminent return motivated them to begin reading the Bible and praying together.

Dr. Morris was active in the Gideon ministry.

Soon both were teaching Sunday school for children. They became convicted about some of their activities and decided to give up dancing, going to movies, and playing cards because they worried that these activities might hinder their testimony when they tried to tell others about Christ. Henry decided that even if the movies were harmless, they were a waste of precious time.

Gideons and witnessing

Another reason Morris started reading his Bible again was the influence of the Gideons. Morris noticed that the men he admired most in his church were Gideons, and he soon asked to join them. They were a group of laymen who were dedicated to spreading the gospel by witnessing and giving out Bibles and New Testaments. The Gideons encouraged their members to spend time each morning in Bible study, prayer, and Scripture memorization. Morris began waking up early so that he could read the Bible and pray for an hour before the rest of the family woke up.

By now, it was 1942 and many servicemen were going off to war. Many trains of soldiers passed through El Paso. Morris and the other Gideons spent many evenings at the train depot, talking to the men about Christ and giving out New Testaments. The Gideons' goal was to get a

New Testament into the hands of every serviceman before he went off to the war.

Now that World War II had broken out, Rice University, his alma mater, needed engineers to teach the men who were going to war. They invited Morris to come back to Houston to teach. His excellent undergraduate record and his three years of experience working as a hydraulic engineer were considered good enough qualifications to teach engineering. In those days, universities did not insist on Ph.D. degrees in engineering as they do now. The odd thing was that he had never considered being a teacher. But when he agreed to come teach civil engineering at Rice, he began his long career in education.

Morris had recently been approved for the Navy Seabees, the civil engineering corps of the Navy. It seemed that he was headed to the war with the rest of the young men of his generation. But without his knowledge, Rice arranged with the Navy to have him released. The Navy felt that Morris would be more useful training engineers for the them. (Morris agreed and thought he would have made an awful soldier. "I probably would have flunked boot camp!" he said.)

He and his wife moved back to Houston so that he could teach at Rice. When he stood in front of his first class as a novice twenty-five-year-old instructor, the stage-fright was very real. Most of the students were his age or older. He became dizzy and faint, and one of the students had to run get smelling salts for him.

But his teaching ability improved, and he studied hard to stay ahead of his classes. He never considered himself gifted as a public speaker, but he was fair and accessible to the students, and they respected him.

In Houston there were even more servicemen than in El Paso, and he again became involved with the local Gideon camp. (A local Gideon group is called a camp.) Morris would go downtown with the other Gideons in the evenings and on Sunday afternoon to talk to the servicemen and give them New Testaments. They also started a Christian Servicemen's Center. Here they invited the servicemen in for refreshments, singing, and board games or table tennis. Then they would offer the men New Testaments and talk to them about Christ. The men were very open to the gospel, especially the ones who were heading overseas.

Several times Morris got permission to invite all the Navy trainees at Rice to a testimony service. Almost every male student at Rice received a copy of the Bible through this ministry. But after one of these meetings, the Rice administration banned his group from meeting on campus, and they had to meet in a nearby church.

Morris started a Bible study group, and through this witness on campus, many students came to Christ. In Morris's last year, they saw about fifty students come to Christ. This early work in witnessing prompted Morris to write a booklet called "God's Way of Salvation According to Scripture, with Excuses and Objections Considered."

A creationist is born

Most of Rice's male students were in the ROTC[3] and Navy V-12 programs and would be sent to active duty after graduation. *These men might die soon*, Morris thought, *and I want to be sure that they hear the gospel.* His own brother had gone to war as a cargo plane pilot and then died when his plane was shot down, so Morris understood how close these servicemen were to eternity. He passed out Bibles to his students and invited them to his house for Bible studies. Surprisingly, the students and other professors didn't mind his zeal. This was probably because he was a good teacher. He had gained the intellectual respect of his peers, and they were willing to indulge his religious whims.

He soon realized that he needed solid answers in defending the Bible when he witnessed to the students. Most of these students were majoring in engineering or science. They were good thinkers, and they were having the same trouble that Morris had had as a college student. Their biggest doubts centered on the reliability of Scripture, especially the book of Genesis. They reasoned that if Genesis could not be trusted to be historically correct, then how could they trust the rest of the Bible, especially Christ's testimony and teaching? If Genesis weren't correct, then how could Revelation and the coming judgment be correct?

All the doubts, he saw, were rooted in the question of creation. So he began studying everything he could find about the creation-evolution controversy. He still held to theistic evolution, an unhappy compromise that he had settled on during college. The fact that practically all the books in the library supported evolution seemed to Henry to be a strong argument in favor of it. But he couldn't see how the mechanism of natural selection adequately explained evolution.

One day when he was busy with paperwork in his office, he was interrupted by the buzzing of the insects that flew in through the open window. There was no air conditioning in his building, and he often kept the window open to get a breeze. As he got up to shoo them out, he paused to watch the insects buzz around his office.

Of course, he had seen flying insects all his life, but now with an engineer's eyes, he watched the yellow jackets fly around. *What a complex engineering feat these flying creatures are*, he thought. His main interest up to this point had been structural design; he understood that even in a relatively simple building project there was a tremendous amount of intricate analysis and design in order to balance the stresses and strains. *How much more care and intelligence must have gone into the design and construction of living systems!* he thought.

He knew complex machines were the product of careful design and execution, and he had never yet seen a machine evolve. *How could these flying insects just evolve?* he wondered. He concluded that it was clearly improbable that evolution had produced these complex insects, complete with functioning flying gear. Henry knew that the Bible argues for special creation, but as he watched the yellow jackets, he saw how nature also argues loudly and logically for creation.

The early creationists

Morris found several of the earlier creationist writings at a Christian bookstore. Most of these creationists from the early 1900s taught the gap

He wondered how these flying insects could have evolved.

theory or the day-age theory. For a time, Morris tried using these two theories, but he found that they didn't harmonize with Scripture.

The gap theory allowed for a huge gap of time between verses one and two of Genesis chapter one. This gave time for the long geologic ages that scientists were now insisting on. The other theory, the day-age theory, said that each day of creation was really a long epoch that could have been millions of years long.

Morris thought these theories were the great weakness of the early creationists and quite possibly the reason that they never had much impact. Another weakness was their lack of high-level scientific training, a deficiency that left them wide open for ridicule from the opposite side.

But even with their weaknesses, two creationist writers who had an impact on Morris were George McCready Price and Harry Rimmer. Morris read most of the books written by these two men. Although there were deficiencies in Dr. Rimmer's work, the logic and sound evidence convinced Morris to give up theistic evolution.

George McCready Price (1870-1962) was perhaps the most significant of the early creationists. Even though Price was largely self-taught, he was highly educated in the true sense. He had a broad knowledge of Scripture and science, and he combined these with his careful logic. He was one of the few creationist writers to have his articles printed in the standard scientific journals. When Henry Morris read Price's *The New Geology* in 1943, it changed his way of thinking. It convinced him that Noah's flood explained many of the geological features of the earth. A few years earlier, Morris had attended Rev. Irwin Moon's "Sermons from Science," and what he heard made him think for the first time about the scientific implications of Noah's flood. Morris was fascinated by Moon's sermon about the canopy theory and flood geology.

This was a confusing time for Christians because it seemed that scientific evidence truly supported an old earth. They thought the evidence was stronger than it really is. Christians had been intimidated by the supposed "proof" of the long ages that the geologists claimed because these long geologic ages were now backed up by the new dating methods that were being used. Christians felt they had to account for these long ages, so they dabbled with several theories that eliminated the need for a strict six-day creation period. This way, a Christian could still feel true to the Bible and yet include the long ages found in the evolution models.

God cannot lie

Morris continued to read all the relevant literature he could find on both sides of the creation-evolution question. To be fair, he continued to read books that promoted evolution and attacked the Bible. By now in his study, though, he found the evidence for evolution to be flimsy. His analytical engineer's mind needed better proof.

He decided to study the Bible verse by verse and see what God's Word said about science, nature, creation, the flood, and other related topics. He still wondered about the earth's age. *Certainly*, he thought, *God would give the answer to these questions in His Word. How could it be the infallible Word of God if it was wrong on such a basic issue as this?*

Based on this study, Morris came to the conclusion that God made everything during the creation week, in the six natural solar days that are mentioned, and that this occurred several thousand years ago. The straightforward teaching of the Bible would not allow for any of the theories that try to accommodate the long geological ages. He reasoned: *Since God cannot lie, then the record that He has given us in the Bible is true. If the entire Bible is true, then even the account of God's creating the world in Genesis chapter 1 is true. If God says it took six days, then it took six days.* Once he reached this decision, Morris never wavered from his conviction of the Bible's solid authority.

When Morris found a critique of radiometric dating by a follower of Price, he realized that Christians didn't have to invent some elaborate way of allowing a great age for the earth. He reasoned that if the dating methods were unreliable at best and inaccurate at worst, then Christians could safely ignore this "evidence" for an old earth and calmly rest in God's creation account.

Evolution—how did it really take over?

Evolution did not begin with Charles Darwin and his book *Origin of the Species*. From the earliest days of history there have been men who have not wanted to acknowledge God as Creator, and they have invented other explanations for how the earth got here.[4] Through the ages, though, most scientists have rejected the various theories of evolution. In fact, historically most scientists have accepted the truth of the Bible, even if they were not dedicated Christians. The complexity and order of nature has always argued strongly for a Designer, and this obvious design in nature has been hard for scientists to ignore.

When Darwin's grandfather had published these same evolutionary ideas, the general public rejected them. People still held to the Bible's teaching of an earth that was roughly six thousand years old, and obviously the process of evolution required much more time than that. Even the men who founded the earth sciences believed that Noah's flood had formed most of the earth's geological strata.

Then came the pivotal work of James Hutton (1726-1797) and Sir Charles Lyell (1797-1875). They said that the geological formations of the earth could all be explained by the ordinary processes of erosion and sedimentation taking place over great ages. This idea was called uniformitarianism or gradualism.

When Darwin published his book in 1859, the time was ripe for his ideas. Now that the long ages were accepted, the problem of the time factor in evolution had been solved. Liberal theologians, who took a dim view of the Bible's total accuracy, quickly adopted evolution. But it was surprising that good, conservative Bible-believers were intimidated by evolution and adopted theistic evolution—the idea that God created the world through the process of evolution. These men did much damage because they influenced other Christians to accept theistic evolution. The majority of the preachers did nothing to fight evolution, but there were a few exceptions during this time—D.L. Moody and Charles Hodge in America and Charles Haddon Spurgeon in London.

In fact, the opposition to evolution came at first, not from theologians, but from scientists who did not necessarily believe the Bible, but who were still opposed to evolution for scientific reasons. The opposition was short-lived, however. In a few decades, almost the entire scientific community had accepted evolution. There remained a small group who still believed in flood geology and the literal chronology of the Bible, but they were a feeble minority. And they had to deal with a lot more ridicule than the scientists of the past faced. It was very hard to find scientists with good credentials who were willing to publicly embrace creation. But there was still a "creationist underground" that was laying the groundwork for the creationist revival that would come in the 1960s.

American Scientific Affiliation

In 1948 Morris heard about the American Scientific Affiliation, and he decided that this would give him the contact he longed for with fellow scientists who were Christians.[5] The ASA, as it was called, was sponsored by Moody Bible Institute. Moody's founder, the famous evangelist D.L. Moody, was soundly committed to creationism. Soon after joining, Morris began a friendly debate with the officers because they argued that the earth was old and that uniformitarian principles explained the earth's geology. Morris wanted them to see that flood geology was a better explanation for the earth's features. When he prepared a rebuttal to the society's official attack on flood geology, the society's journal refused to print his paper.

In 1953, in a rare moment of open-mindedness, the ASA allowed Morris to present a paper called "Biblical Evidence for Recent Creation and the Worldwide Deluge." Morris, in his youthful enthusiasm, assumed that his fellow scientists would accept strict creationism and the worldwide flood if they were only presented with the Scriptural evidences. After all, as members, they all had subscribed to the doctrine of Biblical inspiration. But he was wrong. His paper just solidified the prejudice against strict creationism. They had no answer to the Biblical evidences but felt that the so-called scientific evidence had to govern.

In fact, the society sent two men to visit Morris's home to try to persuade him to change his position. The president of the society and Bernard Ramm, who was considered to be Christianity's most promising young intellectual, showed up at Morris's door. Of course, at this meeting Morris didn't budge from his position, and he was unable to persuade Ramm and the president to adopt his position.

As time went by, the association drifted so much that by the 1970s, the ASA *Journal* stressed that evolution was merely God's method of creation. It was tragic to see that this organization, originally planned as a voice for creationism, actually became an opponent of creationism. It influenced Christian colleges and seminaries to compromise. Over the years, many of the true creationist scientists dropped out of the ASA in disgust and disappointment, but Morris optimistically remained, hoping that the society could be reclaimed some day. He finally had to admit, though, that nothing could stop the ASA's drift into full-fledged theistic evolution.

By now the evolutionists smugly thought they had won the war with creationists. It seemed that the entire world had capitulated to evolution, and the evolutionists gleefully pointed out that even the Christians believed in evolution. It seemed that they were right because even this organization, supposedly evangelicalism's scientific voice, embraced evolution. Among scientists, creationism seemed dead. But there were a few lone voices among Christians, still crying for a literal acceptance of Genesis and the creation model.

A book for college students

As Morris witnessed on the campus, the anti-religious atmosphere disturbed him. He saw how astute professors presented seemingly intelligent arguments against the Bible. The students were confused and frustrated and many chose to give up on the Bible.

Morris felt strongly that some mature Christian should write an easy-to-understand defense of the Bible. If young people knew they could trust the Bible, and not be swayed by the pseudo-scientific arguments they heard, then their faith would not be shaken so easily.

Finally Morris decided to write the book himself since no one else was doing it. When he was twenty-eight years old, he wrote *That You Might Believe*. (It was later revised and called *The Bible and Modern Science*. The current title is *Science and the Bible*.) The book covered the inspiration of the Bible, the truth of Christianity, and God's way of salvation. Morris said, "There was a tremendous need on campuses around the world for a clear, reasonable, and convincing presentation of the Lord Jesus Christ and His claims to a generation of college men and women who don't know Him."[6]

Finding a publisher was difficult because Morris was an unknown author with only a B.S. degree. When he finally found a publisher, they would accept his manuscript only if he would pay for the first five hundred copies. He couldn't afford this, but one of his friends from the Gideons, Mr. W. S. Mosher, lent him the money.

When the book was published in 1946, Mr. Mosher refused to accept repayment. He told Morris to give away the five hundred copies to people who promised to read it. So Morris gave copies to all the Christian students in the campus organizations that he worked in and then offered copies to students who would come to his office and request one. (The students already knew that they could come to his office and request Gideon Testaments.)

The response to his offer totally surprised Morris. Students regularly came to his office asking for the book. A number of students came to Christ through this book. Even some of the faculty members appreciated it. Many years after it was written, Morris says, "I have continued to receive many letters through all these years telling how this first book of mine has changed lives. The credit must go to the Lord, of course. It was only 156 pages long, written by an unknown author without credentials, and published as a first venture by a small religious company. The book certainly was not very promising. It was amateurish in many ways, and it presumed to go against the all-but-universal opinion of the scientific and educational establishments. Yet with all its faults, the Lord wonderfully blessed it."[7]

Graduate work in Minnesota

By the time the war was over, Morris felt that God had called him to be a teacher so that he could witness for Christ in the scientific and educational worlds. But to continue in teaching, he would need a Ph.D. Now that he was fascinated with the Genesis flood and the effects of water in the earth's history, he decided to pursue a graduate degree in hydraulics, with minors in geology and mathematics. "I was convinced," he said, "that expertise in these subjects would give me the equipment to develop a sound system of deluge geology, and that this, in turn, had to be the key in a genuinely Biblical doctrine of creationism."[8] He saw that the creation argument centered on the evidences of the Genesis flood. If the flood were true, then the fossil evidence was explained logically by the flood, not by evolution.

He decided to study at the University of Minnesota because they had the best faculty and facilities to study hydraulics. By this time the Morrises had two children, and three more were born while he was getting his degrees. There was no government aid available to him, so he had to teach full-time to support his family. On top of his teaching and graduate work, he worked in his church's visitation program, taught the college Sunday school class, and taught a Bible class for the engineering students. He saw several students come to Christ through this Bible class.

While he was getting his degree, he taught many different engineering courses. In each course, he let the students know about his personal Christian convictions, and he unobtrusively mentioned the evidences for creation and the truth of the Bible. Occasionally students came to his office later to talk to him, and he could witness further.

A few months after he arrived in Minnesota, Morris attended an evangelistic meeting where Dr. Arthur Brown had been invited to preach. Dr. Brown had left his medical practice in Vancouver, B.C., and become a Bible-conference speaker. He had written several books and tracts, including some anti-evolution booklets. After the meeting, Morris made an appointment to talk to Dr. Brown. Dr. Brown was happy to talk with him because he had been recommending Morris' book *That You Might Believe* as the best book of its kind.

Morris sat in Dr. Brown's hotel room after that meeting and shared his confusion with this godly man. Morris didn't know what he should do at this point in his life. He had been wondering whether he should leave graduate school to enter the ministry full-time. He knew that he needed his master's and doctoral degrees to stay in teaching. But it seemed that the end of the world was approaching because the first atomic bomb had just been dropped. He thought perhaps the years spent getting a secular education would be wasted years. He wondered whether he should become a full-time missionary and devote the rest of his life to witnessing for Christ.

Morris fully expected Dr. Brown to encourage him to leave his secular studies and devote himself to the ministry, just as Dr. Brown had done. But Dr. Brown surprised him. He urgently counseled Morris to complete his graduate degree and to continue in his scientific vocation. Brown knew that Morris could have a greater impact as a scientist than he could as a minister. "We have no way of knowing when the Lord will return," he said. "Right now the world needs dedicated Bible-believing scientists—scientists who are willing to undertake hard training and study. Science, with all its tremendous influence over the minds of men and women, must be brought back to God!"[9]

Morris followed this advice and finished both his master's and his doctorate in less than five years. By 1950, he had earned his Ph.D. from the University of Minnesota and had encountered no outright prejudice for his creationist views.

When their third child, John, was born during the first year of Morris's graduate work, Morris didn't know how he would pay the hospital bill. They had no insurance at the time, and his income was lower than when they lived at Rice. The day before John came home from the hospital, Morris received his very first royalty check. He hadn't been expecting it, and it took him completely by surprise. The amount was for one dollar more than the hospital bill! "God answers prayer," Morris said simply. He always prayed about each decision and need, and over and over again, he has seen God answer prayer. With his low salary and a growing family, he said, "Making ends meet each month was always quite an adventure of faith and frugality."

He attended all church services while he was in graduate school, even though he was working full time and studying full time. He had worried that his graduate work would interfere with his Christian activities. "It's hard to explain how it was possible," he said, "but the Lord seemed to give me plenty of time for these as well. What He did in my case, I'm sure He can do for others at least as easily, so I have little patience with Christians who use their studies or work as an excuse to neglect spiritual needs and responsibilities, or who use the latter as an excuse for poor work at school or on the job. Both aspects of the Christian life are vital, and the Lord always provides the means for accomplishing what He asks."

There were many foreign students in the engineering program, and Morris invited them to church with him. Often he had eleven people squeezed into his little 1941 Chevrolet coupe. Morris saw several of these students come to Christ.

Possible mission work

The contact with foreign students made him think seriously about foreign missions. He considered teaching in a foreign university where the field was closed to traditional missionaries. At different times he was offered overseas jobs in Afghanistan, Israel, and India. The plan was for Dr. Morris to help set up an engineering department in these countries, and at the same time, he would be an unofficial missionary.

But the offers fell through before the Morrises actually got there. He felt that God wanted them to be willing to go and had used these offers as a means to bring them to a complete dedication to His will. Morris even considered enrolling in Bible college to prepare for a pastoral ministry, thinking that that would be more "spiritual" than what he was doing. But God had a ministry for him right where he was, in the secular colleges where he taught.

Dr. Morris's qualifications

Dr. Morris received his doctorate in hydraulic engineering. This field is based on the sciences of hydraulics and hydrology. Hydrology deals with the natural water distribution found in the earth—precipitation, groundwater, and streamflow. Hydraulics deals specifically with flowing fluids and the frictional resistances and forces associated with the fluids.

Hydraulic engineers study erosion and sedimentation (the process of how sediment deposits) in great detail. The sediment can silt up canals and harbors, and erosion can cause banks to cave in and undermine the stability of structures that are built beside the water. These are very real and costly problems that the hydraulic engineer faces. Hydraulic engineers use a mathematical and quantitative approach to study sedimentation. (Most geologists, on the other hand, prefer a descriptive, qualitative approach in their study of sedimentation.)

Since fossils are now encased in sedimentary rock, understanding the process of sedimentation becomes crucial to the interpretation of the fossil record. Obviously, it is impossible to go back in time and reproduce these events. But an understanding of present-day sedimentation processes gives us reasonable and probable answers as to how the fossil-bearing sediments were originally deposited.

As an engineer, Dr. Morris developed the habit of requiring satisfactory evidence and proof for everything that he accepts as fact. Engineers are trained to combine common sense with a critical and investigative attitude. And Dr. Morris has brought that investigative attitude to his study of the flood and creation. As a student of hydrology, hydraulics, and geology, Dr. Morris has a firm grasp of the mechanics involved in flood processes. "Geologists in general had little knowledge or appreciation for the hydraulic phenomena that had produced their cherished sedimentary rocks, and this seemed to be the main weakness in their system of Uniformitarianism," he said.

His scientific work has centered on his studies in hydraulics and sedimentation because he finds these topics relevant to the creation issue. His conclusion is that "study of many of the earth's sedimentary strata in light of known principles of hydraulics shows they must have been formed rapidly and continuously in a great cataclysm. They do not give evidence of quiet deposition in stationary bodies of water."[10]

Teaching in Louisiana

After he received his doctorate, Dr. Morris worked for six years as head of the Civil Engineering Department at the University of Southwestern Louisiana. Working there was a definite change. After being in one of the nation's best universities, he now found himself at a small nonaccredited engineering school. Dr. Morris reorganized the faculty and the curriculum, adding additional courses and expanding the laboratory facilities, even though the funding was limited. In a few years, the engineering school was accredited.

The move to Louisiana was also a change spiritually. In Minneapolis, they had been living in a city with several good evangelical churches. But when they moved to Louisiana, they found a place that was seriously lacking in Bible knowledge. The area was predominately French Catholic, and the Catholic priests didn't let the people read the Bible. The Morrises were surprised to find that most of the Catholic people had never read a Bible or even seen one!

Dr. Morris felt that the main reason God had led them to this area was to witness for Christ. He decided that the first priority should be to get the Word of God out as widely as possible because the Scriptures are essential in salvation. So he started a Gideon camp in his city. These Gideons met for a 7:00 a.m. prayer breakfast every Sunday morning. Their first project was to get Bibles in all the hotel rooms and to get New Testaments by each hospital bed.

There was opposition, though, in this area. After they gave New Testaments to the ROTC units, the local chaplain made the men return their New Testaments. Once they dumped them on the porch of the Baptist Student Center building. The schools, too, were closed to the Gideons. They wanted to give out Youth Testaments in the schools, but the school boards were dominated by Catholics, and they refused to let the Gideons in.

However, one school district that was less Catholic than the rest allowed the Gideons to leave New Testaments at the school office, and the students could come and ask for them if they wanted them. After the announcement was made, the students mobbed the office. All the Bibles were taken, and many students read them. But the next day, the local priest had a Bible burning with the Bibles that he had asked his parishioners to turn in.

One of the Gideons had the idea of offering the children a choice: a Gideon Testament or the Catholic-approved New Testament that was a decent translation with only a few erroneous explanatory notes. The Catholic bishop approved of this offer, and the public schools suddenly opened up. The Gideon administration would not have approved, but Morris's local group figured it's always easier to get forgiveness than to get permission. (They used their personal funds for this instead of the Gideon funds.) Several years later the Catholic attitude toward the Bible changed, and the Catholics were allowed to read the Gideon New Testaments.

By now, the Korean War had started and Dr. Morris obtained permission to have a special meeting each month with the servicemen. He would read Psalm 91 and pray for the men. Then he gave them a New Testament if they promised to read it.

While they were in Louisiana, Mrs. Morris started a child evangelism class in their home. There were usually about twenty children attending. This ministry helped their six children grow in Bible knowledge and gave them a chance to invite their friends and to be good witnesses.

They also had a campus outreach ministry, but they didn't see the same fruit that they had seen at Rice. The ministry in Louisiana was mainly a sowing ministry, getting the Word of God out. Dr. Morris became well-known in the area for his witnessing and his stand on creation. He was elected the state president for the Gideons and had many opportunities to speak at churches and colleges all over Louisiana about the

Gideon ministry. By now, his ministry with the Gideons had included writing the study helps that are printed at the beginning of the Gideon Bibles. He received a few threatening letters and phone calls, and a group of men visited his pastor at the Baptist church saying that Henry Morris must stop his witnessing or they would stop him. But Morris never took the threats seriously and just kept on with his Gideon activities and his church and campus outreach ministries. And nothing happened to him.

Virginia Polytechnic Institute

In 1957, Dr. Morris moved to Virginia Tech (officially called the Virginia Polytechnic Institute and State University). Once again he was head of the Civil Engineering Department and professor of Hydraulic Engineering. He had taught most courses in the civil engineering curriculum at some time in his career, and he found that this broad knowledge helped him now when he was the department head. When Dr. Morris interviewed for the job, he told them about his Christian convictions and his belief in special creation. He assured them that even with his strong convictions, he could get along well with everyone. They were not worried about his views and were eager to have him come work there.

Under Dr. Morris, the engineering department grew in size and prestige. While he was there at Virginia Tech, a new civil engineering building and lab were built. He developed a Ph.D. program and added many graduate-level courses. He expanded the faculty to triple its original size (twenty professors instead of the original seven) and most of them held Ph.D. degrees. Although Dr. Morris didn't require his professors to accept his beliefs, all of them sympathized with Biblical Christianity and supported Dr. Morris and his activities. (A third of the professors were Bible-believing Christians.) This grew to be the third largest civil engineering department in the nation.

Since his specialty was hydraulics, he concentrated on this field and established M.S. and Ph.D. programs in hydraulics and water resources. He had published a study in the *Journal of Engineering Education* in which he showed statistically that hydraulic engineering played a much larger part in the career of the average civil engineer than most colleges realized.

There were no textbooks for these graduate courses in hydraulics that he introduced, so he wrote notes to give to the students. Finally, in 1963, he published these notes in a textbook called *Applied Hydraulics in Engineering*. It was a large undertaking and required a thorough command of the material. It has been used by more than fifty colleges and universities. It is still in print after thirty-eight years—very unusual for any engineering textbook.

During this time, Dr. Morris was active in the American Society of Civil Engineers, presenting several papers and serving on the research committee. He made many contacts with other scientists while he was in this position, and as his reputation grew, his work was recognized nationally with several honors. He became a Fellow of the American Association for the Advancement of Science and received three grants from the National Science Foundation for further studies. He says that these honors were "much more an indication of the Lord's blessing than of my abilities."

Entering the creationist movement

In 1954, Bernard Ramm had published his book *The Christian View of Science and Scripture*. He implied that "science" should dictate what we believe about Scripture. Ramm was now a leader in a movement in Christianity that believed that Christians should not be so strict and should not insist on interpreting everything in the Bible so literally. These liberals were popularizing an idea called "progressive creationism." This idea says that God used evolution to create the world, but that He had to step down from heaven at times to intervene in His evolutionary process. This allowed God to create various entities along the way, particularly at strategic points where there are gaps in the fossil record.

Ramm was a leading spokesman for this odd mix of creation and evolution that allowed evangelicals to accept evolution and at the same time say that God is the Creator of the world. Ramm's book argued for progressive creationism and a local flood, and his teaching completely undermined the authority of the Bible. Dr. Morris realized the grave error of Ramm's thinking. Morris knew that someone should respond to this book on both a scientific and a Biblical basis, but he was very busy at the time. A few years earlier, while he was doing his graduate work at Minnesota, he had started a book on the topic of creation and the flood. There he had the use of an excellent library, especially the geological library. But with all his other responsibilities, his book moved slowly.

The Genesis Flood

One of the students who received a free copy of *That You Might Believe* was John Whitcomb, a science student at Princeton University. (When Henry Morris's pastor in Houston moved to New Jersey, he took some of the books to give away.) Whitcomb appreciated the book and had met Morris at the ASA meeting when Morris had read the unpopular paper on recent creation. Whitcomb was one of the few men there who agreed with Morris, and the two men began corresponding.

Several years later, John Whitcomb wrote his Th.D. dissertation about the effects of the worldwide flood. Moody Press had tentatively accepted Dr. Whitcomb's dissertation for publication, but Whitcomb needed scientific credentials to make his work believable. He wrote to Morris, convincing him to coauthor the book. Whitcomb covered historical and Biblical aspects of the flood, and Morris wrote the scientific chapters.

When the final draft was ready, now with the weight of Morris's scientific contribution, Moody Press became worried about the reaction to the book. According to them, the book was too lengthy, too controversial, and too literal in its interpretation of the Bible. The controversy arose because the authors insisted on a literal six days of creation and a worldwide flood that had completely rearranged the earth's geological structures. Since Moody didn't want the book, the authors finally published with Presbyterian and Reformed Publishing Company. This publishing arrangement worked out beautifully, and the book reached a wide audience.

Impact of *The Genesis Flood*

The Genesis Flood has gone through more than forty printings. It continues to sell well, even though it needs updating. (Since 1961, more evidences for creationism have been uncovered.) But the authors have never had time to update the book. The fame that resulted from this book caused their schedules to change irrevocably because both the authors were in demand to speak on this topic.

In retrospect, *The Genesis Flood* was the catalyst to start the Modern Creationism revival. There were other creationists around, of course, and the ideas of special creation and a global flood were not new. George McCready Price had written some of these same ideas, but no one took him seriously because he was a self-taught geologist and because he was not from a mainstream religious denomination. The few men who believed in creation had no coherent movement and they were discouraged and disorganized. In the years since the publication of *The Genesis Flood*, there has been a revival of belief in a literal creation week and a global flood.

A historian of science observes that "the testimony of countless converts suggests that the lion's share of credit—or blame—for the popularity of flood geology must go to John C. Whitcomb, Jr., and Henry M. Morris."[11] He says that "it is still too early to assess the full impact of the creationist revival sparked by Morris and Whitcomb, but its influence, especially among evangelical Christians, seems to have been immense."[12] Creationism was now an international movement.

The Genesis Flood was written by Christians for Christians. The goal, of course, was to call Christians back to a literal acceptance of God's infallible Word and to embrace the historical reality of a recent creation and a worldwide flood. According to Morris and Whitcomb, the long geologic ages taught by the evolutionists are really a gross misinterpretation and distortion of the geologic data. A worldwide flood is really the cause of many of the earth's geologic formations.

Life for Dr. Morris was never the same after *The Genesis Flood*. In the past, he had traveled just within his state for Gideon activities. But now he had invitations from all over the nation. Many different denominations became interested in creation and the flood. Numerous universities invited Dr. Morris to speak, and many of the Christian universities invited him to teach. (But few Christian schools had engineering departments.) Many of these lectures and messages were later compiled into books.

He traveled mostly by train in the early days, or by car if it was close enough. He often picked up hitchhikers on his trips because he remembered the days when he didn't have a car. He tried to witness to these hitchhikers and leave them with a Gideon Testament or a tract. One day when he was traveling with a friend, he picked up two hitchhikers. They got into the back seat and began speaking in Spanish to each other. As Dr. Morris drove on, his friend, who understood Spanish, turned around and began talking to the men in English. When an exit came up, his friend told him to pull off at the gas station so that they could let the men out. When the two men had walked away, his friend turned and told Dr. Morris what had happened. "Those men were planning to pull a knife and take over the car. I kept them talking so that they wouldn't have time to do anything." After that, Dr. Morris decided it was too dangerous to pick up hitchhikers.

Because of time constraints, he finally decided to use airplanes. His first attempt at flying gave him a tremendous headache and earache. When he arrived at his destination, he sent a telegram to his wife: "Flying is for the birds!" And he took the train home.

But it became impossible to keep up with his speaking engagements using the trains, and he reluctantly began to fly. To this day he dislikes flying. But he always put the time to good use. He would take a stack of his yellow legal pads and sit in the airport lounge writing on his next book project. (He has always preferred to write than to have hobbies. When other men take vacations or go golfing or hunting, he prefers sitting in his office, filling his yellow legal pads with his neat longhand.)

Negative reaction

To balance the positive reaction to *The Genesis Flood*, though, there was a distinctly negative reaction from the entrenched scientific community and from the Christian liberal camp. Obviously these groups did not want to examine their position on evolution, and, instead of actually addressing specific points they disagreed with, they just rejected the book outright or ignored it. They usually commented that the research was impressive, but the conclusions were completely unacceptable.

Perhaps the most disheartening reaction was from Dr. Morris's own pastor. He refused to read the copy that Dr. Morris gave him, saying, "All the scientists couldn't be wrong!" The Morrises had known that the church was a bit liberal when they began attending, but it was the best church that they could find in the community.

This pastor worried that the creation/flood issue was so explosive that it might divide the church, so he asked Dr. Morris not to teach the college Sunday School class any more. When that happened, Dr. Morris knew it was time to go. He realized that it would be impossible to win this pastor back to a more Biblical position.

Since the Morrises couldn't find a church of likeminded believers, they joined with a few other families to start their own. The church met in the Morrises' basement for a while. In the early days before they could afford a pastor, Dr. Morris did much of the preaching and visitation and taught the adult Sunday School class. Many of the messages he preached here became the fodder for later books. Several of the students and faculty at Virginia Tech became Christians through the ministry of this little church. They called it College Baptist Church at first. Later it became Harvest Baptist Church and is now a thriving Bible-centered church in the community.

Repercussions in the academic world

But the negative reaction to *The Genesis Flood* went beyond Dr. Morris's church life. It invaded his academic life. Shortly after the book was published, Dr. Morris's immediate superior died, and the new dean of the College of Engineering did not support Morris's beliefs. Also a new president had come in a year earlier, and he did not appreciate Morris's testimony as the previous president had.

Dr. Morris's growing profile in the creationist movement embarrassed the faculty members in certain other departments. Dr. Morris wrote a weekly column in the local newspaper called "The Bible Has the Answer," and these articles bothered his colleagues. Twice they sent delegations to the school's president, asking for Dr. Morris to resign. Since Dr. Morris's department was thriving, the administration really could find no reason to dismiss him. But they hoped he would resign.

At this same time, Dr. Morris received offers from other engineering schools as well as from several prominent Christian universities. Dr. Morris wondered whether, in light of the opposition, it was the Lord's will for him to leave Virginia Tech. He finally left in 1970, but he later said that all the negative circumstances were really God working for good. Now he decided to devote his limited resources of time and ability to defending and proclaiming his faith.

Family life

The spiritual training of their six children was always the dominating priority in the Morris family. There were times that they couldn't find good Christian friends for the children in the places where they lived, and there were damaging influences in the public schools they had to attend. The Morrises started Bible classes for children and later held youth meetings when their children were older so that they could gather other Christian young people for fellowship.

The Morris family enjoyed singing hymns around the piano. Dr. Morris and his wife couldn't play any instruments, but each of the children learned to play an instrument. The family read the Bible and prayed each morning after breakfast and each evening after supper. The children also memorized Bible verses with their parents. Dr. Morris wanted his children to have the same treasury of Scripture that he has. He had begun memorizing verses when he was twenty-four, and now he has a rich store of Scripture that he can glean from when he is witnessing and writing.

Dr. Morris credits his wife's faithful instruction and influence in the home as the most important factor in the spiritual development of his children because he was so busy most of the time. Dr. Morris often took one of his children with him on trips when he had to travel to speaking engagements or engineering meetings. Sometimes he took the entire family with him, and they made it into a family vacation.

When their youngest son Andy was thirty-nine, he was diagnosed with an aggressive type of lymphoma and died after three months. This has been the greatest sadness of Dr. Morris's life. But he is comforted knowing that Andy died with a calm trust in Christ and a strong Christian testimony. All his other children are now strong believers, active in Christian service. With the growing number of grandchildren and great-grandchildren, Dr. Morris likes to call his family the Institute for Procreation Research![13]

Conferences and speaking engagements

Dr. Morris has carried on an effective speaking ministry, even though he never considered himself gifted as a speaker. Even personal witnessing has not been easy for him because he has always been shy and had difficulty entering into conversations. But he did his speaking and witnessing for the Lord's sake, and the Lord blessed his efforts, even though it was difficult and unnatural for him to do.

He has spoken in hundreds of churches all over the United States and in several foreign countries. When he spoke to church groups, he could bring in the full weight of Scripture, and there was usually a warm reception. Speaking to secular college students and scientific audiences was more difficult because they were usually hostile audiences. In these lectures he focused on the scientific evidences for creation. Many students have been won to creationism and some have even come to Christ after their consciences were awakened and they understood that God was their Creator.

Debates

Dr. Morris hates to argue, so he finds it odd that he has been involved in three dozen debates on the creation-evolution question. He never sought out these debates and didn't enjoy them, but his colleague, Dr. Duane Gish, enjoyed these confrontations with evolutionists. At first Dr. Morris questioned the value of creation-evolution debates. He noticed, though, that the crowds were much larger for a debate than for a lecture. If they were to have a creationist lecture on a secular campus, they might draw a crowd of three hundred. However, if they were to have a debate with the evolutionists, several thousand might come.

Usually, the audience thinks that the creationists have won the debate. "We win," says Dr. Morris, "not because we are better debaters, but because creation is true, evolution is false, and real science confirms this."[14] These debates have been hosted in several foreign countries and in numerous prestigious secular universities.

Creation Research Society

Interestingly, *The Genesis Flood* had the effect of rallying creationists to form their own society. Some of these scientists had reviewed the manuscript before it was published, and others read it after it was printed. And they realized that there was still a strong minority willing to defend strict creationism.

In June of 1963, the Creation Research Society began with ten members. (It was hard to get scientists to come out publicly for strict creationism in those days. Several scientists backed down when they realized their names would appear on the letterhead of the CRS stationery.) After this small start, the CRS (as it is called) has grown into a thriving society that accepts voting members and sustaining members. Voting members must hold a master's or doctor's degree in science and agree to the statement of faith. Sustaining members are those who agree with the statement of faith but don't have the degrees in science.

The goal of the new group was to challenge the theory of evolution at a technical level. They wanted to give a research and publishing outlet for those scientists who believed in strict Biblical creationism and the historical reality of Noah's flood. All other scientific journals, even the ASA's, were notoriously closed to any papers on these topics. (Dr. Morris had found that out firsthand.)

The mission of the society is to show that there is a more plausible explanation for nature than evolution, and that is recognizing the planning of an intelligent Creator. They wanted to bring creationism into the classroom, not ban evolution. Creationism is robust enough to stand beside evolution and to be accepted on its own merits. (Their mission is not political, and they are not trying to outlaw evolutionary teaching in the schools.) Dr. Morris served as president of the CRS for six years. Although he was very busy at the time, he accepted the presidency because he was afraid that the society might waver from its strong creationist position.

Leaving the secular academic world

By now, Dr. Morris had spent thirty-five years in secular universities, first as a student and then as a teacher and administrator. When he left Virginia Tech in 1970, six Christian colleges offered him positions. But they didn't want to establish a center for creation research on their campuses, and this was one of Dr. Morris's dreams. He felt that the Lord was leading him to a full-time ministry getting out the creation message. He believed that the most strategic need in the Christian world was a return to genuine Biblical creationism.

From all his years in secular education, Dr. Morris believed that evolution was the foundation of the false teaching in all disciplines of study. It permeated every subject and was the basis for humanism and atheism. Of course, Dr. Morris expected to find these false teachings when he visited secular schools, but he was alarmed to find diluted brands of evolution even in the Christian schools where he spoke. Perhaps this was inevitable because Christian schools were forced to use the secular textbooks that promoted evolution.

When Dr. Morris decided to dedicate his time and abilities to defending his faith, he went to California to start the Christian Heritage College and a creation research center that would be connected with the college.[15] After a decade of administrating and teaching apologetics and creation studies, Dr. Morris resigned from the college to devote himself fully to the creation center.[16] Since 1972, the center has operated under the name Institute for Creation Research, often called ICR for short. Today ICR is funded by donations and income from literature. Over the years, it has had a significant worldwide impact. The radio ministry and now the website have a worldwide audience.[17]

The goal of ICR has been to bring science and education back to God. Teachers who had been taught the evolution model needed to be completely retrained. ICR seeks to retrain teachers by giving seminars, rewriting textbooks, and providing a graduate school in four scientific disciplines. Other Christian colleges do not have graduate programs in the sciences, and the students have to get their graduate degrees from secular universities that are steeped in evolutionary thought. ICR's graduate school (now nationally accredited) is Dr. Morris's answer to this problem.

ICR doesn't advocate getting creationism into schools using lawsuits. Although other creationist organizations have tried this approach, Dr. Morris has never liked this method. "We prefer the approach of education and persuasion to that of legislation and coercion," he said. "Persuasion is more effective in the long run than coercion."[18]

Publications

The main emphasis of the ICR ministry focuses on writing because Dr. Morris believes that distributing appropriate literature results in the most lasting effects. He points to Darwin's *Origin of the Species* as an example of the power of literature.

When Dr. Morris first began ICR, most publishing houses were unwilling to promote creationist books because they doubted that there was any profit in this type of literature. So Dr. Morris and several friends formed a publishing company called Creation-Life Publishers. The company was not profitable financially, but it was run as a ministry, providing an outlet for creationist books.[19]

Dr. Morris is the most prolific writer at ICR. He believes that the main gift the Lord has given him is the gift of writing. While he was teaching, he did most of his writing at night or on weekends; then later when he was traveling, he wrote in airport lounges and motel rooms. He has published over fifty titles and written hundreds of articles, mostly on the themes of Christian apologetics, Christian education, and the creation question. He believes it is important to present the creation message in each of his books because it is foundational to all of the Christian life.

Dr. Morris is credited with popularizing the term "scientific creationism," and the majority of his writing is devoted to this topic. "Creationism," he says, "can be taught without reference to the book of Genesis or to other religious literature or to religious doctrines." He argues that evolution and creation are equally "scientific" and equally "religious."

Dr. Morris has written several books showing that the Bible is correct in matters of science. "The Bible is not an embarrassment that needs reinterpretation in the light of modern science," he says. "On the contrary, the Bible provides the believing scientist with the very principles and basic reference points that he needs to properly interpret data pertinent to the origin and history of life on earth."[20] He believes that the Bible is without error, even scientific error. "Whenever a Biblical passage deals either with a broad scientific principle or with some particular item of scientific data," he says, "it will inevitably be found on careful study to be fully accurate in its scientific insights. Often it will be found even to have anticipated scientific discoveries."[21]

Dr. Morris doesn't have a degree in Bible, but his many hours of Bible study have prepared him to write about the Bible. He has written hundreds of devotional meditations for *Days of Praise*, a booklet that ICR publishes. He has also written commentaries on seven books of the Bible. He says his commentary on Genesis was probably his most enjoyable project. He believes Genesis is foundational to understanding the entire Bible and the message of salvation. His most ambitious project has been his annotated reference Bible, *The Defender's Bible*, that has 6,400 footnotes and eighteen major appendices.

He confesses to a certain lack of patience with Christians who dismiss the entire creation issue as "unimportant" and think we should be concentrating our efforts just on evangelism. "How can a Christian say the doctrine of special creation is unimportant when it is foundational to every other doctrine in Scripture?"[22] To him, the message of creation does not detract or distract from evangelism. It is foundational to it.

Witnessing

Dr. Morris believes that Christians must study and be prepared to witness intelligently. "All Christians," he says, "should be ready to give a systematic, scientific, legal defense of our Christian faith to anyone who raises questions about the logical and sound basis of that faith. And they should do so in a gentle, respectful, reasonable manner." He bases that admonition on I Peter 3:15.

Dr. Morris sees that one of the greatest difficulties in witnessing is the fact that most people no longer believe the Bible. That makes it difficult to reason with them from the Scriptures. For an example of how to witness to these unchurched people, Dr. Morris points to the Apostle Paul. Paul reasoned with the Gentile pagan idolaters who didn't know the Scriptures, and he showed them the evidence of the Creator in His creation. Showing them the strong case for special creation by the omnipotent God set the groundwork to introduce them to Jesus Christ.[23]

This, Morris believes, is the correct approach to take with young people who reject the Bible and are ignorant of its teaching. Since they have been indoctrinated with evolution and humanism, they must first be approached on the common ground that we all share—the evidence of the Creator in His creation. Then they can be introduced to Jesus Christ through the Holy Scriptures, the inspired Word of the Creator.

Much of Dr. Morris's writing centers around evidences that the Christian faith is true and that the Bible is true. "Indeed, very often it is impossible today even to obtain a hearing for the Gospel unless the ground has been prepared by clearing away some of the stones of misinformation about the supposed errors in the Bible and fallacies of Christian doctrine."[24] His purpose in using these Christian evidences is not to win arguments but to win souls. He warns, though, that "skill at persuasion and argumentation is no substitute for prayer and sincere concern for souls, and certainly no substitute for the use of the Word of God itself. . . . Christian evidences can never replace the convicting and illuminating work of the Holy Spirit."[25]

Criticism

Dr. Morris has found that there is definitely a downside to being so prominent in the creation movement. Since he is thought of as the "Father of the Modern Creation Movement," he has had to weather the brunt of the criticism directed against the creationist movement. Of course, he expects to feel the backlash from the humanists and evolutionists, but it disturbs him to receive it from Christian intellectuals at prominent Christian colleges and seminaries who oppose him for holding to a young earth.

Critics say that the creation movement has been plagued by a lack of scientific expertise and a lack of theological agreement. The lack of theological agreement is understandable because creationists come from such varied denominational backgrounds. Dr. Morris has tried to counteract the charges of shabby scientific expertise in the creation camp by hiring only Ph.D.s to teach in the graduate school at ICR.

Critics also say that creationists are deaf to the unpleasant noise of criticism—that they just tune out the criticisms. Dr. Morris denies that charge and says that the criticisms have already been answered in creationists' books. Creationists are also criticized for undertaking "creation research," a phrase that other scientists derisively refer to as an oxymoron. "How can you possibly research something that isn't taking place?" they say. Creationists answer that they can do field studies, looking, for example, for anomalous fossils (fossils that are "out of place") and studying sedimentary sequences; but most creation research is library research, finding already published studies that might have relevance to the creation question. Most of the data in these studies have been interpreted in the framework of evolution. It is possible to take the same measurements, the same observations, and reinterpret them in a creationist framework.

Critics say Dr. Morris and his colleagues at ICR have misquoted evolutionists, using their own words against them. In his writings, Dr. Morris deliberately chooses quotes written by evolutionists that are unflattering to evolution. But he denies misquoting and says it is impossible to include the entire context when quoting—you can't quote the entire book.

Within his own camp, some fellow creationists criticize him for still favoring the canopy theory, even though calculations have shown difficult scientific problems with the theory. That theory was made popular with *The Genesis Flood*. Dr. Morris believes that the problems are not impossible to overcome and that there is still good Biblical and scientific evidence for supporting the theory. However, he has always considered it only as a possible explanation, and he is not dogmatic about it.

Creationist organizations

Since the early days of the twentieth century when there were just a few spokesmen for creationism (and those were mostly preachers), the creationist movement has mushroomed. Today there are now thousands of scientists who are willing to publicly embrace the truth of special creation. Now there are well over a hundred organizations that are working to get the creation message out. They come from many different denominational backgrounds and have various levels of scientific expertise.

Dr. Morris is pleased with this growth and does not view the organizations as competitors. There is more than enough work for everyone, he says. He believes that it is healthy that they are not all controlled by a central organization. "At the human level at least," he says, "the proliferation and decentralization of the creation movement actually constitute its greatest strength."

Until Christ comes

Dr. Morris has been defending the faith for over fifty years. He is now a great-grandfather and has slowed down his pace, no longer traveling or lecturing. He divides his time between his office at ICR and his home, where he takes care of his wife, who is in poor health. His son, Dr. John Morris, is now the president of ICR, so Dr. Morris no longer has administrative duties there. But he still writes prolifically. He can't stop, he says. It is an occupational disease that he contracted years ago when he wrote *That You Might Believe.*

He waits expectantly for the Lord's return, and for many years he has kept a plaque on his wall that reads "Perhaps Today." He continues to stay busy in the Lord's work, waiting until the Lord comes again or calls him home. When he looks back over his life and he remembers all that God has done through him, Dr. Morris's explanation is "This is the Lord's doing: it is marvelous in our eyes" (Psalm 118:23).

---

[1] Julian Huxley was the grandson of the famous biologist T. H. Huxley, who opposed Lord Kelvin over the geological ages.

[2] Henry M. Morris, *A History of Modern Creationism* (San Diego: Master Books, 1984), first edition, p. 74.

[3] The ROTC is a program that enables college students to qualify to serve as officers in the military. The initials stand for Reserve Officers' Training Corps.

[4] See Romans 1:18-32. Instead of worshiping a Creator, evolutionists worship the forces and systems of nature. Many of the world's religions—Hinduism, Shintoism, Buddhism, Taoism, Confucianism—are based on evolutionary thought. (From *A History of Modern Creationism*, second edition, p. 21)

⁵ An earlier society that he had joined, the Creation-Deluge Society, had collapsed after a group of disgruntled members took over the society and removed it from its Scriptural standards.

⁶ Paraphrased with the author's permission from *That You Might Believe,* (Chicago: Good Books, Inc., 1946), Preface pp. iii, iv.

⁷ Paraphrased with the author's permission from *A History of Modern Creationism,* pp. 98-99.

⁸ Paraphrased with the author's permission from *A History of Modern Creationism,* p. 147.

⁹ Paraphrased with the author's permission from *A History of Modern Creationism,* p. 102.

¹⁰ Paraphrased with the author's permission from *The Biblical Basis for Modern Science* (Grand Rapids, Michigan: Baker Book House, 1999), p. 319.

¹¹ Ronald Numbers, *The Creationists* (New York: Alfred A. Knopf, Inc., 1992), p. 338.

¹² *A History of Modern Creationism,* p. 293, quoting Dr. Ronald Numbers.

¹³ He and his wife have been married for over 61 years and have six children, 17 grandchildren, and (so far) 8 great-grandchildren.

¹⁴ *A History of Modern Creationism,* p. 265.

¹⁵ Dr. Morris was one of the founders of the college, along with Dr. Tim LaHaye and Dr. Art Peters. Dr. Morris is no longer associated with the college.

¹⁶ When Dr. Morris was at Christian Heritage College, all students took twelve hours of apologetics in the courses called "Practical Christian Evidences" and "Scientific Creationism." In the latter course, Dr. Morris tried to bring creationism away from a strictly Biblical defense and place it on scientific footing. The notes for these classes were published into the books *The Bible Has the Answer, Many Infallible Proofs, The Troubled Waters of Evolution,* and *Scientific Creationism.*

¹⁷ For more information on ICR and its various ministries, visit their website at www.icr.org.

¹⁸ *A History of Modern Creationism,* p. 244 and from the tract "Creation and its Critics" published by Institute for Creation Research.

¹⁹ It was later renamed Master Books and was broadened to include other sound Biblical writings that were not just creationist or apologetic in nature.

²⁰ Henry M. Morris and Don Rohrer, *Decade of Creation* (San Diego: Creation-Life Publishers, 1981), p. 225.

²¹ Henry M. Morris, *The Biblical Basis for Modern Science,* p. 20.

²² Henry M. Morris and John D. Morris, *Society and Creation* (Green Forest, Master Books, 1996), p. 188.

²³ For more on this subject, see Dr. Morris's article "Creationist Approach to Missions" and his book *The God Who Is Real* (Grand Rapids, Michigan: Baker Book House, 1988).

²⁴ Henry M. Morris, *Many Infallible Proofs* (San Diego: Creation-Life Publishers, 1974), p. 3.

²⁵ Ibid., pp.4,6.

Dr. Walt Brown (1937-   )

DR. WALT BROWN
(1937-   )

Mechanical Engineer
Air Force Colonel

Finally, my brethren, be strong in the Lord, and in the power of
his might. Put on the whole armour of God, that ye may be
able to stand against the wiles of the devil.
Ephesians 6:10-11

*The doctor pulled the stethoscope out of his ears and left it dangling
around his neck. He told fourteen-year-old Walt to button his shirt and
come to his desk. He looked at Mr. and Mrs. Brown and then at Walt before he spoke. "Yes, I hear the murmur," he said. "But we heart specialists
see these cases. You can still have a full life, Walt, just not as active as the
rest. Why, we have similar cases on record of people who have lived to
be thirty-six years old!" he said, trying to encourage them. But his words
fell flat. The Browns had hoped for better news than this. Well, Walt
thought to himself as they left the doctor's office,* at least I have about
twenty years left.

His heart murmur had been diagnosed when he was a toddler, and he
was tired of the restrictions that had gone on ever since. He had always
had to sit out of physical education classes at school. When he played
baseball with his friends, he was allowed to swing the bat, but someone
else had to run the bases for him. Sometimes, when he thought his parents wouldn't find out, he would run the bases himself. The most vigorous
activity that his parents allowed him was a game of golf, which he played
often and well.

Walt enjoyed competition and had found he could compete in other
areas besides sports. He became a good public speaker and won several
state contests while in high school. At first he was so scared when he
spoke in front of people that he had to wear baggy pants to hide his shaking legs.

While the other boys were spending their time at sports practice, Walt
participated in the high school Chess Club. He had taught himself to play

chess when he was in fifth grade. He had been too sick to go to school one day, so he sat in bed, thumbing through the *World Book Encyclopedia*. He stopped when he came to the "Chess" entry and saw the picture of the chessboard. After reading about chess, he figured he could play it. He got a piece of paper and made a crude chess board by drawing eight columns and eight rows. Then he tore out pieces of paper and made pawns, kings, queens, knights, rooks, and bishops.

Now in high school, chess was his passion. He would spend Friday and Saturday evenings playing chess with friends. He wasn't much of a reader, but he often went downtown to the library to find chess books so that he could improve his strategy.

The chess coach was also the geometry teacher, and Walt was his top math student. This teacher pushed Walt with extra challenges. He also encouraged his bright students to go on to one of the military academies. But that was out of the question for Walt because of his heart condition.

When Walt was seventeen, he went for his annual checkup with Dr. Miller. "I can't hear the murmur!" the doctor said. So he lifted the restrictions on sports. After seventeen years of little physical activity, Walt reveled in the freedom. He tried boxing and running and found to his surprise that he was a good runner. He could easily run five miles and leave his athletic running partners huffing behind him. Now he realized that he just might be able to go to a military academy.

Walt's family

Walt was born in Kansas City, Missouri, the oldest of three children. When Walt was in elementary school, the family moved to Toledo, Ohio. Mr. Brown was a salesman for Hallmark greeting cards and later a real estate agent. Walt's family was a typical American family of the mid 1900s. Mr. and Mrs. Brown, both graduates of a Methodist college, were well read and well liked by all. They encouraged their children to pursue their individual talents.

The Browns attended a Methodist church each week and brought up their two sons and daughter with Biblical ethics and attitudes. When Walt was a teenager, he met people who were preaching the gospel, and their words slowly registered with him. His decision to follow Christ was actually made over a period of time. As time passed, his conviction and faith in Christ grew stronger.

Applying to the military

One Saturday when Walt was a senior in high school, he was walking downtown with his friend Dave. They had just stopped by the library, and Walt had checked out a few more chess books.

Dave and Walt were headed back home when they walked by the office of Congressman Frazier Reams. They suddenly remembered an announcement at school that Congressman Reams was accepting applications to the military academies. "Let's check it out," Dave said.

So, a month later, they were taking several tests with another hundred applicants. With the combination of the written and oral tests, Walt ended up in first place. So he got to choose which military academy he wanted to attend—Army, Navy, Air Force, or Coast Guard.

For Walt the choice was obvious. The challenge and prestige of West Point, the Army's academy, had always attracted him. He wanted to go to West Point because he felt it was the best, the most rigorous and most challenging. But he still had to pass West Point's physical test, mental test, and medical test. The mental test was no problem for him; he worried, though, that the military might not accept him because of his history with the heart murmur. Walt informed the military doctors of the earlier diagnosis, but they thoroughly checked him and said it was no problem.

West Point

Walt Brown entered West Point on July 5, 1955. After he had been there for one hour, he thought he had made the biggest mistake of his life! What a shock this was for a seventeen-year-old boy who had never been away from home. Where was the "glory and the honor of the Corps" that he had heard so much about? He wished he could just walk away from this "nightmare." *What am I doing here?* he wondered. Whenever the question arose, he reminded himself that he was here in the military to help his neighbors—those who were subjected to bullies.

The first two months were called "Beast Barracks"—a fitting name, he found out, for the two months of drills and grueling physical workouts before academics began. He had so much to learn and couldn't seem to do anything right. Taking apart a rifle was a mystery. And he had to do it quickly in total darkness.

Even marching was difficult. Sometimes he couldn't react to the commands fast enough and was left behind. "Mr. Brown, get with it, dumb smack!" the upperclassman barked. "You need more practice, so instead of having free time, I want you to report to my room, and we will work on it."

There was never enough time to do what he needed to do. His math courses came easily, but he had difficulty with the courses that involved long reading assignments. He had to read the *New York Times* every day and keep current with the news in case he was asked to recite the news at meals. If he didn't know the news, he would have to visit each upper-classman who sat at his table and recite the news.

This plebe system was a merciless plan to heap stress on the new cadets, or "plebes" as they were called. (*Plebe* means "common people" in Latin, and it was used in a derogatory sense at West Point.) The upper-classmen would make a plebe feel inadequate and clumsy. If he did something wrong, then everyone would look at him and would find something else wrong. It was a vicious snowball effect, and inexperienced plebes found themselves sleep deprived and buried in demerits.

Walt racked up demerits right and left—having lint in his rifle, not getting a haircut that week, failing room inspection, having dusty shoes or dirty fingernails, hiding clean laundry instead of taking the time to fold it neatly and stack it in his locker. Later Walt realized this constant nit-picking was good preparation for what was ahead in the Army, because there would be situations in which he would have to function under even greater stress.

Plebes were allowed a certain number of demerits each month, but after that, each demerit meant one hour of walking "punishment tours." Many times Walt had to walk tours—walking back and forth in a lane, one hour at a time, in his full uniform carrying his rifle. At one point he had thirty hours of tours to walk. Fortunately, a visiting European prince saved his skin by pardoning all cadets' offenses. (West Point allowed visiting royalty or heads-of-state to "pardon" cadets serving punishments.)

He wanted so badly that first semester to resign or be kicked out. He watched with envy when a classmate failed or resigned and had to leave. One thousand cadets had started in his class, but only six hundred would finish four years later. He was sorely tempted to deliberately fail Russian, his worst subject, so that he would be sent home. He knew he could do well in all other subjects, but if he failed one subject, he was out. As much as he wanted to go home, though, Walt could never bring himself to put down a deliberately wrong answer. When his grades were posted at the end of the first semester, he was very disappointed to see that he had passed Russian. He had passed with the lowest possible grade. One more wrong answer and he might have been sent home.

A welcome rest

Late in his first semester, Walt was helping build a "Beat Navy" sign for the upcoming Army-Navy football game. The makeshift platform he was standing on gave way, and he fell ten feet onto a concrete porch, fracturing his pelvis.

The doctor determined that he didn't need a cast, but he would have to spend two months in bed. Normally, two months in bed would have been torture; but Walt found they were a blessing, a welcome vacation from the oppressive plebe system. Now he could get plenty of sleep and eat peaceful meals. He didn't have to worry about eating properly—sitting on the first three inches of his chair, his back perfectly straight, looking down at his plate unless he was being spoken to.

And he finally had time to study, because he wasn't earning demerits and walking tours. His professors were surprised that he now did better in his schoolwork even though he couldn't attend classes. Walt's stay in the hospital refreshed him. When he got out, he could keep up with his academics, and he wasn't overwhelmed by the plebe system.

A paratrooper and a ranger

After he graduated from West Point, Walt had his heart set on being an Air Force pilot. But he failed the eye exam. It was a huge disappointment when he wasn't allowed to fly, and he had to settle for going into the Army. Months later, he found out that his vision had improved considerably. He had just been suffering eyestrain from all the studying, and it disappeared when he was away from the books. But God used this disappointment with the eye test to change the course of Walt's life. Naturally, he couldn't see through the disappointment into the future to see how God would use him in the Army and prepare him to serve Him in a different capacity.

Fresh out of West Point, Walt went to Fort Benning in western Georgia and learned to be a paratrooper—to jump out of a plane in full fighting gear with a parachute on his back. He started out jumping off thirty-four-foot towers with a harness attached to him. He learned the crucial tuck position so that he wouldn't get whiplash when he jumped out of a plane and the winds hit him at one hundred miles an hour. But that was an easy course compared to what followed.

Next he went to Ranger School. There Walt learned hand-to-hand combat and went through challenging obstacle courses. The Rangers are the Army's most elite, trained to act and react effectively under intense combat stress. The goal of Ranger School is to develop leaders who are mentally and physically tough and self-disciplined. *Surrender* is not a word in the Ranger vocabulary. The training is so realistic that a trainee might lose his life. Several rangers drowned during training a year after Walt was there.

Whenever a dangerous mission needs to be accomplished swiftly, the Army calls on the Rangers. A Ranger mission is typically behind enemy lines. It is obviously dangerous and might involve raids, ambushes, prisoner snatches, or disrupting enemy communications and supplies. The classic WWII Ranger mission was to scale the cliffs of Normandy and knock out guns that would be firing on the Allied landing craft.

After the classroom training came the jungle phase and then the mountain phase of Ranger School. For the jungle phase, they went to northern Florida to learn how to fight and survive under harsh conditions. It was winter, and temperatures were sometimes below freezing. Walt got an average of two hours of sleep a night and half a meal a day during the three-week jungle phase. Rangers had to function far beyond their natural stamina and abilities.

During the jungle phase, Rangers learned to cross rivers using a special technique. Each six-man team picked its best swimmer to cross the river with a rope tied around his waist. He found the tallest, sturdiest tree and tied the rope as high as he could. Then the men on the other shore pulled the rope tight and tied it around another tree. These team members then "monkeywalked" across the rope, carrying the swimmer's clothes and weapons to him.

Walt, unfortunately for him, was the best swimmer of his team. He had swum competitively at West Point and had turned down an opportunity to train with the Olympic team in the Pentathlon event. Right now, northern Florida was experiencing a sudden cold spell, and the wind-chill temperature was seventeen degrees. Standing in front of the swiftly flowing Yellow River, he suddenly wished he weren't such a good swimmer.

It was an exhausting swim as he bucked the current and hauled the rope, but he completed it successfully. His only comfort was knowing that one of his teammates would do the return swim when it came time to repeat the technique back across the river.

But when the time came, all his teammates insisted they couldn't make the swim. "I'm no good, Walt. I'd never make it," they all said. So again, Walt started swimming across the Yellow River—believing he would probably be killed.

By this time, he had been in the freezing water for five hours, and he was overcome by the cold current and by exhaustion. He was swept down river where another team was doing the same drill. *This is it,* he thought. *I'm going to die.* But at that moment he saw the other team's rope. He reached up, grabbed it, and slowly worked his way to shore.

An instructor, immaculately dressed, was standing on the shore, waiting to chew him out for doing the drill incorrectly. As Walt stood shaking in the freezing water, relieved to be alive, the instructor yelled, "Ranger, stop shivering! It's all in your mind!"

Marriage

Walt was beginning to think girls were a nuisance—they were silly and just took up his time. But that changed suddenly and permanently when he met Peggy Hill during his last year at West Point. Walt married Peggy twenty months later, in June of 1960. They went to live at Fort Bragg, North Carolina. She was a Christian and had grown up in a military family. Her father, an Army Colonel, was in charge of Army Space Projects at the Pentagon.

Peggy understood the nature of Army life, and she cheerfully accompanied Walt on the frequent moves. They moved fourteen times in seventeen years. Meeting so many interesting people and experiencing new things more than compensated for the inconveniences of moving so often.

People think of the Army as a place for hard-drinking, loose-living men. But the Browns always found themselves in a wholesome environment, living near other Army families who were friendly and supportive, even if they weren't Christians. At most bases where they lived, there was a good group of Christians they could fellowship with. Walt found that his policy of never drinking alcoholic beverages was not a hindrance in the Army. It brought him a certain respect, not disdain.

Getting a master's degree

Brown chose to transfer into a technically oriented branch of the Army—the Ordnance Corps. This branch dealt with the Army's equipment, and he felt sure he could find interesting things there.

He was excited to learn that the Ordnance Corps would send him to get a master's degree. Engineering fascinated him, so he went to study mechanical engineering at New Mexico State University. At New Mexico State, he found that his mechanical engineering courses were interesting but not difficult, so he also took many physics and math courses.

Overcoming a reading problem

Although technical courses came easily to him, he had always been bogged down by courses that demanded a lot of reading. While he was at New Mexico State, he stopped by the reading laboratory and took a free reading test that he saw advertised. They told him, "Young man, you will have trouble finishing college." Brown laughed and told them he had already finished college. But he realized now why reading assignments had always been a burden and why he had to get a running start on the weekends.

He also found that he was very weak in vocabulary because he had avoided reading in the past. With his characteristic self-discipline, he overcame this reading deficiency. He took several reading courses and added 6,000 words to his vocabulary by studying the dictionary.[1]

White Sands Missile Range

Right after he got his master's degree, Brown went to White Sands Missile Range to oversee testing of three of the Army's missile systems. It was located just over a mountain pass, about forty miles from New Mexico State. Before he arrived, the testing at White Sands had revealed a horrible problem with the Littlejohn missile. Every tenth missile or so would fall several miles short. Of course, it was intolerable to have a nuclear weapon miss its target by a couple of miles, especially falling short, because it might fall on the heads of your own troops.

At the time, the Littlejohn missile was the Army's best hope of blunting a Soviet attack. This was the early 1960s, and tensions in Europe were mounting. Something had to be done to keep Russian tanks from rolling across Germany. And it seemed that the Littlejohn would keep them at bay. But until the "short round" problem was fixed, the missile could not be used. Over the last two years the Army had spent millions of dollars trying to figure out the cause of the short rounds. All the civilian scientists and engineers that had been called in to help were baffled. It seemed that millions more would be needed for testing different possible causes.

One morning Brown was on the firing range a few hours early because he was in charge of firing that day. He noticed two men setting up an elaborate camera system. Out of curiosity, he went over to talk to them and found that they were part of a civilian engineering firm that was developing a new type of camera. They explained their photographic technique to Brown and invited him to come by their office and look around.

A few weeks later, he walked by their office and remembered their invitation to stop by. As they were showing him around, they mentioned in passing that something strange had shown up on the film they had taken that day—some fuzzy stuff was below the missile.

Brown asked them to enlarge the picture. He took into account the distortion from the experimental film and was able to calculate the size of the largest fragment of the fuzzy stuff. It was a hexagonal nut that must have fallen from the missile's shoe. The shoe was a big block of metal that guided the missile along the launch rail. When the missile ignited and shot off the rail, the shoe was supposed to kick off.

He called his office and had them look in the records to find out whether anything strange had happened that day. It turned out that the photographed missile was one of the short rounds. As he walked back to his office, he wondered what the relationship between a short round and a missing nut was. Brown called in his chief engineer, who explained how losing the nut would keep the missile's shoe on. If the nut were missing, the spring that ejected the shoe wouldn't activate. The shoe would stay attached. Brown thought maybe the missile was carrying this shoe downrange, causing the missile to fall several miles short of its target.

He had his office look back at the records of the recovery crew to see whether shoes had been found for the short rounds. (Shoes were generally found about a hundred feet downrange whenever the missile flew correctly.) Just as he thought, whenever there was a short round, they did not find a shoe.

The next day Brown had a crew dig the short round out of the ground at the point of impact. Was the shoe still attached? No. But everyone could see the hole in the missile's skin where the shoe had been attached. It had been ripped by the great aerodynamic forces that had torn the shoe off during flight.

So in less than two days, Brown solved the problem, and the two-year testing program was terminated. He had found that when the Littlejohn missile was shipped in a crate from the manufacturing plant, vibrations sometimes loosened the nut. If the nut fell off, the shoe didn't eject. The missile then had to carry this nonstreamlined hunk of metal downrange, and the extra drag caused the Littlejohn to fall miles short.

The fix was so simple that it cost less than a nickel per missile. When the nut was screwed on at the manufacturing plant, they had to make sure it could never come loose. They took a hammer and "pinged" the nut so that it was permanently attached. As a double check, launch crews checked the shoe and its nut just before launch.

The Littlejohn missile was returned to the troops in Europe immediately. Brown didn't think much about solving the short-round problem because it happened so fast. But his superiors noticed how quickly he had solved this problem that had stumped the best engineers for two years. And they saw that he had saved the Army a good deal of money. The short-round incident went on his Officer Efficiency Report and the Army would later reward him with an early promotion to Major.

Ph.D. in the Army?

One day the thought occurred to Brown that he could get a Ph.D. in engineering. He didn't care about the degree or the prestige, but the subject matter fascinated him. He knew that the two best science and engineering schools were Massachusetts Institute of Technology (MIT) and California Institute of Technology (Cal Tech). He wanted to study at one of them.

But the Army had never assigned an officer to get a Ph.D. The Air Force and the Navy had, but not the Army. The Army's philosophy was that when a Ph.D. was needed, they would hire a civilian. Brown figured that if he got a fellowship that paid for the schooling and was accepted at one of the world's two best graduate schools, then the Army couldn't refuse. As required, he asked for permission from the Army to apply for the National Science Fellowship.[2] This fellowship, while not as prestigious as the Rhodes scholarship, was far more valuable financially.

This was such a new idea for the Army—an officer asking to get a Ph.D. using a National Science Fellowship—that they sent out a high-ranking official from the Pentagon to interview Brown. This official liked the idea and decided to approve.

So Brown applied and scored in the 99.9 percentile in the quantitative part of the National Science Fellowship test. Fellowships were awarded based on ability, and Brown certainly had the ability to handle the subject matter. Meanwhile, both MIT and Cal Tech had accepted him. Brown picked MIT because he thought it was the best science and engineering school in the world.

MIT

The Army gave the final permission, and the Browns moved to Boston so that he could study at MIT. They arrived with two children; two years later another baby was born.

He finished his Ph.D. in record time—two and a quarter years. Most people took three to five years to finish a doctorate. Brown was in a hurry because he knew the Army was losing patience with him. A Pentagon personnel officer would often call and say, "Brown, when are you going to finish up there? We are having to send some officers back to Vietnam for the third time. Here you are having a nice time going to school. We want to send you to Vietnam. You need to get back into a proper career pattern."

"I'll do the best I can, sir," he promised. "I'm working as hard as I can." And he was. Since arriving at MIT, he had stopped watching television and reading the newspaper and worked at an intense pace.

Vietnam

When he finished at MIT, he knew he was going to Vietnam. It was the only assignment in his career he didn't get to pick. But he didn't mind going. He realized how terrorized the South Vietnamese people were. Much controversy surrounded America's involvement there, but Brown saw it as a simple question of helping his neighbor. He knew the atrocities that the Viet Cong soldiers were inflicting on innocent villagers.

Brown was stationed at Cu Chi, thirty-five miles northwest of Saigon. But the Army didn't know what to do with a Ph.D. in the middle of Vietnam. Brown had little actual experience in the Ordnance Corps because he had been going to school. They scratched their heads and ended up giving him a staff position—being a Division Material Officer.

When Brown reported to his unit, the Colonel commanding his brigade interviewed him. The Colonel looked up after reading Brown's record. "I have never in my life seen anyone so ill-prepared to take the job you've got!" he said, unable to hide his disgust. "You have no experience at all. I can't understand why you were sent here. Brown, you better hit the ground running hard!"

Brown did his job well, and this Colonel quickly became one of his biggest supporters. As the Division Material Officer, Brown had five captains and several other men working for him. Their job was to make sure that all the equipment of the division worked. They had to keep everything in repair—tanks, rifles, artillery, helicopters, radar, and radios. And they had to coordinate getting replacement parts shipped over so that few pieces of equipment would be sidelined for a lack of spare parts.

One morning, the division commander called him in and showed him a dozen muddy rifles on the floor. "We had a patrol out last night. They were ambushed, and eight men were killed because their rifles did not work. This is happening all over Vietnam. Fix this problem, Brown!"

And so Brown, the cadet who had trouble taking a rifle apart, had to identify the problem. He did a lot of testing. He found that the rifle was actually a good weapon, but different cleaning techniques were needed. Brown conducted dozens of classes for key maintenance people who then taught their soldiers these cleaning techniques. Reports of jammed rifles ceased.

Each day there were new problems for Brown to solve. He found that Vietnam was a demanding assignment. The first several months he got four hours of sleep a night and ended up in the hospital with pneumonia. While recuperating, he noticed what an outstanding hospital they had—much like the M.A.S.H. unit that was popularized by the television series. *These doctors and dentists are usually underutilized,* Brown thought. *Why not use them to help the local people?*

He mentioned it to his boss, who was enthusiastic about the idea. So, every Wednesday that year, Brown gathered a group of doctors and several soldiers for security, and they headed down the road to the village of Phouc Hiep.[3]

At night the Viet Cong terrorized this village. The village chief had to sleep in a different bed every night because he was never safe. His son had been killed one night—his throat slit while he was sleeping in bed.

Only one young man in the village spoke English, a grade school teacher named Lam Van Hai. (In Vietnam, the names run backwards, so his first name was "Hai.") The villagers looked forward to the weekly visit from the Americans, and Hai, Brown's translator, organized little programs for the kids to perform for the soldiers. Hai and Brown became friends, and Peggy wrote several letters to Hai so that he could practice his English.

One day the doctors were busy with other patients and asked Brown to help a little girl with a fever. "Here, take this little girl and give her a cold bath," a doctor said. Brown picked her up and gently lowered her into the cool water. She screamed, and her cry sounded just like his daughter's when he had given her a cool bath for a fever. As he held this little girl, he thought, *We are just like these people. We laugh alike, and we cry alike.*

As Brown got to know the Vietnamese people, he came to love them. He saw that racial distinctions were artificial. He realized that there is only one race—the human race.[4] And he found that the stereotypes about Southeast Asians were false. It was completely false that they thought life was cheap, that they somehow didn't hurt as much as we did when one of their own died.

Brown organized a medical team to help in a Vietnamese village.

Inventions

The Viet Cong soldiers would hide underground in tunnels, and this was a serious problem in Vietnam. Cu Chi, where Brown was stationed, was famous for its tunnels. The Americans were afraid the Viet Cong soldiers would tunnel into their compound at night. The tunnels were such a problem that Brown spent a lot of time thinking about it and came up with a way to detect them.

It was such a simple idea that anyone could learn to do it in five minutes. He took about fifteen feet of long, skinny cleaning rods for rifles. (Thousands of them were sitting in the warehouses he supervised. They were about a foot long and could be screwed together to any length desired.) At the end of this fifteen-foot rod, he had machinists fabricate a large, sharp tip. A soldier would push the rod into the ground, and if a tunnel was underneath, there would suddenly be no resistance and the rod would pop through. A tunnel was confirmed by squirting in water from a hand-operated fire extinguisher and listening for the splash of water on the bottom of the tunnel. If the water squirted back in one's face, it wasn't a tunnel.

Another of Brown's inventions was an anti-mine device. He saw the gruesome destruction from the mines that the Viet Cong planted in the roads. He was haunted by the sight of an armored personnel carrier blowing up with eleven men inside and seeing the flesh hanging from the walls of the wreckage. *Something has to be done about the mines,* Brown thought. With the help of some welders in the unit, he built a device to be pushed by a tank recovery vehicle. The mine was set off by the device—not a tank or person. The device was heavy enough to set off a mine, but weak enough to break cleanly at a few joints so that the mine damaged only part of the device. Then the soldiers could rebuild it quickly with spare parts that they carried.

This anti-mine device was getting better with each prototype Brown built. But a new commander came in and told him to stop his side projects. Brown wasn't neglecting any of his duties, and he felt that this mine detector was very important. But the commander thought Brown was eating up resources and needed to focus on his assigned duties.

It was a great disappointment for Brown to give up those projects. Sometimes he felt he should have stayed in Vietnam and perfected his anti-mine device and taught more units to detect tunnels. Some encouraged him to volunteer for a second year and go to a unit that did nothing but scientific work. But Peggy was home with the three little children, and Brown needed to go home. He also wondered how many other superiors would squelch anything innovative or want him to do only what made them look good.

So he left Vietnam after his one-year assignment, but he could never get the people out of his mind. Later when America pulled out of Vietnam, Brown was troubled. He worried about Lam Van Hai because he had been friendly to the Americans. Brown knew about the concentration camps for those who helped the United States. He would often talk to Peggy about Hai and wonder what had happened to him. Year after year he couldn't get him out of his mind. But there wasn't any word from Hai.

Bible study

After coming home from Vietnam, Brown spent a year at the Command and General Staff College at Fort Leavenworth, Kansas—a school for majors and lieutenant colonels who were expected to advance.

Brown 287

He was one of the youngest officers selected for this school. Here, for the first time, the Bible came alive for him. There had usually been a strong Christian influence on the bases where the Browns lived, and they had always attended church and Bible studies; but Brown had not studied the Bible for himself. His family had not read the Bible together when he was growing up, and he had not formed the habit of personal Bible study. When he did read the Bible for himself, he usually read the New Testament. He felt comfortable in the New Testament, but the Old Testament troubled him, so he rarely read it.

One of the things that stirred his interest in the Bible was a sermon he heard a classmate preach at the base chapel. The sermon, entitled "It Is Written," described many of the Bible's fulfilled prophecies. This impressed Brown, and he began to study the Bible. The chaplain there encouraged him in his Bible study and gave him a set of commentaries. As he studied, Brown became fascinated with the Bible. It was no longer a dry book, but the vibrant, life-changing Word of God. A few years later he began teaching an adult Sunday School class.

Benét Labs

After Fort Leavenworth, he was invited to be the Director of Benét Laboratories near Albany, New York. This was one of the Army's research, development, and engineering laboratories that was responsible for developing complex armament systems. As the supervisor of 450 people, Brown had to make sure these civilian scientists and engineers were doing work helpful to the Army. Many of them, because of the highly technical nature of their work, were not used to being supervised. It was a busy, challenging job that he enjoyed.

But one day Brown decided he wanted to try teaching. He had always thought that he would enjoy teaching, but he had never had a chance to do it. He called a friend at the Air Force Academy and asked whether there were any openings. The next day he got a call from the personnel director of the math department saying that he was hired. Usually they would have flown him out for an interview, but they recognized that his background was very appropriate. So the Browns moved to Colorado.

What about Noah's Ark?

Whenever the family moved, Peggy would take the kids to visit grandparents. Then Brown would report to the next assignment, sign in, begin work, and wait for quarters. It would have been too difficult and expensive to live in motels with the children.

So in 1970, he put Peggy and the kids on a plane and drove from Albany, New York, to the Air Force Academy in Colorado. Driving across Kansas, he was getting sleepy and bored. The roads were flat and straight, and there was nothing to grab his interest in the passing scenery. He turned on the radio and flipped through the stations. He stopped the dial when he found a Christian station talking about Noah's Ark. The program featured interviews with people who claimed that Noah's Ark had been sighted on Mount Ararat, which rises almost 17,000 feet above sea level. As he listened, he thought, *How in the world could Noah's Ark reach that elevation?*

The Rocky Mountains were just beginning to come into view as he drove along. He tried to imagine an object large enough to fill a football stadium sitting up there on one of the summits because it had floated there. Impossible! When the program ended, he pulled off the road and jotted down the name and address of the radio station.

The very first night he was at the Air Force Academy, he wrote a letter to the radio station asking who their sources were and how he could reach them. Within a few weeks, they wrote back and gave him names and addresses. He called one of the contacts on the list, Jim Lee, a man who traveled across the country giving lectures about the effort to find Noah's Ark.[5] Brown invited him to stay at his home whenever he was passing through.

Jim Lee visited the Browns several times. He and Brown would stay up late into the night talking about the possibility that the Ark could be there. The logistics of it all stumped Brown's engineering mind. "Where did all that water come from?" Brown asked Jim. "You've got to be lame in the head to think that all the mountains were really covered with water."

"Well, I don't know," Jim said. "Maybe the water came from outer space."

"Maybe so," Brown said. "But then where did all the water go afterwards?"

Brown saw other problems. How could so many animals fit in the Ark? How could the freshwater fish survive if the flood waters were salt water? And how did the plants survive?[6]

Why, that part of the Bible has to be wrong, he thought. The Old Testament troubled him because there were parts of it that didn't seem scientifically sound. The New Testament made a lot of sense to him, and he heartily accepted Christ's teaching. (It never dawned on him, though, that Christ himself had talked about Noah as a literal historical figure.)

For the next two years, he read everything he could find about the Ark and talked to many "Ark hunters." The possibility that Noah's Ark was actually buried on Mount Ararat and that the global flood had occurred was growing in his mind.

He had always thought the fossil record was the strongest evidence for evolution—which he had passively accepted. But now he began to wonder whether perhaps the flood had laid down the fossils. If water sloshed all over the earth for a year, that would explain why fossils of sea life are at the tops of all the major mountain ranges—something geologists had known for more than two hundred years. If fossils had been laid down rapidly in Noah's flood, then fossils were no longer evidence for evolution. (In fact, fossils *must* be buried rapidly or else the animal or plant's shape won't be preserved.)

What then was the evidence for evolution? he wondered. The more he struggled with this question and studied it, the more amazed he became at the lack of evidence supporting evolution. To his surprise he found that the scientific evidence actually supported creation. By 1972, Brown was convinced that creation and a global flood were the only logical positions.

The Bible's accuracy

The first eleven chapters of Genesis, which had been so discredited by the world, and even unfortunately by some modern Christians, were now firmly established as truth in Brown's mind. He now saw Genesis as accurate history, describing major events and real people.

He believes that the entire Bible, in the original, is accurate in every detail and that God put every detail there for a purpose. He is fascinated by the analogies to Christ throughout the Bible. His favorite is the parallel between Christ and the Ark. They were both designed by God as perfect provisions freely available to sinful people. And they both provided the only escape from a terrible judgment. Tragically, though, people scoff today at their need of salvation in Jesus Christ, just as the people scoffed in Noah's day at the thought of water falling out of the sky.[7]

Completing the family

While in Vietnam, Brown had seen orphans sleeping on the street on pieces of cardboard. His heart had gone out to them. Later, when he and Peggy decided they were ready for another child, they began the adoption process—the interviews, the home study, the paper work. They initially thought God would lead them to a child from Southeast Asia. But God had other plans for them and gave them a baby girl from Colorado.

The adoption process never worried the Browns. They knew they were not at the mercy of a social worker or government agency. They were confident that God would give them the child He wanted for them. They saw how God orchestrated every amazing detail, and, through their move to the Air Force Academy in Colorado, He put their family together.

As a teacher

At the Air Force Academy, Brown was an Army major teaching on an exchange program. (The Army had lent him to the Air Force.) After a year, the Air Force Academy invited him to stay on as a tenured professor. He quickly accepted. The family was very happy there even though their living quarters were cramped with four children and a dog. This was a wholesome place to raise a family, and they enjoyed good Christian fellowship.

But there was a hitch to the offer. He would have to leave the Army and be permanently assigned to the Air Force. This required an interservice transfer and high-level maneuvers in the Defense Department. If Brown had initiated it, it would have never gone through. But the Air Force Academy had clout and generally got what it wanted. So one day Brown was told to hang up his green uniform and start wearing a blue uniform. Soon he was placed in charge of thirty-five professors who were teaching calculus to freshmen. He felt at home in the Air Force because the two services were similar.[8]

Three years later, the Air Force sent him off to the Air War College for a year so that they could get him current with what the Air Force was doing. He was wearing a blue suit now and had an impressive background, but how much did he really know about the Air Force? The officers who are sent to the War College are the ones they think might become generals. Brown finished at the War College as a distinguished graduate.

The next year the Air War College invited Brown back to give a lecture on operations research, sometimes called systems analysis. These are the mathematical techniques that the military was starting to use to make important decisions. (This is not to say that all decision making is purely mathematical, but there are often quantifiable aspects that can be worked through before experience and subjective factors are considered.)

Brown changed from Army green to Air Force blue when he taught at the Air Force Academy.

Brown was now in charge of the Operations Research Division at the Air Force Academy, and he understood these techniques and their applications well. The War College liked his lecture so much that he was invited to join the faculty. So after five happy years in Colorado, he left his tenured position at the Air Force Academy and moved the family to the War College at Maxwell Air Force Base in Alabama. Peggy's father had died recently, and this move would bring the Browns closer to Peggy's mother.

Air War College

The Air War College was one of five war colleges in the United States. Their mission was to prepare the world's best strategic leaders by stimulating innovative thinking on critical military issues. All military services sent their best senior officers to one of the five. Also present were senior officials from other federal agencies and outstanding officers from forty other nations. Each student brought diverse experiences and backgrounds. National figures lectured each day—a Marine general, a senator, or the Deputy Secretary of Defense. These lectures were followed by thought-provoking discussion groups.

Brown was thirty-nine when he came to teach at the Air War College. Almost all the students were older than he. Brown was in charge of the curriculum concerning science, technology, and decision making. He also lectured on operations research and taught an elective course in computers. He had never had a course in computers, but he had always kept current with computer technology. Brown had often learned a new computer system because he could see how it would help him at a new job.

Getting into the creation movement

In the evenings when supper was over, Walt and Peggy would stay at the table talking. Walt would share with her the amazing things he was discovering in his search for the truth about creation. Peggy listened quietly but didn't share Walt's enthusiasm about his new hobby, even though she could see how compelled he was by the scientific evidence.

She knew many fine Christians who believed in evolution. In fact, she and Walt had believed in theistic evolution all these years, assuming that God had used evolution to create the universe. Theistic evolution had been a comfortable compromise. It gave a sense of scientific respectability and, at the same time, it satisfied an inward conviction that there must be a Creator.

After one of their evening conversations, she asked, "What difference does it *really* make?"

So Walt addressed the theological implications. "Why do we need a Savior?" he asked.

Peggy replied, "To save us from our sin."

Then Walt explained, "If evolution happened, death was already occurring before man evolved. But if death came *before* man, and was not a consequence of Adam's sin, then sin is a fiction. And if sin is a fiction, then why do we need Christ to save us from our sin?"

Suddenly, it made sense to Peggy. It seemed so obvious, but she had never considered it before. Like many others who passively accept theistic evolution, she had not realized the theological implications. But now she saw how evolution completely undermines the need for a Savior. And she saw what an unsatisfactory compromise theistic evolution is. If the Genesis account is not a factual depiction of events, then the entire Bible is not completely true, and that means that it is not the ultimate authority. From then on, Peggy was an eager supporter of Walt's creation study.

Brown had been teaching at the War College for several years and was offered a splendid job as the Director of the Air Force Geophysics Laboratory near Boston. He seriously considered this job because it would put him around experts in geology and geophysics, even if they were evolutionists. Brown was now very interested in geology because of his study of the global flood. His investigation of creation and the flood had started as scientific curiosity, but as he saw the implications, it grew into a passionate hobby.

Unexpectedly one day, Brown's superior, a two-star general, called him into his office to sign papers that would send him to the laboratory. Brown had to think fast. He had reached full colonel rapidly.[9] But he wanted more time to devote to his creation study, and he wanted to help get the creation message out. He politely turned down the offer to go to the Geophysics Laboratory and asked to get out of the military at the first opportunity. So in 1980, after twenty-one years in uniform, he retired from the Air Force as a full colonel.

Dr. Brown was astonished to see that much scientific evidence was poorly disseminated and that young people were taught such erroneous science about origins. He saw that critical thinking skills were not being fully developed in the classroom. Students were being told *what* to think, not being taught *how* to think. Science lost its excitement in this stifling atmosphere. Dr. Brown had seen for himself that the scientific evidence overwhelmingly favored creation and a global flood. If thinking people were allowed to see all the evidence, they could reach their own logical conclusions.

Dr. Brown's Hydroplate Theory

As Dr. Brown thought about the feasibility of the flood, he realized that the Genesis flood was literally an earthshaking event, far more catastrophic than almost anyone had imagined. He was startled by the violence of the event.

When he first thought about the flood, he had been stumped by the mechanism of it all. Yet he saw that the geological evidence corresponded to a devastating, worldwide flood. So where did so much water come from? And where did it go?

As he pondered these questions and studied the Biblical and scientific details, a theory for the mechanism of the flood began to gel in his mind. It became clear to Dr. Brown how the gigantic flood of Noah's day would explain many mysterious features on earth—features that few people realize are not explained by current science. Many of these major features fit into place beautifully if the flood waters came from under the earth's crust—from worldwide, interconnected chambers that erupted violently as *"the fountains of the great deep."*

Dr. Brown calls his theory of the flood the hydroplate theory. It is a mature and detailed theory, complete with many predictions of what science should uncover in the future if his theory is correct. Some of Dr. Brown's published predictions have already come true. He believes that successful predictions are the best test of a theory's strength and fruitfulness; scientists who are unwilling to make and publish predictions show a lack of scientific rigor and confidence. "A weak theory will produce few predictions," he says. "If theories could not be published unless they included numerous details and specific predictions, we would be mercifully spared many distractions and false ideas."

In 1993 Dr. Brown was asked to narrate a five-minute animation of his hydroplate theory for CBS television. CBS television executives had noticed the interest that the public has in Noah's Ark, and they aired a two-hour special on Noah's Ark. That program was seen by 43 million Americans and Canadians. Feedback from Dr. Brown's portion of that program was overwhelmingly positive.

Seminars and debates

After retiring from the military, Dr. Brown moved to the Chicago area and began giving creation seminars and debating evolutionists. He prepared strenuously for his seminars and debates. He always assumed that several people in the audience knew more about a topic than he did, and he didn't want to disappoint them. He forced himself to be very broad because people would ask questions concerning the Bible, genetics, astronomy, physics, geology, or chemistry. Dr. Brown's training as an engineer gave him the tools to explore many disciplines. Engineers ask questions and look for realistic solutions. By definition, engineering—sometimes called applied science—deals with making science useful to people. And that is exactly what Dr. Brown did in his seminars.

His main challenge was to present technical matters understandably to a general audience. He applied the same techniques he had used when he taught math and walked his students through complicated equations. He used demonstrations and simple thought experiments to get his points across.

Dr. Brown's purpose in debating evolutionists is to try to get the real scientific evidence aired. A month ahead of time he sends a summary of everything he plans to say so that the evolutionist will be prepared. If necessary, Dr. Brown is willing to be embarrassed in a public forum if an opponent can catch him saying something wrong. Then he will be able to correct it, and his case is strengthened. Dr. Brown does not have contempt or disdain for those who believe in evolution. On the contrary, he has great compassion for them, because he was once in their shoes.

In his debates, he never uses the word *prove.* Unlike mathematics, science cannot prove something because all the evidence is not in. But he can raise or lower the plausibility of an idea. So the debate topic is simply "Does the scientific evidence favor evolution or creation?"

For seminars, Dr. Brown traveled across the United States and Canada driving a van and pulling a trailer full of seminar props. He received hundreds of invitations to speak at schools or on radio and television, but to save travel time, he generally accepted only those in the city hosting the seminar. One school appearance near Seattle was vigorously opposed by the American Civil Liberties Union (ACLU), an organization famous for its antibiblical efforts. His appearance generated a media ruckus throughout the western United States. When Dr. Brown showed up to speak and saw the reporters gathered, he smiled at the many TV cameras and said, "I want to thank the ACLU for doing such a good job of promoting this program."

The seminar work was encouraging. Dr. Brown was surprised to see what an effective preevangelistic tool the creation science topic is for unbelievers. Many people have told him they had a real problem with origins, and they did not believe the Bible was credible. But the seminars removed those obstacles. For some, this confidence in the Bible leads to the understanding that Scripture is reliable and pertinent. For others, it leads to salvation.

Crossroads

The seminar program was gaining ground until another creationist organization published an inaccurate account of Dr. Brown's work. Unfortunately, there has been much division within the creation movement and instead of concentrating their criticism on the opposition—the theistic evolutionists and the atheistic evolutionists—they have splintered into factions and often undermine each other's work. This hostility from fellow creationists has baffled Dr. Brown. It usually turns out that these critics have not bothered to study his hydroplate theory. They are just repeating what they heard someone else say.

Since the interest in seminars was waning, Dr. Brown saw no need to remain in Chicago. He was there because it was centrally located for his seminar travels. So in 1985, he moved his family to Phoenix, Arizona, where they could be closer to his parents. This was a discouraging time in his life as he wondered how he would support his family and what he would do next.

He decided to devote himself to studying geology from the evolutionists' perspective. He realized that most creationists don't study what the evolutionists are saying—seeing their reasoning and going through their calculations. He knew that a good lawyer knows the other case as well as the opposing lawyer knows it. A solid knowledge of geology would help him build a stronger case for creation.

So Peggy found a teaching job, and Walt signed up to study geology at Arizona State University. Dr. Robert S. Dietz, one of the world's leading geologists, taught there. Several years earlier in 1981, Dr. Brown had given a lecture on creation at Arizona State after the university had been unable to find an evolutionist debater. Days before the lecture, Dr. Dietz asked if he could comment after the lecture. He talked for ten minutes giving his reasons why he thought Dr. Brown was wrong. Then Dr. Brown challenged him to a written, purely scientific debate—no religion allowed. Earlier that day when Dr. Brown had had lunch with Dr. Dietz, Dr. Dietz had flatly refused to participate in a written debate. But now that he was in front of this large audience, he agreed. The audience applauded, and the newspaper featured the upcoming written debate.

Dr. Brown and Dr. Dietz exchanged a few cordial phone calls, working out the rules of the written debate. A month later, though, Dr. Dietz called. "I've tried writing something on this," he said, "and there is no way you can avoid religion. I can't do it."

"Are you backing out, Dr. Dietz?"

"I guess so," he said. "You can't deal with the subject without getting into religion."

"You sure can," Dr. Brown said. "I will." But Dr. Dietz backed out. (Since then, no evolutionist has taken up Dr. Brown's well-known offer for a written, publishable, purely scientific debate.)

Learning geology

Now that Dr. Brown would be walking the halls of the geology department, he decided he had better say hello to Dr. Dietz. By now, Dr. Brown knew exactly who Robert S. Dietz was. He was the leading atheist of the Southwest, completely hostile to creationists. He was also a world-famous geologist, one of the founders of the plate tectonic theory— one of the most significant theories of the twentieth century in the opinion of most scientists.

Dr. Brown went to Dr. Dietz's office and told him he was there to learn geology from Dr. Dietz's perspective. Oddly enough, that was the beginning of their friendship. Dr. Dietz offered to meet with Dr. Brown each Wednesday afternoon for several hours of discussion. They spent hundreds of hours discussing geology, comparing Dr. Dietz's plate tectonic theory and Dr. Brown's hydroplate theory. After their private sessions, they went down to the Wednesday afternoon geology forum and listened to a visiting geology speaker. Sometimes Dr. Dietz would invite Dr. Brown out to eat with the guest speaker.

In private, Dr. Dietz would give straight, honest answers. He would say things that he would never repeat publicly. When he saw a draft of Dr. Brown's book, he went through every point and acknowledged, "Yes . . . that's a problem for evolution. Well, we might have an answer to this point. Yes . . . there are gaps in the fossil record."

But when they were on radio programs together as creationist versus evolutionist, Dr. Dietz couldn't be trusted. Once Dr. Brown brought up the gaps in the fossil record. "Oh, that's not a problem at all," Dr. Dietz said. "We've got lots of intermediate forms."

During the commercial break, when Dr. Brown reminded Dr. Dietz that he *knew* there were many gaps, Dr. Deitz just laughed.

Geology

Dr. Brown spent several years studying geology. His background in engineering gave him a strong grasp of the math and physics involved in geological processes. He found that while geologists are skilled at describing what they see, most don't pause to figure out the mechanics and the feasibility of their theories. They talk about long periods of time and think that the sheer amount of time glosses over the mechanical difficulties of what they are describing. They don't concentrate on energy, forces, causes, and effects. But Dr. Brown brought a fresh mindset to his study of geology. He thought as an engineer, a mathematician firmly grounded in physics.

There is also a not-so-subtle arrogance in the entrenched geology establishment. They resent an "outsider" intruding in their field. This sounds similar to the criticism that Lord Kelvin received when he waded into the geological age controversy with the geologists of his day. Interestingly, the founders of modern geology, men who have contributed greatly to conventional geological thinking, were not even trained as geologists.[10]

Since the 1800s, geologists have tried to rule out *all* global catastrophes. Actually, they were opposed to the Bible, but they didn't want to seem closed-minded by disallowing only a global flood; so they ruled out all catastrophes. They proposed a principle of gradualism (uniformitarianism) that said only gradual processes going on today could tell us about the past. But by ignoring the possibility of a global catastrophe, they have stifled true study of the facts.

Grand Canyon

Dr. Brown lived near the Grand Canyon and frequently took trips to study it. He also studied the Grand Canyon with a leading expert at Arizona State, but this professor preferred not to deal with the origin of the canyon. Dr. Brown often pondered the mechanism that must have formed this great canyon, one of the seven wonders of the natural world. He studied maps of Utah and Arizona and suspected that a huge lake, or a series of lakes, had breached their natural boundaries and carved the canyon in a few weeks. He realized that a fault had to be in a certain place if he was correct, but the state geologist, a man Dr. Brown once had supper with, checked his files and found no fault was there. (A fault is a crack in the ground along which the opposite sides have slipped in relation to each other.)

"This is going to ruin Meg's wedding"

Dr. Brown became very excited when he found an obscure geologic map that showed a fault there—"19-mile fault" it was called. (Now, some jokingly call it "Walt's Fault.") He wanted to go right away and see the fault and trace it from one cliff system to the other. The family was preparing for his daughter's wedding, so no one could go with him. His son begged him not to go alone. He had been in this area before with his dad and knew it was a dangerous, unforgiving place.

But Dr. Brown wouldn't listen. He had to go see this fault right away. He kissed Peggy goodbye early the next morning and told her to ask the park rangers to send out a search aircraft if he wasn't back by noon the third day. He arrived at the canyon at sunrise and stopped at the park ranger's office where he filled out the forms to get permission to go into the "backcountry."

He parked his van near the rim of Ryder Canyon, a remote side canyon of the Grand Canyon. He soon found the fault he was looking for, but he wanted to trace it from one cliff system, down across the Colorado River, through Ryder Canyon, and up to the cliff system on the other side. He worked his way along the fault, down a deep slit in the ground, and descended into Ryder Canyon. He was loaded with his backpack, his camera, and his drinking water. He had brought gallons of water—more than the park rangers recommended. He spent a strenuous day taking pictures and exploring along the dangerously steep side of the canyon.

Late that hot June afternoon, he decided to head back. He had taken longer than he intended because he was so fascinated by what he was discovering. His water had run out hours before, and he was very thirsty. He turned around, found the slit, and headed back up. But after half a mile, the slit came to a dead end. It was a box canyon, not the incline he remembered coming down. *What went wrong?* he thought. *How did I ever get here?*

Several times he retraced his steps and tried to find where he had made the wrong turn, but he couldn't figure out what had happened. *Am I losing my mind?* he asked himself. He walked back and forth in the box canyon, wondering how he was going to get out.

It seemed that he was not going to find where he had made the wrong turn. So he considered two options. Should he lie down in the shade, try to minimize his growing dehydration, and spend the night in the canyon, hoping that the rescue aircraft would spot him late the next day? Or should he try to retrace his path along a very strenuous, steep slope and risk falling off a cliff? By now, his tongue was sticking to the sides of his cheeks, and his legs were shaking from dehydration.

He thought about his daughter's wedding in a couple of days. *If I don't get out of here, this is really going to mess up Meg's wedding.* He thought of Psalm 23 as he paced back and forth, and the words "Yea, though I walk through the valley of the shadow of death" began to take on a grim reality. He went through the psalm many times and found comfort in the phrase "for thou art with me."

I need to find a way out, he decided. In his backpack was fifty feet of rope that he had purchased at a hardware store several days before. He took the rope out to see whether he could use it to get out of this canyon. He saw an overhanging rock and thought that perhaps he could hook the center of the rope around it. After several throws, the rope finally hooked around the rock. Then he grabbed both ends of the rope, put his feet on the side of the canyon, and "walked" up the vertical side. When he got out of the box canyon, he looked around, and everything made sense. Thirty feet away was the parallel slit he had gone down. An hour later, he rested by his van, drinking water and thanking the Lord for making a way out of this valley of the shadow of death.

He got home in the wee hours of the morning. Peggy woke up and asked how it went. When he told her what had happened, she said, "Walt Brown! You have to promise me that you will *never* do that again!"

"I promise," he said solemnly. He knew that he had been unwise to go exploring alone. He had been so excited about the fault that he had disregarded the Ranger buddy system, always to be with a friend in case one needs help. But his other Ranger training had helped him get out.

In 1988, Dr. Brown confirmed his theory about the origin of the Grand Canyon with other field studies. The huge lakes, whose waters suddenly broke through their natural dam and carved the Grand Canyon after the flood, no longer exist. But northeast of the canyon Dr. Brown found unmistakable traces of the water and its rapid escape.[11]

In the Beginning: Compelling Evidence for Creation and the Flood
Dr. Brown's move to Phoenix was a crucial turning point in his life. If he had continued with the seminar work full-time, as he had originally hoped, he wouldn't have had time to study geology and work on his book. Although his seminars had been useful in getting out the creation message, Dr. Brown's book has reached a much wider audience.

He paced back and forth, wondering how to get out of the canyon.

His book, *In the Beginning: Compelling Evidence for Creation and the Flood*, more closely resembles an encyclopedia than any other kind of book. Here he summarizes the evidences for creation and explains his hydroplate theory of the flood. Based on this theory, he has found that twenty-five major features of the earth can be explained logically. Scientists who have taken the time to understand the theory have often converted to flood geology, because Dr. Brown gives them a scientifically acceptable approach that is intellectually satisfying. Scientists are struck by the diverse problems the hydroplate theory solves.[12]

Dr. Brown has a vital function in the creation ministry. He keeps current with the latest scientific data and analyzes the implications for creation and publishes it in a format that lay readers can understand. Early on he decided not to write a lot of books. He felt he needed to improve and expand his original book that had started out as a guide for those attending his seminars. In this guide he had summarized the evidences for creation and against evolution so that people weren't frantically taking notes. Then people who hadn't been to the seminar started asking for copies. So every few years, Dr. Brown has had to publish a new edition. Each edition has been larger and more popular.

In the Beginning has now reached the seventh edition and is widely in demand because it is the most complete reference work covering the broad subject of origins from a scientific standpoint.[13] For scientists who want to follow his calculations, he has included technical notes explaining how he arrived at his conclusions. But the pictures and graphics make it interesting for young people, and the explanations are understandable to lay people. The entire book is meticulously footnoted so that a reader can delve into the sources and not just take Dr. Brown at his word.

His book is on his website, and anyone can access the complete volume from there or print it out at no cost.[14] When people ask Dr. Brown how he can earn any money if he makes his book free to everyone, he replies, "My purpose is not to make money. My purpose is to get the information out. Nothing could make me happier than if this evolution problem ended and I was unemployed. I would probably take up golf again."

Dr. Brown receives much mail from people who have read his book or visited his website. About five percent of the feedback is negative, and Dr. Brown carefully considers each hostile letter to see whether it is pointing out an error of his. If it does, he is grateful for the helpful criticism. But the vast majority of the mail is encouraging and motivates him to continue with his ministry.

One day while opening the mail, Dr. Brown found a letter from Hai Lam, his friend from Vietnam! Thirty-three years after Walt Brown left Vietnam, Hai found him! He had suffered a great deal because of his involvement with the Americans. After two failed attempts to escape Vietnam, Hai did finally make it to America and was living in California with his wife and three children.

In his letter to the Browns, Hai enclosed a water-stained picture that he had kept all those years. It was a picture of himself and Dr. Brown standing in the village of Phouc Hiep. A few months later, Hai sat in the Brown's living room, smiling at his long lost friend, saying, "I so happy. I so happy."

Too busy to retire

Dr. Brown is the proud grandfather of eleven grandchildren and enjoys a close relationship with his four children, his parents, and his large extended family. He lives in Phoenix, Arizona, the home of many retirees. He is at the age when he could retire and spend his time traveling or playing golf like many of his generation. But he is much too busy to sit back and relax. Every day he is in his office, reading science journals, researching, corresponding, and meeting with visitors. He is always adding to his book, strengthening and clarifying his case.[15]

His wife Peggy has always been a supportive companion, but now she has become his most valuable asset in his work. When she saw that he was getting buried by his correspondence and not having time to devote to study, she resigned her teaching job to take care of his office work.

A different battle

Where is the creation-evolution controversy headed? According to Dr. Brown, "The battle will be won by 'grass roots' science education, not in courts, legislatures, boards of education, or church councils. Yes, today evolutionists generally control higher education, science journals, and the media. But the scientific evidence overwhelmingly supports creation and a global flood. Throughout the history of science, whenever controversies have raged, the side with scientific evidence has always prevailed. Our task, then, is educating the public. What we have to do to win this battle, is not to preach to people who already believe as we do, but to people who have questions, people who disagree."[16]

Dr. Brown continues to "fight the good fight of faith." He marvels at how God uses every experience in our lives to equip us for His service. Looking back, he realizes that West Point, Ranger School, and MIT each taught important lessons for his present work. Who would have ever thought that infantry training had anything to do with telling the world about the Creator? Yet the skills and discipline he learned from his military training have prepared him to be a soldier in a different battle. He is a living example of God's warrior in Ephesians 6, strong in the Lord and in the power of His might, equipped with the whole armor of God so that he can stand against the wiles of the devil.

---

[1] He bought *Thorndike's Most Frequently Used Words*, a book that categorized words by how frequently they appeared in print. With it, Walt quickly spotted the most frequently used words that he didn't know, and he marked them in his unabridged dictionary with a paper clip. He kept 100 paper clips in his dictionary, and every day he flipped to each paper clip and studied the words. He added new words as soon as he mastered the old ones.

[2] National Science Foundation Graduate Fellowships are awarded to study physical, biological, and social sciences; mathematics; engineering; and the history and philosophy of science. The fellowships lead to a master's or doctoral degree that is research-based.

[3] Pronounced "Fu-KEP."

[4] Walter T. Brown, Jr., *In the Beginning: Compelling Evidence for Creation and the Flood,* seventh edition (Phoenix, Arizona: Center for Scientific Creation, 2001), p. 269.

[5] Jim Lee was a Seventh-Day Adventist. The Adventists were very strong in the creation movement, long before it became popular in mainstream Christianity. They were also active in the hunt for Noah's Ark.

[6] See Dr. Brown's book, *In the Beginning: Compelling Evidence for Creation and the Flood,* for answers to these questions.

[7] For more parallels between Christ and the Ark, see *In the Beginning,* p. 284.

[8] The Army is more manpower oriented and the Air Force is more technically oriented. The Air Force grew out of the Army. It was the Army Air Corps during WWII.

[9] The Army and Air Force have the same rank designations.

[10] James Hutton, considered the father of uniformitarian geology, trained as a medical doctor. Sir Charles Lyell, who popularized the idea of long geological ages, studied law.

[11] For over a hundred years, geologists have known that if a large lake begins to erode a point on its rim, canyons can be carved in days. Another geologist had similar ideas. He published Dr. Brown's data on the elevation, name, location, and breach point of Grand Lake without proper crediting and then backdated his publication to a year before Dr. Brown's publication. This geologist also claimed that an even earlier, obscure publication of his contained this explanation for the Grand Canyon. It does not contain this explanation. The claims of this geologist have caused confusion as to who first published the data and who first set forth this explanation for the formation of

the Grand Canyon. Careful examination of the evidence indicates that Dr. Brown was the first.

¹² Brown, p. i from endorsement page and p. v from the Preface.

¹³ Brown, p. i from endorsement page.

¹⁴ Dr. Brown's website is www.creationscience.com. Brad Anderson, a science education major and now a computer expert, set up the website because he wanted more people to know about Dr. Brown's work.

¹⁵ Dr. Brown has a tremendous range of contacts. He met many influential people when he worked at the Air Force Academy, the Air War College, and Benét Labs. He finds that other scientists are happy to talk to him when they see his interest, even though he is a creationist.

¹⁶ Brown, p. v from the Preface and personal communication with the author.

CONCLUSION

Several common themes stand out in the lives of these Christian men of science. First of all, they were rightly oriented to the study of science. There is nothing inherently wrong with the study of science, but it can be carried out in a correct way or an incorrect way. Since God told man to "subdue the earth," the pursuits of science are both legitimate and necessary. The scientist should study God's creation so that he can master it and use it for our good and God's glory. A broad view of science history shows that the sovereign God is at work, directing the development of science and technology to aid in building His church and preaching His gospel.

The correct study of science—the way these men studied science—brings glory to God, not to the scientist. It declares God's wisdom, not man's wisdom. As the student of science describes God's wonders in creation, he magnifies God's power and deity. Scientists who are Christians are, in fact, the best-prepared to interpret God's creation correctly, the best-equipped to see God's glorious revelation in His Creation. But even with a correct study of science, there is a limit to how much we can learn about God in nature. No human left to himself with only nature to guide him would be able to guess God's plan of redemption. Only in God's Word can we see Christ and His work of redemption revealed. It is refreshing to see that the scientists in this book understood the limitations of God's revelation in nature. They never elevated scientific revelation to take the place of the Bible. The Bible for them was God's supreme, inspired, authoritative word. They clearly saw that their scientific studies supported the truths of the Bible, but they didn't need science to prove God's Word.

In contrast to the God-centered science of the men in this book, there is definitely a wrong way to study science. Unfortunately, for the most part, modern man now studies science this way—without considering God. Since the discipline of science demands keen, logical, analytical minds, many people assume that scientists have the definitive word in any discussion, even in matters of faith. When today's scientists exclude God by saying that evolution explains the universe, uninformed people blindly follow them. But taking God out of the study of science has led to abundant misinterpretations. Scientists are only human and are subject to faulty observation and prejudice, which can lead to misinterpretation of evidence. As a result, man no longer sees the wonderful design God created into the universe and has substituted an evolutionary explanation for what he sees. Man has always had the tendency to worship the creation, rather than the Creator, and today it is no different. Now modern man is so busy with his cars, televisions, and computers (the products of advanced scientific technology) that he has no time for God. He is still worshiping material things instead of the Creator.

The men featured in this book studied science correctly, and they made significant contributions. But their scientific work is not the most important theme in their lives. The most outstanding feature of their lives is the fact that they believed the gospel of Christ revealed in God's Word. But what exactly is this gospel that these men believed? It is the good news that Christ has paid for our sins. These men saw themselves as sinners, deeply in need of God's forgiveness. They repented of their sins and trusted Christ as their Savior from sin. This is tremendously good news for all of us, no matter what vocation we have. No longer do we have to live under God's wrath, because Christ's sacrifice provided perfect payment for our sins. Now, those who repent and believe in Christ are new creatures, free from the bondage of sin and free to enjoy fellowship with God. All of us—plumbers, housewives, accountants, biophysicists, children, young people, and adults—need to have our sins forgiven. No matter what intellectual equipment we have, we all have the same basic need for Christ's forgiveness. At the end of life, when all is said and done, our talents and intellect will not matter. The only important thing will be whether we have looked to Christ to save us.

What would these men want from us, the readers? Would they want us to be in awe of their intellectual abilities and their contributions? No. They understood how temporary this kind of recognition is. They would want us to follow their example and look to Christ for salvation. They would want us to know "the mystery of God, and of the Father, and of Christ; in whom are hid all the treasures of wisdom and knowledge" (Colossians 2:2,3).

A Word About the Author

I believe that my dad was uniquely qualified to write this book because he was both a humble Christian and a competent scientist. He was born in Syracuse, New York, in 1932. His mother was a professional pianist, and his father was a composer and a piano professor at Syracuse University. The Mulfingers carefully cultivated the intellectual and musical talents of their three sons. Dad studied piano with his parents when he was very young and then started playing cello when he was thirteen years old. His talent was such that his training included lessons with the renowned cellist Orlando Cole.

His brilliant scientific mind was evident as a teenager. He had earned his ham radio operator's license by the time he was fourteen, and he would spend all his money to buy parts to build radios and other electronic equipment. Once he installed a microphone in his parents' music room, hiding it inside a cut-out encyclopedia. With this, he secretly made recordings of his mother as she taught piano.

Dad occasionally attended gatherings of shortwave radio operators. They would camp by a lake, and each man would bring along his own radio equipment. They often had to install antenna wires to get better reception. One night Dad climbed a tall tree to put up his antenna. As he was pulling the antenna tight, it crossed the path of a live electrical wire, which he hadn't seen because it was dark. When his antenna touched the wire, it emitted a terrific spark, and all the electricity at the houses around the lake went off instantly. There was a moment of deathly silence; then one of his friends on the ground said slowly, "George? Are you still alive?" He had sustained a shock, but he was unhurt. (Later, when he became a Christian, he recounted this incident and said that God had miraculously spared his life.)

As a teenager, he attended church with his parents fairly regularly, and he was the Sunday school pianist for five years. But, unfortunately, at this liberal church he learned to question the Bible. The minister convinced him that the miracles of the Bible were not really miracles. If that is the case, Dad thought, then how can I believe the rest of the Bible? He decided that he couldn't believe God at all since the Bible wasn't true—it contained fairy tales.

When he went to Syracuse University in 1949 to study chemistry, he was a brilliant student. One of his professors said, "If you can't prove anything with an equation or a slide rule, don't believe it." Obviously, Dad couldn't prove God's existence that way, so he decided that God doesn't exist. He joined a clique of atheists on the campus. They said that religion is childish and that they had matured beyond that foolishness.

One day an atheist friend pointed out a fellow from the Inter-Varsity Christian Fellowship. "There goes a fundamentalist," he said in scorn.

"What's that?" Dad asked.

"That's someone who believes the Bible is God's Word."

Dad shook his head in disgust. "It's hard to believe anyone is dumb enough to believe that!" he said.

His intellectual pride was well-founded. He was always at the top of his class, and he graduated *summa cum laude*. By the time he entered graduate school, he was a complete atheist. He had the pride of an atheist and was sure that he didn't need God. But that changed when he was hospitalized during grad school. His roommate, Pete, was a Christian from an Ivy League university. Dad was convinced by then that faith in Christ was for the mentally weak. But Pete was a real intellectual, the type Dad always admired, so he listened to him. Pete talked with Dad about Jesus Christ and the claims He had made for Himself. They discussed whether or not Jesus fulfilled Old Testament prophecies.

"Jesus could have just read the Old Testament prophecies and then fulfilled them," Dad said.

"But how did he arrange to be born in Bethlehem?" Pete asked. "Micah the prophet predicted that the Messiah would be born in Bethlehem—some seven hundred years before his birth." Then Pete mentioned Christ's resurrection and other prophecies that came to pass after the death of Christ, things over which no ordinary man would have had control.

Those fulfilled prophecies made Dad think. He started to read the Bible that his family had brought to the hospital for him. Pete's daily witness and the reading of God's Word were a potent combination. The Holy Spirit opened Dad's eyes, and he saw that he was one of the worst sinners because he had completely denied God. One night in March of 1955, he slipped out of bed when everyone else in the hospital was asleep. He knelt by his bed and asked God to forgive his sins.

Soon after that, he renewed his acquaintance with a childhood friend, Joan Wade. She had graduated from Eastman School of Music with a degree in violin and had recently come to Christ through the testimony of the Inter-Varsity group on campus. Dad had been praying for a Christian wife, and she was the answer to his prayers. They fell in love and were married a year later.

They found a Bible-believing church and began to learn what walking with Christ meant. Dad was still a young Christian, but he knew so much about the Bible that they soon asked him to be the teacher of the young adult Sunday school class. From then on, he was often asked to teach Sunday school, and he later served as an elder in his church.

Dad demonstrated early on that professional prestige was not important to him. When the family was still young, Dad relocated to Bob Jones University in South Carolina because he wanted to use his talents to serve the Lord in a Christian ministry. In the move he gave up prestige and salary, but he never seemed to mind.

By this time, he had completed the course work for a combined Ph.D. in physics and chemistry—an unusual degree that was offered only at Syracuse University. When it came time to write his dissertation, his adviser died. At that point, the administration unexpectedly changed the requirements and said that Dad would have to take additional course work. This would mean moving the family back to New York. At that time there were five children in the family, and they couldn't find housing. Perhaps if he had been more ambitious and proud, he would have left the family in South Carolina and found a way to get the work done. But he firmly believed that professional success is meaningless if it is achieved at the expense of one's family. So for the rest of his life, his title remained "Mr. Mulfinger." But many people instinctively felt that he should be called "Dr. Mulfinger."

Scientific work

Dad cultivated a broad background in the fields of science teaching, scientific journalism, and research. He taught many subjects—physics, chemistry, astronomy, geology, logic, and philosophy. His areas of research were experimental electronics, Biblical science investigation, and the history of science. He received research grants from the National Science Foundation to study the desalination of seawater and from the Creation Research Society to investigate the precipitation of calcium carbonate dissolved in water. He undertook this research with several other creation scientists, and their results were important in interpreting dripstone formations in caves. Their conclusion was that dissolved limestone could produce stalactites and stalagmites in caves much more quickly than scientists previously thought.

He also studied astronomy and was an expert stargazer. One evening he noticed something new in the sky. He was the first in the Western Hemisphere to spot this nova, but a Japanese astronomer had spotted it a day earlier.

Creation work

Dad was one of the early members of the Creation Research Society, during the first decade when it was certainly not a status symbol to be associated with the creation movement. He was one of the few astronomers in those days who was willing to speak out strongly for creation, and he often lectured and wrote about the fallacies of the different theories of stellar and galactic evolution. He taught logic, and he could quickly spot the logical errors in the evolutionists' thinking. He complained that astronomical theories had such a short life expectancy that when he was critiquing these stellar evolutionary theories, he had the distinct feeling that he was trying to nail Jell-O to a wall. He contributed chapters to several creation books and wrote several articles for the *Creation Research Society Quarterly*, the first technical journal for creationists. For a time he served as chairman of the Publications Committee for the society and edited their monograph on astronomy. He also wrote two tracts that are still used today, "How Did the Earth Get Here?" and "The Flood and the Fossils."

The evolution issue concerned him greatly because he understood just how dangerous the teaching of evolution is. He carefully scrutinized all the books that came into the house and even took White-Out to our books and changed the "millions of years" to "thousands of years." It was a long time before he found an encyclopedia set that he would have in the house. It wasn't completely without evolution, but from his research he concluded that it had the least in it.

He was very upset that there were Christian schools using textbooks that taught evolution as fact. He often said that "someone should do something about this." He turned out to be that "someone." He certainly didn't have the time to add major textbook writing projects to his schedule as a university professor, but since that someone else never showed up, he decided to do it. Along with Dr. Emmett Williams, he organized the projects and found coauthors to work with him. When he and Dr. Williams finished the first textbook, *Physical Science for Christian Schools*, Dad chose Revelation 4:11 as his dedication verse: "Thou art worthy, O Lord, to receive glory and honour and power: for thou hast created all things, and for thy pleasure they are and were created."

This high school science textbook was the first textbook published by the Bob Jones University Press. Dad coauthored an entire series of creationist science textbooks, ranging from the elementary school level all the way to the high school level. Years after the other authors had moved to computers, Dad still wrote his first drafts in longhand on his clipboard, using his black Bic pen and his trusty bottle of White-Out.

Many of the works to which he contributed contained brief biographies of Christian men of science. He wanted others to know the amazing testimonies of some of the great names in science. He had a solid grasp of the history of science, both of the men and the theories, and he believed it was important to understand the personalities behind the scientific theories.

Achievements

Dad was recognized nationally as a scientist and as a musician. He appeared in an impressive list of Who's Who books, ranging from *Leaders in American Science* all the way to *International Who's Who in Music.* These books gave his long list of achievements as a scientist, university professor, textbook author, and musician. But when he introduced himself, he skipped all his professional credentials and just said that he was the father of eleven children. He considered his eleven children to be his greatest accomplishment. Dad did the usual things that good fathers do—attend painful recitals and boring ball games, keep track of schoolwork and music lessons—but multiplied by eleven. To Dad and Mom, good parenting was not a method or formula. It was a matter of genuine Christian character. What you are in the home is what you really are. There is no faking.

Dad didn't delegate our Christian training to the Sunday school teacher. Each evening after supper, he gathered the entire family for family devotions. We suspended all activities and schoolwork for half an hour while we read the Bible and prayed. Often during devotions he would read us missionary stories or the biography of his great-grandfather, who had been a German Methodist circuit-riding preacher. Dad had painstakingly translated this biography from German and written a children's version to read to us.

As far as I know, my father never missed a church service, even though he was an incredibly busy man. For almost twenty years, Dad and Mom played the cello and violin along with the hymns at church because they wanted to use their musical abilities to worship the Lord. They wrote original hymn arrangements long before it became popular with other Christian musicians.

I hear parents say today that they can't get their teenagers to come to church with them. It never occurred to us children to refuse to go to church. Perhaps if Dad's faith had been for Sunday only, we would have rebelled. But his faith permeated every area of his life and was so genuine and attractive that we wanted to be like him. To children, the true measure of a man is not the mark that he makes in his public life. It is the way he behaves himself in private with only his family watching. What we saw of my father's private life gave us the greatest respect for him.

Professor of science and music

Dad was my cello teacher and my physics teacher. As a professor, I found him to be the same as a father—funny and compassionate. He was a softie and known to extend deadlines for overwhelmed students. His former students remember him with admiration and fondness because he made his subject matter understandable and enjoyable. His lectures were full of his dry humor. He used to say that his idea of a controlled experiment was one that stayed off the ceiling. To illustrate the remarkable faith it takes to believe in evolution, Dad made up this humorous definition of hydrogen: "Hydrogen is a colorless, odorless, tasteless gas, which, given a few billion years or so, turns into people." He enjoyed the Murphy's Law brand of humor and had invented several "Mulfinger Extensions" to the laws. ("Any material can conduct electricity if you get the voltage across it high enough.")

He continued to teach cello and perform in chamber groups and orchestras throughout his life. His performing career included principal cellist of the Syracuse Symphony, cellist with the Krasner String Quartet, and principal cellist with the university orchestra where he taught.

Dad never forced us to follow his footsteps and study science or music. He waited until we showed an interest in an instrument, and then he would encourage us to pursue it. "Children should learn an instrument," he would tell other parents, "so that they can stay out of trouble when they are teenagers." Most teenage mischief comes from boredom, he thought, so he kept us busy and content with daily practicing and music activities. Eventually, all eleven children learned to play an instrument, and we formed a family orchestra. Today, all of the children have graduated from the university where he taught. And we still play music—all play for church and several have become professional musicians.

Home life

Dad was strict and old-fashioned in a good sense. He never went to movies or allowed a television in the house. For entertainment he played board games with us. On special occasions he would sit down and tell us stories—original detective stories with elaborate plots. These stories featured a family that owned a private UFO that could travel anywhere in the world in a few hours.

Dad was humble enough to sign himself up for dish duty twice a week so that my mother wouldn't have to wash dishes in the evenings. And he took the trash out every day—a significant chore in a household of thirteen people. He referred to it as his "trash ministry."

He never outgrew his teenage love for electronics and radios. The back half of his desk was full of his radio equipment that he used as a ham radio operator. He installed a speaker system in the entire house, and he could sit at his desk and make announcements to the entire family with the flick of a switch.

When I was in college, I noticed that Dad had less energy, but he brushed it off and said he was just getting old. We never imagined that he was terminally ill. He was diagnosed with colon and liver cancer in the spring of 1987. He still taught that fall, but with a lighter schedule. He died a few days before Christmas of 1987, when he was fifty-five years old. He had shown us how a Christian lives and how a Christian dies. He had used his many talents to serve the Lord faithfully, never seeking the limelight. His godly influence lives on in our family, and the influence of his science textbook ministry continues. Now it is gratifying to see his *Christian Men of Science* finally come into print.

The artist, Mark Mulfinger, is the third oldest of George Mulfinger's eleven children. Mark holds a master's degree in art. He specializes in oils, linocuts, and batiks. He has a studio in Greenville, South Carolina, where he lives with his wife and three young children.

Julia Mulfinger Orozco is the sixth child of George Mulfinger. She holds a degree in Humanities and has taught English, elementary school, and music. She is now a homemaker living in Mexico where her husband pastors a church.

Bibliography

Agassi, Joseph. *Faraday as a Natural Philosopher*. Chicago: University of Chicago Press, 1971.

Allen, Donald S., and Richard J. Ordway. *Physical Science*. 2nd ed. Princeton, N. J.: D. Van Nostrand Co. 1968

Arons, Arnold B. *Development of Concepts of Physics*. Reading, Mass: Addison-Wesley, 1965.

Austin, Steven A., editor. *Grand Canyon: Monument to Catastrophe*. Santee, California: Institute for Creation Research, 1994.

Barker, William P. *Who's Who in Church History*. Grand Rapids, Michigan: Baker Book House, 1969.

Baumgardt, Carola. *Johannes Kepler: Life and Letters*. New York: Philosophical Library, 1951.

Bell, E. T. *Men of Mathematics*. New York: Simon & Schuster, 1937.

Bixby, William. *Great Experimenters*. New York: David McKay Co., 1964.

Blow, Michael and Robert P. Multhauf. *Men of Science and Invention*. New York: Harper and Row, 1960.

Bolton, Sarah K. *Famous Men of Science*. New York: Thomas Y. Crowell Co., 1960.

Boreham, F. W. *A Handful of Stars*. London: The Epworth Press, 1930.

Boyle, Robert. *The Sceptical Chymist*. London: J.M. Dent & Sons Ltd., 1911. (Original in 1661.)

Boyle, Robert. *The Works of the Honourable Robert Boyle*. Vol. 1, to which is prefixed the life of the author. Bristol, England: Thoemmes Press, 1999. Reprinted from the 1772 edition.

Brewster, David. Report to the British Association for the Advancement of Science, 1844.

Brown, Walter T., Jr. *In the Beginning: Compelling Evidence for Creation and the Flood*. 7th ed. Phoenix, Arizona: Center for Scientific Creation, 2001.

Butterfield, Herbert. *The Origins of Modern Science*. New York: Collier Books, 1962.

Cairns, Alan. *Dictionary of Theological Terms*. Greenville, S.C.: Ambassador-Emerald, Intl., 1998.

Campbell, Lewis, and William Garnett. *The Life of James Clerk Maxwell*. London: Macmillan, 1882. Electronic version by James Rautio, Sonnet Software, Inc., 1997.

Cane, Philip. *Giants of Science*. New York: Pyramid Publications, 1962.

Caspar, Max. *Kepler*. London and New York: Abelard-Schuman, 1959.

Clark, Robert E. D. *The Christian Stake in Science*. Chicago: Moody Press, 1967.

Clark, Robert E. D. *The Universe—Plan or Accident*. London: Paternoster Press, 1961.

Conant, J.B. *Robert Boyle's Experiments in Pneumatics*. Cambridge, Mass.: Harvard University Press, 1950.

Crowther, J. G. *Men of Science*. New York: W.W. Norton & Co., 1936.

Davis, Audrey W. *Dr. Kelly of Hopkins: Surgeon, Scientist, Christian*. Baltimore: The John Hopkins Press, 1959.

de Vaucouleurs, Gerard. *Discovery of the Universe*. New York: Macmillan, 1957.

DeVries, John De. *Beyond the Atom*. Grand Rapids, Mich.: William B. Eerdmans Publishing Co., 1950.

Drummond, Robert J. *Outcasts of Rome or Four Foes of the Papacy*. London: Samuel Bagster & Sons, Ltd.

Dugan, James. *The Great Iron Ship*. New York: Harper and Brothers, 1953.

Erdman, Walter C. *Sources of Power in Famous Lives*. Nashville, Tenn.: Cokesbury Press, 1936.

Everitt, C.W.F. *James Clerk Maxwell: Physicist and Natural Philosopher*. New York: Charles Scribner's Sons, 1975.

Faraday, Michael. *The Chemical History of a Candle*. Atlanta, Georgia: Cherokee Publishing Company, 1993.

Fleming, John Ambrose. *Memories of a Scientific Life*. London: Marshall, Morgan & Scott. No date.

Gladstone, John H. *Michael Faraday*. New York: Harper & Brothers. No date.

Goldman, Martin. *The Demon in the Aether: The Story of James Clerk Maxwell*. Edinburgh: Paul Harris Publishing, 1983.

Gordon, Margaret Maria. *The Home Life of Sir David Brewster*. Edinburgh: Edmonston and Douglas, 1870.

Greene, Jay E., ed. *100 Great Scientists*. New York: Washington Square Press, 1964.

Hall, A. Rupert and Marie Boas Hall. *A Brief History of Science*. New York: Signet Science Library, 1964.

Hall, Marie Boas. "Robert Boyle." *Scientific American*, 217, No. 2 (August 1967), pp. 96-102.

Hawkins, Gerald S. *Splendor in the Sky*. New York: Harper & Brothers, 1961.

Hunter, Michael, ed. *Robert Boyle Reconsidered*. Cambridge: Cambridge University Press, 1994.

Hunter, Michael. "Casuistry in Action: Robert Boyle's Confessional Interviews with Gilbert Burnet and Edward Stillingfleet, 1691." *Journal of Ecclesiastical History*, 44, No.1, (January 1993).

Ihde, Aaron J. *The Development of Modern Chemistry.* New York: Harper & Row, 1964.

Jones, Bence. *The Life and Letters of Faraday.* 2 vols. London: Longmans, Green & Co., 1870.

Kelly, Dr. Howard A. "I Believe," tract printed by the Maryland Tract Society, Baltimore, Md. No date.

Kelly, Howard. *A Scientific Man and the Bible: A Personal Testimony.* New York: Harper & Brothers, 1925.

Koestler, Arthur. *The Watershed: A Biography of Johannes Kepler.* Garden City, N.Y.: Anchor Books, Doubleday and Co., 1960.

Latham, Jean Lee. *Trail Blazer of the Seas.* Boston, Mass.: Houghton Mifflin Co., 1956.

Latham, Jean Lee. *Carry On, Mr. Bowditch.* Boston, Mass.: Houghton Mifflin Co., 1955.

Latham, Jean Lee. *Young Man in a Hurry: The Story of Cyrus W. Field.* New York: Harper and Brothers, 1958.

Lewis, Charles Lee. *Matthew Fontaine Maury: The Pathfinder of the Seas.* Annapolis: The United States Naval Institute, 1927.

Lodge, Sir Oliver. *Pioneers of Science.* New York: Dover Publications, Inc., 1960. (From the 1926 edition, originally published in 1893 by Macmillan and Company)

Lubenow, Marvin L. *From Fish to Gish: Morris and Gish Confront the Evolutionary Establishment.* San Diego, California: CLP Publishers, 1983.

Mabee, Carleton. *The American Leonardo: A Life of Samuel F. B. Morse.* New York: Knopf, 1943.

MacDonald, D. K. C. *Faraday, Maxwell, and Kelvin.* Garden City, NY: Doubleday, 1964.

Marcus, Alan I. and Howard P. Segal. *Technology in America: A Brief History.* New York: Hardcourt Brace Jovanovich, Publishers, 1989.

Maury, Matthew Fontaine. *The Physical Geography of the Sea.* 8th ed. Cambridge, Mass.: The Belknap Press of Harvard Univ. Press, 1963.

Meyer, Jerome S. *The ABC of Physics.* New York: Pyramid Publications, 1962.

More, Louis Trenchard. *The Life and Works of The Honourable Robert Boyle.* Oxford: Oxford University Press, 1944.

Morris, Henry M. *A History of Modern Creationism.* First and second editions. San Diego, California: Master Book Publishers, 1984.

Morris, Henry M. *Biblical Cosmology and Modern Science.* Grand Rapids, Michigan: Baker Book House, 1970.

Morris, Henry M. *Biblical Creationism: What Each Book of the Bible Teaches about Creation and the Flood.* Grand Rapids, Michigan: Baker Books, 1993.

Morris, Henry M. *Defending the Faith: Upholding Biblical Christianity and the Genesis Record.* Green Forest, Arkansas: Master Books, 1999.

Morris, Henry M. *Many Infallible Proofs: Practical and Useful Evidences of Christianity.* San Diego: Creation-Life Publishers, 1974.

Morris, Henry M. *Men of Science, Men of God: Great Scientists Who Believed the Bible*. San Diego, California: Creation-Life Publishers, 1982.

Morris, Henry M., ed. *Scientific Creationism*. El Cajon, California: Master Books, 1974.

Morris, Henry M. *That Their Words May be Used Against Them: Quotes from Evolutionists Useful for Creationists*. San Diego, California: Institute for Creation Research, 1997.

Morris, Henry, M. *That You Might Believe*. Chicago: Good Books, Inc., 1946.

Morris, Henry M. *The Bible Has the Answer: Practical Biblical Discussions of 100 Frequent Questions*. Nutley, New Jersey: The Craig Press, 1971.

Morris, Henry M. *The Biblical Basis for Modern Science*. Grand Rapids, Michigan: Baker Book House, 1984.

Morris, Henry M. *The Genesis Record: A Scientific and Devotional Commentary on the Book of Beginnings*. Grand Rapids, Michigan: Baker Book House, 1976.

Morris, Henry M. *The God Who Is Real*. Green Forest, Arkansas: Master Books, 2000.

Morris, Henry M. *The Long War Against God: The History and Impact of The Creation/Evolution Conflict*. Green Forest, Arkansas: Master Books, 2000. (Original edition copyright 1989 by Baker Books.)

Morris, Henry M. *Age of an Amazing Book*. Grand Rapids, Michigan: Baker Book House, 1988.

Morris, Henry M. *The Revelation Record: A Scientific and Devotional Commentary on the Book of Revelation*. Wheaton, Illinois: Tyndale House Publishers and San Diego: Creation-Life Publishers, 1983.

Morris, Henry M. *The Troubled Waters of Evolution*. San Diego, California: Creation-Life Publishers, 1974.

Morris, Henry M. and Don Rohrer. *Decade of Creation*. San Diego, California: Creation-Life Publishers, 1981.

Morris, Henry M. and Duane T. Gish, eds. *The Battle for Creation: Act/Facts/Impacts/ Vol. 2*. San Diego, California: Creation-Life Publishers, 1976.

Morris, Henry M. and John C. Whitcomb. *The Genesis Flood: The Biblical Record and Its Scientific Implications*. Phillipsburg, N. J.: Presbyterian and Reformed Publishing, 1961.

Morris, Henry M. with John D. Morris. *Society and Creation*. Green Forest, Ark.: Master Books, 1996.

Morrison-Low, A.D. and J.R.R. Christie, eds. *Martyr of Science: Sir David Brewster 1781-1868*. Edinburgh: Royal Scottish Museum, 1984.

Morse, Edward Lind, ed., *Samuel F. B. Morse: His Letters and Journals*. Vol.1. New York: Da Capo Press, 1914, reprint 1973.

Mulfinger, George and Emmett L. Williams. *Physical Science for Christian Schools*. Greenville, S.C.: Bob Jones Univ. Press, 1974.

Mulfinger, George L., Jr., ed. *Design and Origins in Astronomy*. Norcross, Georgia: Creation Research Society Books, 1983.

Nickel, James. *Mathematics: Is God Silent?* Vallecito, CA: Ross House Books, 1990.

Numbers , Ronald L. *The Creationists: The Evolution of Scientific Creationism.* New York: Alfred A. Knopf, 1992.

Pastore, John O. *The Story of Communications.* New York, N.Y.: Macfadden-Bartell Corp., 1964.

Phillipson, Nicholas. "Sir David Brewster: Some Concluding Remarks," in Martyr of Science: *Sir David Brewster 1781-1868,* A.D. Morrison-Low and J.R.R. Christie, eds. Edinburgh: Royal Scottish Museum, 1984.

Prime, Samuel Irenaes. *The Life of Samuel F. B. Morse, LL.D., Inventor of the Electro-Magnetic Recording Telegraph.* New York: D. Appleton and Co., 1875.

Rice, John R., ed. *The Best of Billy Sunday.* Murfreesboro, Tenn.: Sword of the Lord Publishers, 1965.

Rousseau, Pierre. *Man's Conquest of the Stars.* New York: W. W. Norton & Co., 1961.

Runes, Dagobert D., ed. *Treasury of Word Science.* Paterson, N.J.: Littlefield, Adams and Co., 1962.

Sandfort, John F. *Heat Engines.* Garden City, N.Y.: Anchor Books, 1962.

Schaff, Philip. *The Creeds of Christendom.* New York: Harper & Brothers, 1877.

Sharlin, Harold Issadore. *Lord Kelvin the Dynamic Victorian.* University Park and London: The Pennsylvania State University Press, 1979.

Shiers, George, ed. *The Electric Telegraph: An Historical Anthology.* New York, N.Y.: Arno Press, 1977.

Siedel, James M. and Frank Siedel. *Pioneers in Science.* Boston, Mass.: Houghton Mifflin Co., 1968.

Small, Robert. *An Account of the Astronomical Discoveries of Kepler.* Madison, Wisconsin: University of Wisconsin Press, 1963.

The Defender's Study Bible with annotations prepared by Henry M. Morris. Grand Rapids, Michigan: Word Publishing, 1995.

Thompson, Silvanus P. *Life of Lord Kelvin.* London: Macmillan and Co., 1910.

Tiner, John Hudson. *Johannes Kepler: Giant of Faith and Science.* Milford, Michigan: Mott Media, 1977.

Tolstoy, Ivan. *James Clerk Maxwell: A Biography.* Edinburgh: Canongate, 1981.

Tyndall, John. *Faraday as an Experimenter.* New York: Thomas Y. Crowell Co., 1961.

Wertz, Richard W. and Dorothy C. Wertz. *Lying-In: A History of Childbirth in America.* New York: The Free Press, 1977.

Westfall, Richard S. *Science and Religion in Seventeenth-Century England.* New Haven: Yale University Press, 1958.

Whewell, William. *History of the Inductive Sciences.* London: Frank Cass and Co., 1967. (First published in 1837)

Whewell, William. *The Philosophy of the Inductive Sciences*. London: Frank Cass and Co., 1967. (First published in 1840)

Whittaker, Edmund. *A History of the Theories of Aether and Electricity*. London: Thomas Nelson & Sons, 1951.

Williams, Emmett L., ed. *Thermodynamics and the Development of Order*. Norcross, Georgia: Creation Research Society Books,1981.

Williams, Frances Leigh. *Matthew Fontaine Maury: Scientist of the Sea*. New Brunswick, N.J.: Rutgers Univ. Press, 1963.

Williams, L. Pearce. *Michael Faraday: A Biography*. New York: Clarion, 1971.